PROSPER OF AQUITAINE:
DEFENSE OF ST. AUGUSTINE

Ancient Christian Writers

THE WORKS OF THE FATHERS IN TRANSLATION

EDITED BY

JOHANNES QUASTEN
Catholic University of America
Washington, D.C.

WALTER J. BURGHARDT, S.J.
Woodstock College
Woodstock, Md.

No. 32

PROSPER OF AQUITAINE: DEFENSE OF ST. AUGUSTINE

TRANSLATED AND ANNOTATED
BY

P. DE LETTER, S.J., Ph.D., S.T.D.

Professor of Dogmatic Theology
St. Mary's College
Kurseong, India

NEWMAN PRESS

New York, N.Y./Ramsey, N.J.

De Licentia Superioris S.J.
   Nihil Obstat
            J. Quasten
               Cens. Dep.

Imprimatur:

               Patricius A. O'Boyle, D.D.
                  Archiep. Washingtonen.
                     die 20 Decembris 1962

Library of Congress
Catalog Card Number: 62-21490

ISBN: 0-8091-0263-3

PUBLISHED BY PAULIST PRESS
Editorial Office: 1865 Broadway, New York, N.Y. 10023
Business Office: 545 Island Road, Ramsey, N.J. 07446

PRINTED AND BOUND IN THE UNITED STATES OF AMERICA

CONTENTS

PROSPER OF AQUITAINE: DEFENSE OF ST. AUGUSTINE

INTRODUCTION

St. Prosper of Aquitaine, the author of the *De vocatione omnium gentium*,[1] was the chief opponent of the anti-Augustinian reaction known in history as Semi-Pelagianism.[2] Arising in the south of Gaul during Augustine's last years, the Semi-Pelagian opposition continued unabated till the death of its main representative, Abbot Cassian, in 436,[3] when it subsided for a time, to flare up again twenty-five years later. It is in the first phase of these controversies that Prosper was the acknowledged leader of the Augustinians.

Of his life little is known besides what appears from his own works. Born in Aquitaine, he lived at Marseilles when the controversies broke out.[4] He was a layman connected with the monasteries of Marseilles.[5] After Cassian's death, he left Gaul for Rome, where he seems to have been a secretary at the papal court under St. Leo I.[6] He lived there till after 455. The year of his death is not known.

Prosper was both a theologian, who wrote in prose and verse, and a historian, author of a *Chronicon*.[7] In the present volume we collect his theological works in prose which constitute his defense of Augustine against the Semi-Pelagians.[8]

PROSPER'S CAMPAIGN FOR AUGUSTINE

Augustine's writings on grace and predestination against the Pelagians,[9] with his insistence on the absolute gratuity of grace (if grace is not gratuitous but deserved, it is no longer grace[10]) and on the mysterious ways of God saving the predestined in His mercy and in His justice leaving the nonpre-

3

destined to reap the deserts of the Fall,[11] provoked in the monastic centers of Marseilles a reaction of protest similar to that of the Hadrumetan monks.[12] If anything, the protest was a good deal worse and more obstinate. The Doctor of Grace was suspected of the worst errors: fatalism, Manicheism, predestinationism; at any rate, such errors, it was rumored, were the logical consequence of his teaching. Prosper at this point took up the defense of Augustine in his *Epistula ad Rufinum*,[13] the first document of the Semi-Pelagian controversy.[14]

Who this Rufinus was, is not known. He must have been a friend of Prosper who heard about the rumors spread against Augustine and, knowing Prosper's attachment to the Doctor of Grace, anxiously wondered what his views were on the question. In his letter Prosper proclaims his enthusiastic fidelity to the vanquisher of the Pelagians (3). He is well aware of the two main slanders spread by the monks against Augustine: that he sets aside free will to preach fatalism under cover of grace, and that his views about divine predestination divide mankind into two camps after the fashion of the Manichees (3). But he tackles, and refutes from Scripture, their main principle, which amounts to a denial of the gratuity of grace, namely, that grace and virtue are given in reward for good works and good desires (4-6). All good, he says, is God's gift (7-8), including the true freedom of the will and its perseverance in virtue (9-10). The reason why Augustine's opponents refuse to admit the gratuity of grace is their fear of having also to admit the predestination of a fixed number of the elect. They are right, Prosper says; the two points of doctrine go together. And he gives the proof for predestination (11-12). To the objection drawn from 1 Tim. 2.4, Prosper answers by interpreting the universalism of God's salvific will in a restricted sense; this par-

ticularism, he shows, is borne out by the facts we witness in
the preaching of the gospel (13-16). No less assured is his
answer to the other objections. Grace does not set aside free
will; it heals the will of evil. Augustine does not teach either
fatalism or Manicheism; let them show texts if they can; in
fact, Augustine refuted both these errors explicitly (17-18).[15]

Prosper's assurance in defending Augustine's teaching was
perhaps more apparent than real; at any rate, it did not last
long, if we are to judge from the humble and anxious tone of
his *Epistula ad Augustinum*, written a little later (end of
428).[16] Whether the Massilians knew of his letter to
Rufinus or not, neither this nor Augustine's answer to the
African monks in the *De correptione et gratia*[17] satisfied or
pacified the monks of Marseilles. They rather took occasion
of the new tract to clamor and sharpen their objections against
Augustine's teaching—so much so that Prosper, at the end of
his wits, felt himself compelled to ask Augustine himself for
further light and explanation on how to answer his opponents. A friend of his, Hilary, did the same.[18] Their two
letters are the chief documents about the Semi-Pelagian crisis
of the time.

Prosper, who had never met Augustine in person but had
written to him before (1), explains the objections which the
monks of Marseilles raise against his teaching, even after they
came to know the *De correptione et gratia*: that teaching, they
say, is at variance with tradition and with the Church's doctrine (2). They hold that all men, even after the Fall, are
equally offered a chance for salvation; and they reject predestination as entailing a danger of lukewarmness and being
a cover of fatalism; it is better not to preach about Rom. 9.14–
21, which you interpret, they say, as was never done before
and which no one can understand (3). They even come
dangerously close to the Pelagian heresy when they teach that

man's merit forestalls grace, or when they call free will itself the first grace. That is their way of explaining how all men are called and those who wish are saved, those who refuse are lost (4). To my answer drawn from the salvation or loss of infants, or from the delays in the evangelization of some peoples, they reply by appealing to futurible merits and demerits as the reason for these divine dispositions (5). The reason why they hold that grace follows on free will and does not precede it is their reluctance to accept absolute predestination (6). To answer them fully, I need more light from you, especially as their authority with the people is great, some of them having been made bishops. Please show them the danger for their faith involved in their opinions; explain the connection between God's foreknowledge of man's merits and predestination, and how the doctrine of predestination is no hindrance to effort for virtue and agrees with the traditional teaching (8).[19]

Hilary's and Prosper's appeal to Augustine did not go unheeded. The Doctor of Grace, then seventy-three years of age, replied with a double tract, later known as two separate books: his *De praedestinatione sanctorum* and *De dono perseverantiae*, of the year 428/29.[20] Far from making any concession to the Massilians—their views concerning the universal call to salvation and its incompatibility with the absolute predestination of a fixed number of the elect were not altogether unfounded, even though they based them on an inadmissible principle about the *initium fidei*—Augustine reaffirmed his teaching on predestination as part of the faith and implied in the doctrine of the gratuity of grace, and his interpretation of the divine salvific will in a restricted sense; and he showed this to be the Church's traditional doctrine.[21] Little wonder, then, if the *De praedestinatione sanctorum* was a source of new trouble for Prosper, his defender and "press agent"[22] in Gaul.

From Genoa an appeal came to Prosper for light on some difficult passages in this latest publication of Augustine. Two priests, Camille and Theodore, sent the now-famous lay theologian and leader of the Augustinians a list of ten extracts, seven from Book 1 and three from Book 2, with the request for an explanation. Augustine having died meanwhile, Prosper, a little abashed by the honor of this consultation, replied with his *Pro Augustino responsiones ad excerpta Genuensium*.[23] In it he shows himself the ever-enthusiastic follower of Augustine's teaching. The first five excerpts deal with the *initium fidei*. On this point Augustine corrected his earlier views, when he had held that we can have faith of our own (first three excerpts[24]) and then stated in unmistakable terms that faith, no less than everything else which helps for salvation, is a gift of God: to say the opposite is to deny the gratuity of grace (exc. 4), however mysterious may be the reason why it is given to some and not given to others (exc. 5); that reason is hidden from us (exc. 6), we only know the fact, as we also know, Augustine says, that God makes use of the wicked for His own designs (exc. 7). In his comment on excerpt 8, with Augustine's famous "definition" of predestination ("the foreknowledge and preparation of the gifts by which God saves infallibly all those who are saved"), Prosper says that to reject this is to reject the gratuity of grace and fall into Pelagianism. We must preach predestination, since it is part of the faith, but we must do so in the proper way shown by Augustine—his opponents rather gave a parody of that preaching (exc. 9).[25]

Prosper's charitable explanation may have satisfied his Genoese consultants. In Gaul, however, the opposition to

Augustine's teaching was far from dying out—so much so that his defenders saw no other way out than to appeal to Rome. Prosper and Hilary went to Rome and appealed to Pope Celestine.[26] The Pope met their request with a letter to the bishops of Gaul, *Epistula 21 ad episcopos Gallorum,*[27] in which he commends Augustine, who always was in communion with Rome and was considered by the Roman Pontiffs as one of the great doctors of the time; he urged peace and calm under the lead of the bishops and condemned the novelties that went against the traditional doctrine. The Pope, however, did not give any doctrinal decision in the controversy,[28] nor did he commend Augustine's works in any but a general way; he did not specifically commend Augustine's latest writings, which were precisely the butt of the Semi-Pelagian attacks. And so the Roman move of Prosper and Hilary was only a partial success.

If Pope Celestine's intervention restored peace for a while and to some extent, it was not to be for long. No sooner did the Pope die (July, 432) than the anti-Augustinian party grew more active than ever. Cassian published his thirteenth *Collatio,*[29] Vincent of Lerins his *Commonitorium,*[30] Arnobius the Younger his *Praedestinatus;*[31] pamphlets were spread with a list of propositions that drew the worst consequences from Augustine's doctrine on predestination.[32] Prosper back in Gaul did not remain inactive. He may not have known the *Commonitorium* and the *Praedestinatus,* or have failed to gauge their camouflaged anti-Augustinianism; he certainly knew Cassian's *Collatio* and the slanderous pamphlets against the Doctor of Grace. He turned to these and answered them one by one.

Abbot Cassian's anti-Augustinian ideas, expressed in the conferences he held for his monks, had been rumored about before,[33] but it was not till 432 that the text of the famous

Collatio 13 (*On the Protection of God*) was published and Prosper got hold of the text. The Conference is not the insidious or wicked attack on Augustine which Prosper's treatment of it might make one believe. It follows, in the set of Cassian's twenty-four Conferences, the one about chastity in which he says that chastity is a gift of God and no fruit of mere human effort. In continuation of this, he answers the question about the relation between God's grace and man's effort. Broadening out the topic, he shows that not only chastity but every spiritual good is possible only with God's help. This help, however, is withheld from no one by Him who wishes all men to be saved (7). Nor does it do away with human freedom. Sometimes it awaits, at other times it forestalls, human initiative (12–13). Various are the ways of God's protection, and we cannot understand them. But it remains true that "God works all in all" (18). There is no censure of Augustinian predestination,[34] nor any straightforward denial of the fact that all good comes from grace.

Yet, there was a weak point, an error: Cassian said that grace sometimes awaits the good movement of man's unaided will, and that the will, even after the Fall, is not of itself incapable of every good or salutary act. It is against this "remnant of Pelagianism," which moreover he magnifies by taking it out of its context, that Prosper levels his criticism *Contra collatorem.*[35] This is anything but a charitable fraternal correction.

Prosper picks out of Cassian's text twelve statements, *definitiones,* only the first of which is perfectly orthodox: God is the principle of all good acts, thoughts, and desires; His is the initiative of every good will. The other eleven he then scrutinizes one by one, to contrast them with the first and reveal the Pelagian venom they contain: God fans the spark of good will He finds in us (2); free will can of itself conceive a good desire (3); *velle adiacet mihi* without grace (4); grace forestalls the good will in some and awaits it in others (5); both free will and grace help for virtue (6); after the Fall men kept the knowledge of what is good (7); the seeds of the virtues remain after the Fall (8-9); God at times abandons us to show our weakness (10); the faith of the centurion of the Gospel was not due to grace (11); God is *protector* when He calls men, and *susceptor* when He responds to their good initiative (12).

After close criticism of each of these propositions, Prosper repeats them, annexing to each its "theological qualification." In this treatment he is less than fair to Cassian and rather puts an unfavorable interpretation on sayings which, in their context, could well be understood in an acceptable meaning. He manifestly exaggerates what Cassian says of the not-complete corruption of fallen nature. But he is right in condemning Cassian's ideas about an *initium fidei* which in some cases does not spring from grace but from man's unaided good will. When, however, he pictures Cassian's teaching as a *Pelagianismus redivivus* (20), he draws a caricature rather than a faithful portrait of the *doctrina Massiliensis*.[36]

The *Contra collatorem*, with its highhanded manner of dealing with Cassian's error, its biased reading of the texts, and its rhetorical style, failed to put the anti-Augustinians out of action. It rather made matters worse. If we may believe that it was anterior to the two pamphlets with "objections" against Augustine's teaching, the *obiectiones Gallorum* and the *obiectiones Vincentianae*,[37] it received the rebuttal which in a way it deserved: caricature for caricature. Both of these lists of "Augustinian" propositions are caricatures of Augustine's teaching and a good deal blacker than the caricature which Prosper made of Cassian.

The fifteen *Objections of the Gauls,* though somewhat less violent in tone than those of Vincent,[38] definitely aim at discrediting Augustine's teaching on predestination and on the divine salvific will. They draw from that teaching a series of unacceptable conclusions. Predestination, they say, as taught by Augustine, is fatalism (1); it reduces free will to nothing (6); it is one with God's prescience (15); from the nonpredestined it precludes all grace (2, 3, 10, 12) and certainly the grace of perseverance (7); it drives them to sin (11); they were created only for this world, as a utility for the predestined (13). Augustinian predestination implies that God does not will all men to be saved (4, 5, 14) and that Christ did not die for all (9).

As in his attack on Cassian, so also in his *Responsa,*[39] Prosper in a first section discusses the propositions one by one, intending to answer them by giving Augustine's genuine teaching. Predestination, he retorts, is a Catholic doctrine; the accusation of fatalism is false; as to the nonpredestined, the reason why they are not predestined is, he says (going beyond Augustine, who left it hidden in the mystery of God's secret counsel), that God foresaw their evil deeds. God foresees evil; He does not predestine it. God's salvific will is universal in a sense: He calls all men either through nature or through the law or grace; but in another sense this universalism is a restricted one: He does not, in fact, save all. This rather woolly position leaves it unclear whether or not Prosper keeps to Augustine's particularism.[40] After this discussion, He repeats the propositions in the form of canons with their respective theological note. Five of them are against the Catholic faith: that predestination is fatalism (1), precludes from the nonpredestined the effects of baptism (2, 3), excludes free will (6), drives man to sin (14). Others

are erroneous (5, 11, 12). Others still demand a distinction
(4, 7, 8, 9, 10, 15). One is wrong only in the way of ex-
pressing what it says (13).[41]

The sixteen *Objections of Vincent*[42] repeat in a more
violent way the same distortions of Augustine's teaching on
the restricted salvific will and predestination. They say that
Augustine teaches, in fact, that Christ did not die for all (1)
and that God does not will all men to be saved (2, 7, 8, 9):
He created the greater number of men for perdition (3, 4),
predestination making their free will incapable of good (6).
Thus, God Himself is the author of sin (3), even of the worst
crimes such as adultery (10) and incest (11). Predestination
turns sons of God into sons of the devil (12), withholding
from them the means for repentance and salvation (13, 14,
15). In the Our Father the nonpredestined pray for their
own damnation (16).[43]

Prosper's answer[44] to this "devilish catalogue" shows a
rudeness of expression fitting their violent tenor, but it adds
little or nothing to the matter of doctrine. His stand on the
doctrine of the salvific will remains equally ambiguous, uni-
versalist in appearance and words, particularist in fact. As
to the ungodly conclusions drawn from Augustine's teaching
on predestination, their very exaggeration made the answer
to this *latius hos* an easy one. Prosper's reply is ever the
same: God does not predestine evil, He only foreknows it.
The nonpredestined are so because God foreknows their sins.

After this critical phase, the controversy lost much of its
vehemence. With the death of Cassian in 435, it apparently
died down. Prosper left the scene of his fights for the faith
and went to Rome, where he settled at the papal court for his
remaining years.[45] He did not, however, remain inactive,
though no longer provoked to polemics in the calmer atmos-
phere of the Roman court. It may have been under the

influence of Pope St. Leo I that he came to write, as a fitting
conclusion to the first phase of the Semi-Pelagian controversy,
a syllabus of Catholic propositions, the *Capitula* or *Auctoritates*[46] which he compiled between 435 and 442.[47]   These are
mainly quotations, each prefaced with a brief introduction,
from Pope Innocent I (1–4), from Pope Zosimus (5–6), and
from the Eighteenth Council of Carthage, approved by Pope
Zosimus (7),[48] to which are joined two proofs for the doctrine
of grace drawn from liturgical prayer (8) and from the ceremonies of baptism (9).   Two points are central: the Fall of
man and its consequences for all, and the necessity of grace,
which not only forgives sins but works whatever is good in
men.   No word about predestination, or even about the salvific will; these difficult questions are left aside, and only
what pertains to the faith in the doctrine of grace is here
proposed (10).   Even of the specific points of doctrine
formerly defended by Prosper against the Semi-Pelagians,
about the beginning of faith and perseverance in virtue, there
is hardly an explicit mention (9, 3); but both of these are
included in the repeated insistence that all good comes from
grace (5–6).[49]   This syllabus of Catholic and Augustinian
doctrine on grace (Augustine, however, is not mentioned by
name) sums up what was to be the lasting outcome of Prosper's part in the Semi-Pelagian controversies and his contribu-
tion to Catholic tradition.[50]

The Doctrinal Issues

Prosper's defense of Augustine against the Semi-Pelagians
involves several mutually connected points of doctrine, all of
them centered on the gratuity of grace or on the very idea of
grace as an underserved gift of God.   Augustine's great
triumph over the Pelagians had been precisely the vindica-

tion of this basic notion of the Christian faith, and this was endangered by the error of the Massilians. Their contention that the beginning of faith, or the initiative in the life of grace, including the intellectual assent to the divine call,[51] comes from man's free will and not from grace, or at least could and in some cases did so come, and that both progress and perseverance in grace were in a true sense the fruit of unaided free will and not merely a gift of grace, thus granting to free will a priority or lead over grace all along the development of the life of grace,[52] cut at the root of the very notion of grace. A gift given in answer to merit (however small the merit) is no longer pure grace in the Catholic sense of the term. The Semi-Pelagian position, however far removed from that of Pelagius, is in fact at variance with the teaching of the faith. However slight and out of proportion with what follows it may be the merit of faith which, without the help of grace, initiates the process of the life of grace, it does mar the gratuity of grace: this is no longer a pure gift; it is in a real measure a reward.[53] This cuts at the very root of the gratuity of the life of grace. Prosper was right in upholding, and it is his lasting merit to Catholic doctrine to have upheld, this point of faith for Augustine and against the monks of Marseilles.

But this point of doctrine was set in a context which is rather confused and in which neither of the opposing camps was right or wrong all along the line. The Augustinian insistence on the gratuity of grace was set against the background of the dogma of the Fall. Because of original sin, man's free will can do nothing of its own for the life that leads to salvation; only grace can set the will free and enable it to work as it should. So far so good.[54] But Augustine's idea of the crushing effect of original sin on all men, mankind being a *massa damnationis,* brought in its wake the concept of election and predestination. God could, Augustine taught, have left all men after the Fall to perish forever; that is what all deserve in justice. In His mercy, however, He chooses a number of them for the life of grace and for salvation. This is His gratuitous predestination, uninfluenced by any initiative of fallen men, who are, because of the original fault, unable to make any such move towards what is good or salutary. As to those whom He does not choose, they are left to reap the just punishment due to the original fault.[55]

To this Augustinian concept of the Fall and of predestination and reprobation, the monks of Marseilles objected, and they were to some extent justified in doing so. They objected, first, to Augustine's idea of the Fall. Does original sin really entail the consequence that man unaided by grace is good for nothing but evil? Is every act of his really sinful? If Augustine said so—and, historically speaking, it is hard to say that he did not—then he was not altogether right or he meant something different from what we understand by it today. One need not say that every act of fallen man's unaided will is a sin in the sense of an offense against God. It need not of necessity and without exception be vitiated by sinful self-love,[56] though it may often be so. It can be, later theology would say, a naturally honest or good act, without being positively helpful for salvation. But this perspective lay outside Augustine's horizon. To his mind, even such an act was defective and sterile for salvation, and because of this he called it sinful. It is so only in an improper and diminished sense.[57]

But Cassian and the Massilians went too far in their protest against Augustine's idea of the Fall when they said that without any help of grace free will in fallen man is able, sometimes at least, to make the first move towards salvation, *initium fidei,* or when they taught that the seeds of the virtues which lead to salvation, and of faith in particular, are alive in fallen men.[58] This is an overstatement. Actually, a virtuous move which a man makes unaided by grace is not salutary, it is merely naturally good. And so, natural virtues found in fallen men, for all their being virtues in some sense, are sterile for life eternal.[59] This answer, however, Prosper, faithful to Augustine, could not and did not give. After Augustine, he excluded from fallen man's free will every good initiative, because good for him meant salutary and he never envisaged purely natural goodness. As the Semi-Pelagians went wrong in asserting a salutary initiative without the help of grace, so Prosper himself erred in a way when he implied that without grace every good, even nonsalutary, initiative is impossible.

The strongest protest of the Massilians, however, was against Augustine's teaching on predestination. The idea of the election of a fixed number of the predestined[60] and of the dereliction of the remainder among the *massa damnationis* without any hope or possibility of salvation seemed to them to exclude altogether the universal salvific will, as Scripture (1 Tim. 2.4) and tradition proposes it to our faith. One had to choose, they thought, between the universal salvific will and the limited predestination; one could not hold to both; and they preferred to keep to the teaching of the faith on God's universal will to save.[61]

To this objection Prosper, in spite of some velleity to the contrary, in fact gave no other answer than that of Augustine: after his master, he interpreted the salvific will in the sense of a restricted universality. This answer, however, is unsatisfactory. Neither Augustine nor Prosper after him ever endeavored to show that the nonpredestined also were in fact given a real chance of salvation, and if lost, they were lost because of their failure to take this chance. Augustine's idea of eternal punishment owed for original sin, which in his eyes justified the damnation of the nonpredestined in strict justice, precluded from his reflection any attempt at conceiving such a chance. And it remains doubtful whether or to what extent Prosper freed himself from this Augustinian outlook.[62] It would rather seem that he did not.

At any rate, Catholic tradition corrected Augustine's views by making explicit what he neglected or left implicit: it has shown that even after the Fall, to all men *sufficient* grace is given to take the road to salvation, though not all co-operate with the divine call; their initial lack of co-operation is the reason why they fail to receive *efficacious* grace for salvation. As shown by Karl Rahner,[63] the undeniable harshness of Augustine's teaching on predestination is mainly due to his considering exclusively the efficacious grace which effectively leads to salvation. This, it is correct to say, is not given to all. In this sense it is true to say that the salvific will is not universal, it is restricted. In this context Augustine's restrictive interpretations of 1 Tim. 2.4 were inevitable, and they are correct as far as they go. They require, however, and very urgently, to be completed by a universalistic interpretation which takes into account the nonefficacious grace offered to all[64] (as is commonly held today). Prosper himself made an attempt to do so, but he failed in part. Hardly more than Augustine does he consider sufficient grace offered to all, and without this there can be no universal salvific will.[65] The only explicit softening of Augustine's teaching on predestination which he initiated was his explanation of the nonpredestination or (negative) reprobation of the nonelect by God's foreknowledge of their future sins.[66] This may contain, as in an unopened shell, a very implicit hint at some sort of sufficient grace which is presupposed in the very possibility of these sins (the reprobate were somehow able—thanks to grace?— to avoid these). But not more than Augustine was Prosper

able to envisage this perspective. The shell remained unopened. His position concerning the divine salvific will remains ambiguous.

On the other hand, Cassian and his followers, who took
their stand on the universal salvific will against Augustinian
predestination, overshot the mark when they postulated as its
necessary presupposition that all men, even after the Fall, are
able of themselves to answer God's call to salvation and need
not be aroused to this by God's prevenient grace. Unless
every man can answer God's call with either yes or no, in such
manner that in either case it is his free will that decides the
issue, God's salvific will, they thought, would not really be
universal.[67] They may have been unaware of the implications of this position, especially of what it meant to allow a
real priority of the will over grace; they certainly did repudiate
beforehand the Pelagian consequences Prosper drew from
their premise.[68]   In this, however, they were inconsistent.
Prosper was justified in saying that logically and in principle
the denial of the universal necessity of grace for the *initium
fidei* led to a denial of grace. But it is not so rare that other
considerations than logic command a doctrinal position.
Actually, the universal salvific will does not require that man
should have the initiative in his salvation as in his perdition.
All that it requires is that the sufficient grace without which
that initiative cannot arise be offered to all; that is what today
the theology of the salvific will commonly says. If the Semi-
Pelagians did not say this, it is because their concept of grace
was not different from that of Augustine and Prosper. To
their mind, also, grace meant efficacious grace; once given,
man infallibly or necessarily (if freely) assents; if withheld,
man is unable to make the initial move for salvation (suppos-
ing that grace be required for this). Accordingly, in their
position, a universal distribution of this grace was unthinka-

ble; and the universal salvific will entails that men can make the initial move without grace. With the Augustinian concept of efficacious grace which was also theirs, this was a necessary consequence or postulate of the universal salvific will.[69]

It is perhaps verging on the tragic that historically it is the Semi-Pelagians who upheld in the centuries of the controversies about grace the doctrine of the universal salvific will so dear to contemporary Catholic thought. They defended their position in the wrong manner, and this might well have endangered the very doctrine; apparently it did endanger it to some extent in Augustinian theology.[70] Prosper, and with him the defenders of Augustine, rejected the wrong argument of the Semi-Pelagians (the *initium fidei* without grace), rightfully holding on to the absolute gratuity of grace, without however rejecting the doctrine of the universal salvific will; at any rate, he made an effort, partially successful, not to reject that doctrine explicitly and in fact to state it positively.[71] He did not, however, give the right argument for the doctrine of the universal salvific will; in the perspective in which his concept of grace (all grace being considered as efficacious) placed him, he could not have done so. Thus, his attitude before the doctrine of the universal salvific will naturally remained uncertain—all the more so that for a long time he considered Augustine's teaching on predestination a doctrine of the faith.[72] He therefore hesitated to give up predestination; he hesitated to give up the universal salvific will. By his lingering attachment to the latter he was to prepare the way for a solution. This he did still more when he eliminated Augustinian predestination from the doctrine of the faith and separated it from the dogma of the universal necessity and absolute gratuity of grace, as he did in the *Auctoritates.*[73] Here he prepared the ground for an explicit awareness of sufficient (and not necessarily efficacious) grace, which alone allows a reconciliation of God's universal salvific will, shown in the universal distribution of sufficient grace, and His predestination, revealed in the actual granting to the elect of efficacious grace up to final perseverance.

*   *   *

The present translation was made on the text of Mangeant, reprinted in Migne's *Patrologia latina* 51,[74] except for the *Epist. ad August.*, of which A. Goldbacher gave a critical edition in the Vienna Corpus among the letters of Augustine.[75] No better printed text is available, nor is there, as far as we know, any critical edition in immediate preparation. Cappuyns, in his study of Prosper's Augustinism,[76] lists the chief manuscripts of each of Prosper's works.

As to modern translations, we have been helped by the French translation of Prosper's works by C. Lequeux, *Oeuvres de saint Prosper d'Aquitaine* (Paris 1762).[77] This does not include the *Auctoritates*. The recent English translation of the *Contra collatorem* by J. R. O'Donnell in Vol. 7 of *The Fathers of the Church* (New York 1949) is too defective to be of real help. Of the *Auctoritates,* a good translation of all but the last chapter is found in *The Church Teaches* (St. Louis 1955). We know of no other available modern translation of these works of Prosper. This should, therefore, be the first English translation of his defense of Augustine against the Semi-Pelagians.

LETTER TO RUFINUS

To his lord and dear brother in Christ, the rightly revered Rufinus, Prosper sends best wishes.

I received through our mutual friend[1] the tokens of your brotherly concern for me, and I was glad of this new proof of your sincere and painstaking charity. And lest malicious rumors which cannot fail to reach your ears should cause you fear and anxiety, I have taken care to free you from all uneasiness, in so far as this is possible by letter. I am endeavoring to explain exactly the whole situation. Thus you will be able to learn from myself—since you could not hear every rumor our opponents[2] are spreading—whatever is being bruited about concerning us with an evil but futile intention.

But first I must intimate to Your Holiness the nature of the issue that gives rise to these rumors. You will understand better then the calumnies of our opponents and see what light they try to obscure and with what gloom.

1. The Pelagian heresy and the doctrine by which it began its destructive attack on the Catholic faith and endeavored to poison with ungodly tenets the inner life of the Church and the very vitals of the Body of Christ are too well known to need relating. Among these tenets there is one impious assertion, however, which is the evil and tenuous seed of the others, namely, that God's grace is given in answer to men's merits.[3] The Pelagians first wished to say that human nature is perfectly sound[4] and able to attain the kingdom of God by its unaided free will, the reason being that nature finds help enough in the very gift of creation. Being naturally endowed with reason and intellect, it can easily

choose what is good and avoid what is evil. And since the will is equally free for both good and evil, if men are wicked it is not because they lack the ability to do good but the endeavor to do it. They, then, as I said, pretended that the whole of man's justice comes from his natural rectitude and ability. But Catholic doctrine rejects that statement. Yet, the very opinion which was condemned by the Catholics,[5] the Pelagians afterwards with heretical cunning proposed under many various hues, and they managed to keep it while yet confessing that God's grace is necessary for man to begin what is good, to advance and to persevere in it.[6]

2. But the very grace of God revealed to the *vessels of mercy* the fraud by which the *vessels of wrath*[7] maneuvered to steal into this insincere profession of faith. It was found out and ascertained for the good of the faithful that the Pelagians confessed nothing more than that grace is some sort of teacher of man's free will[8] and that its only function is to instruct the mind from outside by exhortation, law, teaching, contemplation of created things, miracles, threats; so, everyone can by his own free will find if he seeks, receive if he asks, enter if he knocks. They meant to say that what the call of grace does first is to admonish the freedom of our wills; that grace is nothing else than the law, the prophet, the teacher: these take care in a general way of all men, so that those who wish can believe, and those who believe can obtain justification through the merit of their faith and of their good will; that accordingly God's grace is given in answer to men's merits.[9] In this manner, grace is no longer grace, because, if it is rendered for merit and does not itself cause what is good in man, then its name is meaningless.[10]

3. This cunning of the sons of darkness who wished to be taken for sons of light was exposed both by the Oriental bishops,[11] the authority of the Apostolic See,[12] and the African

councils.[13] Augustine also, at the time the first and foremost among the bishops of the Lord, refuted them abundantly and effectively in a number of tracts.[14] Among many other divine gifts showered on him by the Spirit of truth, he excelled particularly in the gifts of knowledge and wisdom flowing from his love of God, which enabled him to slay with the unconquerable sword of the word not only the Pelagian heresy, still alive now in some of its offshoots,[15] but also many other previous heresies. Against this doctor, resplendent with the glory of so many palms and so many crowns which he gained for the exaltation of the Church and the glory of Christ, some of ours, to their own great misfortune, speak and murmur in secret; but we came to know their criticisms. When they find ears ready to listen, they defame the writings Augustine published against the Pelagian error. They say he completely sets aside free will and under cover of grace upholds fatalism.[16] He wants us to believe, they add, that there are in the human race two different substances and natures.[17] Thus, they attribute to a man of such outstanding holiness the ungodliness of pagans and Manichees! If what they say is true, why are they so remiss, not to say ungodly, as not to remove from the Church such a pernicious bane and to oppose such insane preaching, or even to counter in some writing or other the author of such teaching? They would, to their own glory and fame, render a service to mankind if they brought Augustine back from his error! Unless perhaps those unassuming people and new censors, out of veneration and mercy for him, spare an old man once upon a time of so high merit, and keep quiet, certain that no one will approve of his writings! Let them be merciful! Or rather let them learn that not only the Church of Rome and of Africa and all the sons of the promise the world over agree with the teaching of this doctor both in the faith as a whole and in particular in

the doctrine on grace, but also that in the very places where
they arouse remonstrances against him there are, by God's
favor, many people who learn from his enlightening tracts
how to understand the teaching of the gospel and of the
apostles and who rejoice in seeing his writings spread where
Christ gains new members of His Body.[18]   If we deserve
censure, why do they hesitate to accuse us?   If we are not
blameworthy, why this biting secret detraction?

4.   But does not everybody know why they whisper their
chagrin in private and on purpose keep silent in public?
Desirous of taking pride in their own justice, rather than
glorying in God's grace,[19] they are displeased when we oppose
the assertions they make in many a conference[20] against a man
of the highest authority.   They know full well that whenever
they raise a question on the matter, whether in some meeting
of prelates or in some gathering of other people, we could
put before them hundreds of volumes of Augustine.[21]   When
these writings will be read and show eager listeners the unconquerable truth of the Christian faith flooding their minds
with the fountains of the word of God, who of the faithful
and the godly, understanding and believing what are the real
causes of their salvation, will admit that bitter teaching based
on untruth and ending in smoke?   I, for one, hope also for
this from the wealth of God's mercy, that He will not in the
end fully deprive of understanding those whom He now
allows to be deceived by their own free will and to stray from
the path of humility.   I hope He only delays halting their
advance in error in order that the power of His grace may be
proclaimed more gloriously when grace will subject to itself
the hearts of its very opponents; they have run into danger
because of their very zeal for virtue, into peril because of the
integrity of their lives.[22]   Virtue indeed is necessary; but they
make a miserable use of it when they think it is a gift of

nature, or if it comes from grace, then was given as a reward for some previous good work or good desire.[23]

5. Our opponents say this on the strength of some texts of Holy Scripture, but they do not explain these texts in the proper way. To prove a proposition, such texts should be quoted as cannot be understood in another meaning opposed to that proposition, such as do not disagree with the principle for whose proof they are quoted. Now, they say that the following words are addressed to men who should act of their own free will: *Come to me, all you that labor and are burdened, and I will refresh you. Take up my yoke upon you and learn of me, because I am meek and humble of heart, and you shall find rest to your souls. For my yoke is sweet and my burden light.*[24] They say this applies to all men who labor in the uncertainty of this life and are burdened with sins. Those who are willing to follow the meekness and humility of the Saviour and to accept the yoke of His commandments will find rest for their souls in the hope of eternal life; those who refuse to do so are deprived of salvation through their own fault—had they wanted to, they could have attained it.

But let them listen also to the other words our Lord addressed to men who should act of their own free will: *Without me you can do nothing.*[25] And: *No man can come to me, except the Father who hath sent me draw him.*[26] And: *No man can come to me, unless it be given him by my Father.*[27] And: *As the Father raiseth up the dead, so the Son also giveth life to whom He will.*[28] And: *No one knoweth who the Son is but the Father; and who the Father is but the Son and to whom the Son will reveal Him.*[29] Since all these texts are irreformable and cannot be twisted and interpreted in another sense, who can doubt that free will obeys the invitation of God calling only when His grace has aroused in him the

desire to believe and to obey? Else it would be sufficient to
instruct a man and there would be no need to produce in him
a new will, as Scripture says: *The will is prepared by the
Lord*,[30] and the Apostle: *For it is God who worketh in you,
both to will and to accomplish, according to His good will*.[31]
According to which good will, if not the one which God produces in them, so as to give them to accomplish what He gave
them to will?

6. They also quote the story of the centurion Cornelius
as a good example of what free will is able to do.[32] Before he
had received grace, *fearing and praying God, he was*, of his
own accord, *intent on almsgiving, fasting, prayer*.[33] That
was the reason why Holy Scripture praised him and why he
received the gift of baptism. They fail to see that the whole
of Cornelius' preparation for baptism was a gift of God's
grace. For when St. Peter was directed, by the vision of all
kinds of animals, to baptize Cornelius and also anyone of the
Gentiles,[34] and when according to Jewish custom he declined
unclean and *common* food,[35] a voice spoke to him thrice:
That which God hath cleansed, do thou not call common.[36]
This shows clearly enough that it is God's grace which, in
order to purify Cornelius, had initiated all the good works
that preceded his baptism. And so the Apostle had not to
hesitate to give the sacrament of baptism to a man to whom
the Lord had already granted this gift. The beginnings of
this new and still unrevealed call of the Gentiles might have
looked uncertain, had it not been clear from the signs of their
previous good dispositions that God's grace had been at work
in the future converts: *For all men have not faith*.[37] *All do
not obey the gospel*.[38] Believers are led by the Spirit of God;
unbelievers turn away of their own free will. Accordingly,
our turning to God is not our doing but God's gift; as the
Apostle says, *By grace you are saved through faith, and that*

not of yourselves, for it is the gift of God. Not of works, that no man may glory.[39]

7. Let, then, human weakness and all generations of men condemned in the first man acknowledge their true state. When the dead are brought to life, the blind made to see, the ungodly led to justice, let them confess that Jesus Christ is their life, light, justice, and *He that glorieth should glory in the Lord,*[40] not in himself. When he was ungodly, blind, dead, it was from his Saviour that he gratuitously received justice, light, life. He did not practice justice already and then receive an increase in justice; nor did he walk towards God and get strength to continue his course; nor did he love God and receive an increase in the fervor of charity. When as yet without faith, and hence ungodly, he received the Spirit of faith and was made just.[41] *The just man liveth by faith.*[42] And: *Without faith no one can please God.*[43] And: *All that is not of faith is sin.*[44] So, he should understand that the justice of infidels is no justice,[45] because nature without grace is unclean.

8. When man lost his native innocence, he became an exile and a lost man, walking without knowing whereto, straying into ever-deeper error. But he was sought, found, brought back, and led into the way that is truth and life; he was set on fire with the love of God, who loved him first when he did not yet love Him. St. John the Apostle says: *Not as though we had loved God, but because He hath first loved us.*[46] And again: *Let us therefore love God, because God first hath loved us.*[47] And still: *Dearly beloved, let us love one another, for charity is of God. And everyone that loveth is born of God and knoweth God. He that loveth not knoweth not God, for God is charity.*[48] St. Paul agrees to say: *In Christ Jesus neither circumcision availeth anything, nor uncircumcision, but faith that worketh by charity.*[49]

Where does this faith linked with charity come from, if not from Him who gave it, as he shows, when saying: *For unto you it is given for Christ, not only to believe in Him, but also to suffer for Him;*[50] this could not have been done without a great charity. And again: *The charity of God is poured forth in our hearts by the Holy Ghost, who is given us.*[51] Without charity, the Apostle testifies,[52] neither faith, nor knowledge however great, neither virtues, nor efforts, nor works of any sort profit anything. That means: there may be many praiseworthy and admirable works in a man, but if they are without the marrow of charity, they have the semblance of holiness, not the reality.[53]

9. No man, therefore, is of himself found worthy of the great and unspeakable gift of charity. Whosoever is an elect of God is made worthy of it, as the Apostle says: *Giving thanks to the Father, who hath made us worthy to be partakers of the lot of the saints in light; who hath delivered us from the power of darkness and hath translated us into the kingdom of the Son of His love.*[54] And to Timothy he writes: *Labor with the gospel, according to the power of God, who hath delivered us and called us by His holy calling, not according to our own works, but according to His own purpose and grace, which was given us in Christ Jesus before the times of the world.*[55] And to Titus: *We ourselves also were some time unwise, incredulous, erring, slaves to diverse desires and pleasures, living in malice and envy, hateful and hating one another. But when the goodness and kindness of God our Saviour appeared, not by the works of justice which we have done, but according to His mercy, He saved us.*[56]

Accordingly, whomsoever God's grace justifies, it makes them, not better from good, but good from bad. Later, when they make progress, it will make them better from good, not by taking away their free will but by setting it free.[57] When

free will was unaided by God, it was dead to justice and living
for sin. But when the mercy of Christ enlightened it, then
it was brought out of the kingdom of the devil and became
the kingdom of God. And to continue in this happy state,
man's free will is not sufficient unless he be also given perseverance by Him who gave him that diligence.[58]

10. A proof of this is St. Peter's faith, which, however
ardent, would have given way in his temptations had not the
Lord prayed for him;[59] so the Evangelist discloses in these
words: *And the Lord said: Simon, Simon, behold, Satan hath
desired to have you, that he may sift you as wheat. But I
have prayed for thee, that thy faith fail not; and thou, being
once converted, confirm thy brethren.*[60] And: *Pray, lest ye
enter into temptation.*[61] To prove better still that free will
can do nothing without grace, to the same Peter who had
been told: *Confirm thy brethren,* and: *Pray lest ye enter into
temptation,* and who had answered: *Lord, I am ready to go
with thee both into prison and to death,*[62] the Lord foretells
that before the cock crows, he will disown his Lord thrice.[63]
What else does this mean but that he will be wanting in
faith? Certainly, our Lord had prayed for Peter, that his
faith might not give way; nor had He prayed in vain, for His
action is one with that of the Father to whom He had prayed.
But Peter, who had made so great promises on his own, is
allowed to run into danger, lest one should think he stood
firm of his own free will. And after he is shaken and is
giving way, he is looked on and restored by Him without
whom no one can be steadfast in virtue or persevering.

11. From this profession of faith in God's grace some
draw back for fear lest, if they accept the doctrine on grace as
shown in Holy Scripture and manifested by the effects of its
power, they be compelled to admit also that of all men born
in the course of the centuries the number of the predestined,

chosen according to the design of God's call, is fixed and definite with God.[64]   But it is as much against holy religion to deny this as it is to gainsay grace itself.[65]   For it is no secret, but evident to all who open their eyes, how for so many centuries countless thousands of men were left to their errors and impieties and died without any knowledge of the true God. This is shown, in the Acts of the Apostles, by the words of Barnabas and Paul, who told the Lycaonians: *Ye men, why do ye do these things? We also are mortals, men like unto you, preaching to you to be converted from these vain things to the living God, who made the heaven and the earth and the sea and all things that are in them, who in times past suffered all nations to walk their own ways. Nevertheless, He left not Himself without testimony, doing them good, from heaven giving rains and fruitful seasons, filling your hearts with food and gladness.*[66]   Certainly, had natural reason or the use they made of God's gifts been enough for them to attain eternal life, then in our day also the light of reason, the mildness of the climate, the abundance of crops and food would be able to save us,[67] because making a better use of nature than they did, we would serve our Creator in gratitude for His daily gifts.

12.   But let such absurd and baneful opinion be far from the minds of Christians redeemed by the blood of the Christ! Human nature cannot be made free apart from the one Mediator of God and men, the man Christ Jesus:[68] without Him there is no salvation.[69]   Just as *He made us and not we ourselves,*[70] so also He remakes us and not we ourselves. And lest man may seem by his natural powers to repay the price of his reparation with his works of justice, at least after he has been restored, we see the riches of God's goodness poured out over the first moments of infants whom God does not choose because of their piety whether before or after their baptism,

in whom He finds neither obedience, nor discernment, nor will. I speak of those infants who are baptized at once after their birth and, taken away from this life, are carried up into eternal happiness. And there is another countless multitude of infants of the same nature and condition as the former who die without baptism and of whom we may not doubt that they have no share in the city of God.[71]

13. What, then, about the trite objection from the Scripture text, *God will have all men to be saved and to come to the knowledge of the truth?*[72] Only they who fail to see its meaning think it goes against us. All those who, from the past ages till today, died without having known God, are they of the number of "all men"? And if it is said, wrongly, that in the case of adults the evil works they did of their own free will were the obstacle to their salvation, as though grace saved the good and not the wicked, what difference in merit could there be between infants that are saved and others that are not? What is it that led the first into the kingdom of God, and what is it that kept the second out of it? Indeed, if you consider their merit, you cannot say that some of them merited to be saved; all of them deserved to be condemned, because all sinned in Adam's sin. The unimpeachable justice of God would come down on all of them, did not His merciful grace take a certain number unto Himself. As to inquiring into the reason and manner of this discrimination hidden in God's secret counsel, this is above the ken of human knowledge, and our faith suffers no harm from not knowing it,[73] provided we confess that no one is lost without his fault, and no one saved for his own merit, that the all-powerful goodness of God saves and instructs in the knowledge of the truth all those whom *He will have to be saved and to come to the knowledge of the truth.*[74] Save for His call, His teaching, His salvation, no man comes or learns or is saved. Though

the preachers of the gospel are directed to preach to all men
without distinction and to sow the seed of the word everywhere, yet *Neither he that planteth is anything, nor he that
watereth, but God that giveth the increase.*[75]

14.   Hence, when the apostles began to preach the gospel
to the Gentiles, Holy Scripture reports of one section of those
who heard them preach: *And the Gentiles hearing were glad
and glorified the word of the Lord, and as many as were
ordained to life everlasting believed.*[76] And elsewhere it says,
when many women listened to Paul's preaching: *A certain
woman named Lydia, a seller of purple, of the city of Thyatira, one that worshiped God, did hear: whose heart the Lord
opened to attend to those things which were said by Paul.*[77]
And again, at the very moment that the preachers of the
gospel were sent out to all the nations, the apostles were
forbidden to go to certain regions by Him *who will have all
men to be saved and to come to the knowledge of the truth,*[78]
with the result, of course, that many, detained and going
astray during this delay of the gospel, died without having
known the truth and without having been sanctified in
baptism. Let, then, Holy Scripture say what happened: *And
when they had passed through Phrygia and the country of
Galatia, they were forbidden by the Holy Ghost to preach the
word in Asia. And when they were come into Mysia, they
attempted to go into Bithynia, and the Spirit of Jesus suffered
them not.*[79] Is there any wonder that at the very beginning
of the preaching of the gospel the apostles could not go
except where the Spirit of God wanted them to go, when even
now we see that many of the nations only begin to have a
share in the Christian grace, while others have not yet got a
glimpse of that divine gift?

15.   Or should we say that the wills of men obstruct the
will of God, that those peoples are of such wild and fierce

ways that the reason why they do not hear the gospel is that
their ungodly hearts are not ready for its preaching? But
who else changed the hearts of believers but He who *hath
made the hearts of every one of them?*[80] Who softened the
hardness of their hearts into willing obedience but He who
is able of these stones to raise up children of Abraham?[81]
And who will give the preachers intrepid and unshaken
firmness but He who said to Paul: *Do not fear, but speak,
and hold not thy peace, because I am with thee and no man
shall set upon thee, to hurt thee. For I have much people in
this city?*[82] I think no one will make bold to say that there is
any nation in this world or any region on this earth in which
the Church should not be established, since God spoke to His
Son: *Ask of me, and I will give thee the Gentiles for thy
inheritance, and the utmost parts of the earth for thy possession.*[83] And again: *All the ends of the earth shall remember
and shall be converted to the Lord, and all the nations of the
Gentiles shall adore in His sight.*[84] And our Lord Himself
says: *This gospel of the kingdom shall be preached in the
whole world, for a testimony to all nations, and then shall the
end come.*[85] Whatever nations then have not yet heard the
gospel will hear it, and *as many* of them *as were ordained to
life everlasting* will believe.[86] For none other will have a
share in the inheritance of Christ than those who before the
creation of the world were elect, predestined, and foreknown,
according to the counsel of Him who *worketh all things
according to the counsel of His will.*[87]

16. Let us, then, praise the works of the Lord and give
glory to His mercies; let us not grow impatient at our ignorance of the choice and the number of the vessels of election.
Even in former ages, when Scripture said of one people: *In
Judea God is known: His name is great in Israel,*[88] the future
election of the nations was hidden; only later did God make

known what He kept secret before.   So the Apostle says:
which in other generations was not known to the sons of men,
as it is now revealed to His holy apostles and prophets in the
Spirit: that the Gentiles should be fellow heirs and of the
same body, and copartners of His promise in Christ Jesus.[89]
And in the Acts of the Apostles he says: *The faithful of the*
circumcision, who came with Peter, were astonished for that
the grace of the Holy Ghost was poured out upon the Gen-
tiles.[90]   If, then, the Lord hid and delayed His design to call
all the nations as long as He pleased and revealed it when He
pleased, yet the ignorance of that mystery was no harm to the
faithful, why should we think it is harmful to our hope not
to know how many and whom God prepares among men as
vessels of mercy for the heavenly glory?   For it is quite
certain that all good men will enter the kingdom of heaven,
and do so by the favor of God's grace, and that none of the
wicked will enter, because they deserve to be cast out for
their sinfulness.

   17.   It is really too silly and thoughtless to say, as our
opponents do, that God's grace leaves nothing to free will to
do.[91]   True, in infants who receive baptism, there is evidently
no act nor desire of their wills; true also, many who have the
use of their free wills but live estranged from the true God
and lead a life of sin, happen to receive grace and to be saved
through baptism as it were at their last breath.[92]   Yet, if we
consider with the eyes of faith that section of the sons of God
who reach the age when they can accomplish the works of a
God-fearing life, do we not see that their free wills are not
suppressed but rather reborn in grace?   When unaided and
left to itself, free will acted only for its own perdition.   It had
turned blind through its own fault; it could not recover the
light by itself.   But now by grace the same free will is turned
back to God, not destroyed.[93]   It is given new desires, new

tastes, new actions; its health is entrusted not to itself but to its Physician.[94] For even now it is not so perfectly healthy as to be proof against what caused its past illness or to be able by its own strength to abstain from what is unwholesome. Accordingly, man who was evil in his free will has been made good in that same free will. Evil he was of himself; he becomes good by God's gift. God restored him to his original dignity by giving him a new beginning: He not only forgave the guilt which man incurred by willing and doing what is evil; He also gave him to will and to do what is good and to persevere in it. For the Apostle James says: *Every best gift and every perfect gift is from above, coming down from the Father of lights.*[95] And he shows clearly the difference between a free will led by human wisdom and one ruled by God, when he says: *But if you have bitter zeal, and there be contentions in your hearts, glory not and be not liars against the truth. For this is not wisdom, descending from above, but earthly, sensual, devilish. For where envying and contention is, there is inconstancy and every evil work. But the wisdom that is from above, first indeed is chaste, then peaceable, modest, easy to be persuaded, full of mercy and good fruits, without judging, without dissimulation.*[96] They who with constancy apply themselves to these virtues follow the light not of their own but of a heavenly wisdom. For *the Lord gives wisdom, and from His face come knowledge and understanding.*[97] And their truest glory is to glory not in themselves but in the Lord.[98]

18. As for the objections—as inept as they are false, yet constantly repeated—that Augustine teaches fatalism and divides mankind into two different substances and natures,[99] they fail to touch him, as in his books he refutes those very errors at length.[100] They do not disturb us either, for we strongly condemn those opinions and their authors. Let

rather the inventors of this silly fiction take care to guard
themselves against the shame which such a calumny may draw
on them if the persons whom they deceive with their talk
take ever so little pains to read the writings of the most outstanding among the defenders of grace.   Or, better still, they
might spare others a long search: they should bring and explain the books of the holy doctor, or at least show some passages which, if only because of their ambiguous meaning,
could be interpreted in their own sense.   But they never
heard from us anything of the sort; they never read in our
writings anything like it; we know and say that no event is
ruled by fatalism but that all things are ordained by God's
decree.   We also know that the nature of all men was created
and is created, not from two different substances or natures,
but from one substance, which is the flesh of the first man;
that this nature fell miserably through the free will of the
first man, *in whom all have sinned;*[101] and that it can in no
way be freed from the debt of eternal death unless the grace
of Christ reforms it after the image of God by a second creation and keeps the free will, moving, inspiring, and assisting
it, and taking the lead till the end.[102]

Your Holiness can see now, at least if my exposition is not
too obscure, that there is no ground for some people to raise
objections against us, and that all their silly accusations are
concocted for the sake of arousing and turning against us the
minds of those whom they wish to bring round to another
opinion.   Trust, therefore, in the power of God's mercy.
This opposition will die down in these regions just as in other
parts of the world.   The teaching of Augustine, the greatest
man in the Church today, may someday be furthered even by
those who oppose it today.   You, my dear and revered
brother, if you wish to be truly informed about these matters,
as it is proper you should wish to be, take the trouble of read-

ing Augustine's own tracts. Concerning the Catholic doctrine on grace, you will draw from them a salutary insight into
the teaching of the gospel and of the apostles.[103]

May the grace of God and the peace of our Lord Jesus
Christ keep you at all times and lead you by the way of truth
to life eternal!

LETTER TO AUGUSTINE

To the most holy lord, Bishop Augustine, wonderful beyond words, honorable without comparison, his most excellent patron: from Prosper.

1.   Though unknown to you by sight, yet, if you remember, known somehow from what I wrote to you (for I sent you a letter and received an answer through my brother in Christ, deacon Leontius),[1] I make bold to write again to Your Holiness, not only, as then, to send you my respects, but also for love of the faith that is the life of the Church.   Your alert vigilance keeps watch over all the members of the Body of Christ; by the power of truth you fight the deceits of heretical doctrines.   So I thought I should not be afraid you would be irked or inconvenienced by a matter that concerns the salvation of many and therefore your own kind charity.   I should rather consider myself guilty if I did not refer to the special protector of the faith such errors as seem to me to be very baneful.

2.   A number of the servants of Christ[2] who live at Marseilles are of opinion that what Your Holiness wrote, in your tracts against the Pelagian heresies, about the call of the elect according to God's decree, is against the teaching of the Fathers[3] and the faith of the Church.   For some time they preferred to blame only their own dullness rather than censure what they did not grasp.   Some of them wanted to beg Your Holiness for a clearer and more detailed explanation of the question.   But by a disposition of God's mercy, it so happened that, when some people in Africa[4] had the same difficulties, you published a book *On Admonition and Grace*, brimful with the teachings of Holy Scripture.   When by an

unhoped-for chance we came to know this book,[5] we thought
it would settle all grievances of our opponents: it gave such
a complete and definite answer to all the questions we had to
ask of Your Holiness, as though you had written it for the
special purpose of settling our differences. Actually, if the
reading of this book of Your Holiness gave much better and
deeper understanding to those who already before followed
the holy and apostolic doctrine which you teach, it increased
the opposition of those whose minds were held by the cloud
of their own opinion. This stubborn antagonism is dangerous, first for the opponents themselves: the spirit of the
Pelagian heresy may deceive these men so renowned and so
outstanding in the practice of every virtue. It is also fraught
with danger for the simple faithful who revere those persons
highly for their virtue and who believe it is perfectly safe for
them to admit what they hear from those whose lead they follow without questioning.

3. The opinion they hold is as follows: Every man has
sinned in Adam, and no one is reborn and saved by his own
works but by God's grace. Yet, all men without exception are
offered the reconciliation which Christ merited by the mystery of His death, in such manner that whosoever wish to
come to the faith and to receive baptism can be saved.[6] God
has foreknown before the creation of the world who they are
who will accept the faith and with the help of further grace
persevere in it. He has predestined for His kingdom those
who, called without any merit of their own, He foreknew
would be worthy of their election and depart from this life by
a good death.[7] Accordingly, every man is urged by the
teachings of Holy Scripture to believe and to work, and no
one should despair of attaining eternal life, the reward prepared for those who serve God freely. But as to the decree
of God's special call by which He is said to have separated the

elect and the reprobate, either before the creation of the world or at the very creation of the human race,[8] and according to His own good pleasure, so that some are born vessels of honor, others vessels of dishonor,[9] this, they say, takes away from sinners an incentive for conversion and gives the pious occasion for lukewarmness. For both of them, exertion becomes superfluous if neither diligence can save a reprobate nor negligence ruin an elect. Whatever way they behave, nothing can happen to them except what God has decreed. With such doubtful prospects no man can follow a steady course of action, since all pains a man takes one way or another are of no avail if God's predestination has decreed otherwise. To teach that the decree of God anticipates the wills of men is to invite them to cast aside all diligence and give up the effort for virtue; it is, under cover of predestination, to set up a sort of fatal necessity,[10] or to say that the Lord has made men of different natures, if it is true that no one can change his condition of elect or reprobate in which he was created.[11] To put their opinions more briefly and fully: the very objections which in your book *On Admonition and Grace* you took from the ideas of your opponents and proposed to yourself, and the objections of Julian also which in your books against him you relate in this matter and which you answered fully, exactly these our good Christians greet with loud approval. When we show them the writings of Your Holiness which abound in countless unanswerable proofs from Holy Scripture, when we ourselves try, after the pattern of your tracts, to construct some new argument to counter them, they take cover for their obstinacy by appealing to the ancient teaching.[12] The text of the Apostle Paul to the Romans, which you quote to prove that divine grace precedes the merits of the elect,[13] they say was never understood by any of the churchmen in the sense in which you take it now. And when we ask them to explain it themselves according to the meaning given by the authors they prefer, they answer that they have found there nothing which satisfies them, and they ask us not to speak about things whose depth no one is able to fathom. Finally, in their obstinacy they go to such length as to assert that what we teach as being of faith is harmful to the spiritual good of those who come to hear of it; and even if it were true, we should not come out with it, because it does harm to preach what will not be well received, and there is no harm in not speaking of what no one can understand.[14]

4. Some of these people actually fail to keep clear of the Pelagian errors. When they are compelled to admit that the grace of Christ forestalls all merits of men—else, if grace were given for merit, its name would be meaningless—then they say this grace is nothing else than the creation of each individual man. By this grace the Creator endows man with free will and a rational nature without any previous merit of his, for he did not even exist, and so enables him freely to discern between good and evil, to acquire the knowledge of God and to keep His commandments, and thus to come to the grace by which we are reborn in Christ, having by his natural powers asked and sought and knocked. For this reason will he receive and find and enter, because, having made good use of his natural gifts by means of that first grace, he deserved to come to the saving grace of Christ.[15]

The whole meaning of the call of grace they reduce to this: God has decreed not to admit anyone into His kingdom except through the sacrament of regeneration and to call to this gift of salvation all men in general, either by means of the natural law or of the written law or of the preaching of the gospel. Hence, any who so desire can become sons of God.[16] Those who refuse the faith have no excuse, and God's justice is manifested in the loss of the unbelievers. His goodness

shines out in this, that He discards no one from eternal life
but impartially wills all men to be saved and to come to the
knowledge of the truth. And to prove this they quote texts
from Holy Scripture which invite and urge men to willing
obedience. Being free, men either do what they are told or
pay no heed. Accordingly, they conclude, just as it is said of
a sinner that he refused obedience because he did not want to
submit, so also there should be no doubt that when a man
comes to accept the faith he did so because he wanted to.[17]
Every man has equal power for the practice of good and for
evil. The soul of man is in a perfect balance between vice
and virtue.[18] When he chooses what is good, he is helped by
God's grace; when he turns to what is evil, he rightfully
deserves to be condemned.

5. We raise before them the objection drawn from the
countless number of infants who have only original sin, with
which all men are born, sharing as all do in the condemnation
of the first man, and can make no acts of their own wills nor
do any works of their own, yet are treated very differently, not
without a divine decree. When taken away from this world
before they can discern between good and evil, some of them
are through the sacrament of regeneration taken up among
the heirs of the kingdom of heaven, others deprived of baptism go to swell the number of those condemned to eternal
death.[19] To this they answer: These infants are lost or saved
according to what God in His omniscience foresaw they
would have been in their grown-up age, had they lived to be
capable of free action. They do not notice that by saying that
grace only helps but does not anticipate human merits,
they make grace dependent on these very wills of infants
which they agree to say, according to their own idea, are
forestalled by grace. But so much do they subordinate the
divine election to some sort of human merits that, for want of

past merits, they imagine future ones that will never exist. By this novel kind of absurdity of theirs it follows that God would have foreknown what will never happen and that what He has foreknown would never take place.[20]

They fancy they have still a better proof to show that the grace of the divine call operates according to God's foreknowledge of human merits when they come to consider those nations which either in past ages were left *to walk in their own ways*[21] or even now are lost in the ungodliness and ignorance of their ancestors: on these no ray of light whether of the law or of the gospel shines as yet, while among other peoples, where the preachers of the gospel found an open entry and a free way, the people of the Gentiles who *sat in darkness and in the shadow of death hath seen a great light;*[22] *that which was no people is now the people of God;*[23] those *on whom He had no mercy have obtained mercy* now.[24] They explain this difference by saying: the Lord has foreseen who are they that would believe, and He has disposed for each nation the time of sending His preachers at the very moment when He knew it would be well-disposed and conceive the desire of the faith.[25] Nor is this explanation of the divine delays against the Scripture text which says that God *will have all men to be saved and to come to the knowledge of the truth:*[26] there is no excuse for those nations, because they could have come to know and worship the one true God by their natural reason,[27] and if the gospel was not preached to them, it is only because they would not have accepted it.[28]

6. Our Lord Jesus Christ, they hold, has died for the whole of mankind. Not one man is excluded from the redemption which He wrought in His blood, even if he lives his whole life long in complete estrangement from Him. The sacrament of the divine mercy is meant for all men. If many fail to be reborn in baptism, it is because God foreknew

that they had no desire to be reborn.[29]   Accordingly, they say, on God's part eternal life is prepared for all men; but on the part of human freedom those only attain to eternal life who of themselves believe in God and through the merit of their faith obtain the help of grace.[30]

Our opponents and contradictors, who formerly were of a different and better opinion, were led to these ideas about grace above all by the following reason: if they were to confess that grace forestalls all merit and even makes it possible, then they would be compelled to say that there is in God an absolute decree depending only on His will; by a judgment of His which remains hidden from us and whose effects only we know, He makes *one vessel unto honor and another unto dishonor;*[31] for according to the above principle, there is no one who is justified otherwise except through grace, and there is no one who is not born in sin.   But that is exactly what they refuse to concede, and they are afraid of attributing the merits of the faithful to the divine action in them.   They do not admit that the predestined number of the elect can neither increase nor decrease.[32]   For if that were the case, they fear there would be no reason for preachers to exhort infidels to accept the faith or the careless to be diligent, there would be no use in commending Christians to be industrious and make efforts for their salvation—their zeal must all the same be futile if they are not among the elect.   Finally, they say, then only does it make sense to invite a man to better his ways or to make progress in virtue, if he is convinced that he can become better by his own effort and that grace will not fail to help his free will if by himself he chooses to do what God commands.   And so, for those who are old enough to act freely, there are two principles which work unto their salvation, namely, the grace of God and the docility of man; but of these, they say, docility comes before grace.   Thus, they wish us to believe that the beginning of salvation comes from man himself who is saved, not from God who saves,[33] that it is man who by the good use of his will gains for himself the help of grace, that it is not grace which submits to itself the will of man.

7. Knowing well, thanks to the light God's mercy grants us and to the writings of Your Holiness, that this is all very wrong, we can indeed keep steadfast in our refusal to accept this teaching, but we are no match for its supporters, who are men of high standing. They far surpass us by the sanctity of their lives. Some of them are also of higher dignity, having recently been raised to the episcopacy.[34] Apart from a few intrepid lovers of the full doctrine of grace, no one is daring enough to contradict the discourses of men who are so far his superiors. Accordingly, with their advancement in honors the danger also has increased, not only for the people who listen to them, but also for these eminent disputants themselves. Reverence for their episcopal dignity restrains many from speaking when it would all the same be useless, or inclines them to give their assent blindly. And the teachers themselves come to consider as perfectly safe what hardly anyone contradicts.

Since, then, these remainders of the Pelagian heresy[35] nurse a germ of no small virulence; if it is wrong to attribute[36] the beginning of salvation to the will of man; if it is against holy religion to give the will of man precedence over the will of God by saying that it is because man first desired what is good that he is helped by grace, and not that because he was helped by grace he came to desire what is good; if it is wrong to believe that one who is a sinner from his very origin initiates a virtuous life by himself and not through a gift from the supreme Good; if it is true that one cannot please God except by His gifts—then, most holy Bishop, the best of fathers, grant us in the present issue the active help of your fatherly kindness. Deign to explain in as clear and detailed a manner as possible what in these matters is more obscure and more difficult to understand.

8. And first of all, since many people do not think that the Christian faith is at stake in this difference of opinions, please show how great a danger is involved in their position.[37] Then, in what manner free will is not hindered by the grace which precedes its activity and co-operates with it.[38] Further, whether God's foreknowledge depends on His decree, so that we must conceive that what God foreknows is what He has decreed; or whether there are any differences in God's decree and foreknowledge according to the various kinds of their objects and the different classes of persons, in such manner that, because men are not all called to salvation in the same way, in the case of those who are saved without any good works of their own the decree of God appears to exist, so to speak, all by itself, while in the case of those who will be saved by their own good works God's decree may be conceived as dependent on His foreknowledge of those good works. Or must we rather conceive things in the same manner for all and say: although we may not conceive any temporal priority of God's foreknowledge with regard to His decree, yet, in our way of conceiving, His foreknowledge supports His decree according to some priority of nature? And just as nothing of any sort happens which God did not foresee in His pre-science, so also there is nothing good we come to share which did not flow from God as from its source.[39] Finally, explain how, when we teach that this divine decree is the reason why they who are predestined to eternal life come to the faith, we place no obstacle in the way for any one of those to whom we have to preach, nor give some people a pretext for carelessness in the practice of virtue if they come to think they are not of

the predestined.[40]   Also, please, have patience with our
ignorance and explain how to answer the difficulty of those
who say that when they go back to the teachings of the early
writers, they find that all of them unanimously hold the same
opinion, namely, that God's decree and predestination are
based on His foreknowledge. God, they say, made some vessels of honor and others vessels of dishonor because He foresaw in what state each of them would die and foreknew what
each one would, with the help of grace, desire and do.[41]

9.   When you will have explained all these points and expounded many others which your deeper insight in the matter
will show you to pertain to the question, then, we believe and
hope, not only shall we ourselves be strengthened in our
weakness by your explanations,[42] but they also who, however
renowned for the sanctity of their lives and the dignity of
their rank, have in these obscure matters been taken in by
that dangerous opinion will come to embrace the true doctrine
on grace in all its purity. Your Holiness must know that one
of them in particular, of extraordinary standing and zeal for
holy religion, saintly Hilary, Bishop of Arles,[43] is an admirer
and follower of your teaching in every other point of doctrine.
Already before, he wished to write to Your Holiness and explain his views on the particular point he calls into question.
But we do not know whether he will do so or for what purpose. All of us here look for relief in this hard trial to your
great charity and learning, knowing that God's grace and
providence send you to be our help in this present day. We
think it necessary and useful that you write again what you
have written already, lest these men come to take these
opinions of theirs lightly when no one reproves them over and
over again. They believe they are in good health because
they do not feel any hurt; they are unaware of the abcess
hidden under the skin. Let them be made to understand

that when a tumor persists, one must finally decide to have it lanced.

May the grace of God and the peace of our Lord Jesus Christ reward you always and crown your progress from virtue to virtue with eternal glory, most holy lord Bishop, admirable beyond words, revered above all, our most excellent patron!

ANSWERS TO THE EXTRACTS
OF THE GENOESE

To the revered Camille and Theodore, priests, from Prosper.

In the books of Bishop Augustine of saintly memory entitled *On the Predestination of the Saints*,[1] some passages have struck you as being novel and not very clear. You excerpted them from their context and sent them on to my humble self. You wish to know how I understand them and what I think of them—as though I had more light to grasp the meaning of those texts than you![2] Had you not better apply your own minds to this study and, if any difficulty stops you, have recourse to *the Father of lights, from whom every best gift and every perfect gift comes down*,[3] who gives the Spirit of wisdom and understanding? Yet, I shall not refuse my services to your request, and with the help of the Lord, who *gives wisdom to little ones*,[4] I shall briefly expound what I think of these passages in agreement with those of our brethren here outstanding in virtue and learning. But please do not take for pretense of learning what is just compliance with your wishes.

These are the first excerpts you submitted in the very words of the holy Bishop Augustine:

EXCERPT 1

"Jacob I have loved, but Esau I have hated."[5] In the process of my reasoning I was led to say: God, then, did not choose men because of their works which are His own gifts but because of their faith which He foreknew; that is, foreknow-

49

ing who would believe in Him, He chose him and bestowed on him the Holy Spirit to enable him then by his good works to attain to eternal life. I had not yet studied more thoroughly nor yet found out what is the true nature of the election of grace."[6]

Excerpt 2

"I then added: Our faith itself is our doing, but our good works are the gift of Him who bestows the Holy Spirit on those who believe. I would not have said that, had I known already that faith itself is one of the gifts God gives by *the same Spirit*.[7] Both faith and good works are ours because of the free act of our wills, yet both of them were given us with the spirit of faith and charity."[8]

Excerpt 3

"And I said further: We cannot even desire what is good unless God calls us. When after being called we do desire it, our good intentions and actions fall short unless God gives us strength to act according to our faith and leads us to the end where He calls. And I added: It is obvious, then, that when we do what is good, this *is not of him that willeth, nor of him that runneth, but of God that showeth mercy*.[9] All this is correct. But I had not explained sufficiently what is the call itself which is according to God's decree. Not all those who are called, are called in that manner, but only the elect."[10]

Answer to These Three Excerpts

Though these three passages taken out of the tract are less clear, separated as they are from their mediate and immediate context,[11] yet we should understand that the author develops one and the same topic. He speaks of those who said that his ideas were more correct in the first months after his conversion, when he believed that the faith which makes us Christians does not spring from grace or is not a gift of God but comes from man himself and from his free will;[12] but now he was mistaken in asserting that faith itself is also a gift of God and that the Scripture text, *What hast thou that thou hast not received?*[13] applies also to faith; and he was not right in ascribing now to God's decree the election of Jacob[14] which formerly he had attributed to His prescience.

It is this difficulty he answers in the present excerpts: Before he had understood the true doctrine on grace and before he was appointed to govern the Church, he had unwittingly erred by holding that opinion. But at the very beginning of his episcopacy, when consulted by Simplician, Bishop of Milan, of saintly memory, about the election of Jacob and the rejection of Esau,[15] he had studied the whole question of those twins with more care and application. Applying all the power of his mind, he had come to the certain conviction that no human merits precede the election of grace; that faith, which is the beginning of all merit, is a gift of God, else *grace would not be grace*[16] if anything precedes it and is the reason why grace is given; that accordingly the text, *Jacob I have loved*, shows the gift which is bestowed on man, and the other, *but Esau I have hated*,[17] shows what man deserves. This point he had explained carefully in the second book of his *Revisions*.[18] When there he examined all his own views with the severity of a censor, he had precisely rejected the opinion to which his detractors now give the preference—an opinion of which he foresaw, even before the Pelagian heresy had arisen, that it would favor the future error, and which he disowned after he had learned from God the true doctrine on grace. Why, then, should we not approve of this declaration of Augustine in which he corrects his mistake and teaches us after his own example to reform our opinions if we happen through imprudence to have taken to erroneous ones? He shows that it is from God that we receive what we are commanded to ask for in prayer.

Let us just examine the reasonings of the Pelagians. What other point do they try to make except to show that the grace of God is given in answer to our merits, in such manner that while saying that grace is necessary, in the same breath they destroy its reality by making it dependent on the merits of the human will?[19] Men who think that faith is not one of God's gifts fall right into that error.[20] Or they may pretend that they include faith among the gifts of God because they say God created nature and endowed it with reason and freedom, which enable every man freely to believe or not to believe; and with these natural gifts which man received in his very creation without any preceding merits he merits the other divine gifts.[21] People who speak thus do, I suppose, agree with us in saying that the nature of all men was vitiated in the first Adam; they do not refuse to say that in the Fall human nature lost its native strength and, unless this be restored by grace, our nature cannot recover it.[22] But why, then, do they refuse to say of faith alone that it was taken away from our nature, when rather, had not our nature lost faith first, it would not have been deprived of all the other virtues? It was by giving credence to the devil's words that Adam ceased to believe in God. Allowing himself to get drunk with the spirit of pride, he turned his heart away from the Lord when seeking to free himself from the law of justice, and he became the slave of the apostate angel. And so, just as we should not have continence did not *God give it*,[23] nor should we love with a saintly love were not *the charity of God poured forth in our hearts by the Holy Ghost who is given us*,[24] nor finally should we have *wisdom and understanding, counsel and fortitude, knowledge and godli-*

ness, and fear of the Lord[25] did not the Holy Spirit grant these gifts: how could the faith which Adam lost be found in any of his sons unless it be imparted to them by the same Spirit who *worketh all in all?*[26] Accordingly, if the posterity of Adam did not lose what he lost, then his sin only harmed him personally, it did not harm the human race. But *all have sinned in one:*[27] in punishment of Adam's sin the whole race was condemned. Therefore, all have lost what Adam lost. He lost faith in the first place; and if faith is the first gift we all lost, it is also the first gift we have to receive again. Let us, then, hold on to the doctrine of grace which says that faith is a gift of God, and we shall be proof against the deceits of the Pelagian error; for it is in order to prove that grace is due to man that the Pelagians refuse to say that faith is a gift of God.[28]

We see, then, that there is neither justice nor reasonableness in the conduct of these objectors who preferred the imperfect knowledge of the young Augustine to the mature learning which he built up later by constant and steady progress and perfected by long years of study. It may be conceded that his inexperienced views of the first years after his conversion would favor the heretics, more than the truth he came to know during his episcopacy could profit the Catholics. It is, therefore, with good reason that the holy doctor censures severely those who take this false pretext to rest content with opinions which he had abandoned long ago; though they took pains to study the whole of his teaching, they refused to follow him in his progress in the truth.[29]

But let us examine the extracts you took from the following chapters.

EXCERPT 4

"Not because it does not lie within the power of a man's

free will to believe or not to believe, but because the Lord *prepares in the elect the will to believe.*"[30]

ANSWER

Let us also quote what follows on this passage, to clarify Augustine's teaching from the context: "Accordingly, the Scripture text, *For who distinguishes thee? Or what hast thou that thou hast not received?*[31] applies also to faith itself, which involves an act of the will. Many hear the truth preached to them, only some believe, others refuse to believe. The first wish to believe, the second do not. Who does not know this? Who would deny it? But as it is the Lord who prepares the will of some and does not prepare that of others, we must distinguish what is due to His mercy and what to His justice. *That which Israel sought, he hath not obtained; but the election hath obtained it. And the rest have been blinded;*[32] according to the Scripture, *God hath given them the spirit of insensibility, eyes that they should not see, ears that they should not hear, until the present day.*[33] And David says: *Let their table become as a snare before them, and as game, and a recompense, and a stumbling block. Let their eyes be darkened, that they see not; and their back bend thou down always.*[34] There you have both God's mercy and His justice: mercy for the elect who obtained the true justice of God, His just judgment of the others who were blinded. Yet, it is certain, the first believed because they wished to believe, the second failed to believe because they did not wish to believe. Accordingly, both God's mercy and His justice are operative in the very wills of men. The divine election is based on grace, not on merits, according to the words of the Apostle: *Even so, then, at this present time also, there is a remnant according to the election of grace. And if by grace,*

it is not now by works: otherwise grace is no more grace.[35]
And so it is in a gratuitous manner that the elect obtained
what they obtained. Nothing on their part preceded which
they could give to God in order to obtain a reward: *for
nothing He saved them.*[36] But the others who were blinded
received, it is said explicitly, a just punishment. *All the ways
of the Lord are mercy and truth.*[37] *Unsearchable are His
ways.*[38] Unsearchable, then, are both God's mercy, by which
He saves gratuitously, and His truth, by which He condemns
in justice."[39]

What is there in all this to give offense to any God-fearing
and Catholic reader or to raise objection? Is it not true that
the will is prepared by the Lord?[40] Are not *whosoever are
led by the Spirit of God . . . the sons of God?*[41] Is it
nature that makes men different from one another, or is it not
rather grace that differentiates a believer from an unbeliever?[42] Can anyone say he has anything which he has
not received, and glory in it as in his own as though he had
not received it? Is there any doubt that when the gospel is
preached, some people believe of their own free will, while
others of their own free will refuse to believe? But since it is
God who opens the hearts of the first and closes the hearts of
the second, we must distinguish between what comes from
His mercy and what comes from His justice. Augustine first
quoted the view of St. Paul, which the Apostle proves from
texts of the prophets, namely, that the elect obtained through
grace the justice of God which Israel sought and did not
obtain, while the rest were blinded by a just punishment.[43]
Does he then not say with perfect truth: "There you have
both God's mercy and His justice: mercy for the elect who
obtained the true justice of God, His just judgment of the
others who were blinded"? And a little further: "And so
it is in a gratuitous manner that the elect obtained what they

obtained. Nothing on their part preceded which they could give to God in order to obtain a reward: *for nothing He saved them*.[44] But the others who were made blind received, it is said explicitly, a just punishment." Who can find here a pretext for objecting, except the enemies of God's grace who say that, unless what God gives gratuitously may be called a reward, the punishment of sin would be unjust? Further, what he concluded from the prophetic words, *All the ways of the Lord are mercy and truth*,[45] who has ever denied that? Or his comment on St. Paul's words, *Unsearchable are His ways:*[46] "Unsearchable, therefore, are both God's mercy, by which He saves gratuitously, and His truth, by which He condemns in justice"? Men in their senses do not object to all this, nor do they concede that the unsearchable ways of God, that is, the gifts of His mercy and the judgments of His truth, can be sounded by Pelagian pride. According to the Pelagians, who say that for all men God's grace and His punishment alike depend on their merits, God's counsel is no longer a mystery nor are the reasons of the divine decrees a secret.[47]

After this you quoted the following:

Excerpt 5

"Accordingly, faith both in its beginning and in its perfection is a gift of God. No one can doubt, without contradicting the most evident texts of Holy Scripture, that this gift is bestowed on some and is not given to others."[48]

Answer

One who does not admit this, what opinion does he hold but that of the Pelagians: the faith that makes me just, I have of my own; this excellent gift by which *the just man liveth,*[49] I did not receive from God's grace, I possess it by nature? But if faith is not a gift of God, then it is senseless for the Church to pray for unbelievers that they may believe, it is enough to teach them the law, of which yet St. Paul has written: *If justice be by the law, then Christ died in vain;*[50] and the same can be said of nature. It is meaningless for the Apostle to give thanks to God for those who accepted the preaching of the gospel,[51] since, according to the Pelagians, their faith is not a gift of God but a fruit of their own will; meaningless also for him to pray for people that they may have peace and charity:[52] the pride of heretics drives them to say not only of faith but also of peace and charity that men have these virtues of their own. But if these virtues are of human origin, what prevents one from saying that other lesser gifts came from the same source, when he is bold enough to ascribe to men the highest gifts, those without which other virtues, however many and however excellent they may be, can serve no purpose?

There is, then, no valid objection against Augustine's statement: "Accordingly, faith both in its beginning and in its perfection is a gift of God." The Apostle says exactly the same: *By grace you are saved through faith; and not of yourselves, for it is the gift of God; not of works, that no man may glory.*[53] And: *Unto you it is given for Christ, not only to believe in Him, but also to suffer for Him.*[54] And again: *Let us run by patience to the fight proposed to us, looking on Jesus, the author and finisher of our faith.*[55] These and a host of other texts of Holy Scripture show beyond any doubt that, as Augustine stated, "faith both in its beginning and in its perfection is a gift of God. No one can doubt, without contradicting the most evident texts of Holy Scripture, that this gift is bestowed on some and is not given to others." We might be led to think that this is not so if all men did have the faith. But when it is clear that some believe and others do not, and when the Apostle says: *All men have not faith*,[56] who could fail to see that the faith which was given to those who have it was not given to those who are without it?[57]

EXCERPT 6

He further says: "The reason why faith is not given to all men should not disturb any of the faithful who really believe that *from one all men* went *into condemnation*,[58] a punishment which was undoubtedly perfectly just. So much so that, even were no one freed from it, we should have no reason for blaming God. It is clear, then, that it is a very great grace of God if many are saved and acknowledge, when seeing the misfortune of those who are not saved, what would have been their own due, so that *he that glorieth may glory*, not in his own merits, which he sees are no better than those of others who remain in that condemnation, but *in the Lord*.[59] As to the reason why God saves one rather than another, *incomprehensible are His judgments, and unsearchable His ways*.[60] In this matter also we better listen to St. Paul and say with him: *O man, who art thou that repliest against God?*[61] rather than make bold to speak about this mystery, as though we had knowledge of what God, who could not will anything that is not just, wanted to be hidden."[62]

ANSWER

If all this is wrong, then God's judgments are comprehensible and His ways searchable; then it is no longer mysterious why this man is saved in preference to another; and he who is found worthy of the divine election, while others perish through their own fault, will glory in himself rather than in the Lord. And so it will no doubt be in justice that many are damned, but it will not be by grace that many others are saved from damnation.[63] God forbid that this should ever enter Catholic minds! God forbid such ungodliness that we should ever think that anyone *is delivered from the power of darkness and translated into the kingdom of the Son* of God[64] by an adoption which is a reward he deserved and not a pure grace! Adam was lost by a grave sin of his, and all men were lost in him. Eternal perdition is what is owing in Adam to every man who is born from this cursed stem. And just as we have no right to complain because in past ages God left all nations to walk in their own ways,[65] so also we would have no reason for complaint if God even now withholding His grace allowed us to perish together with those whose condition is the same as ours. But as in those times grace saved a few the world over, so in our day it saves us in countless numbers from all parts of mankind, *not according to our works, but according to His own purpose and grace, which was given in Christ Jesus before the times of the world.*[66]

EXCERPT 7

Next you added a text taken from much further: "It lies in the power of the wicked to commit sin, but it does not lie in their power to control the particular effects of their sin, but in the power of God who governs darkness and light and so disposes things that in their very revolt against God's will the wicked fulfil nothing else but the designs of that will."[67]

ANSWER

This passage is so obviously true that I wonder why you

picked it out as though it were obscure, and did not see that its context is of a nature to dispel any indecision of the readers. Consider what follows: "We read in the Acts of the Apostles," he says, "that when the apostles were dismissed by the Jews and came back to their brethren, when *they related all that the chief priests and ancients had done to them, the brethren with one accord lifted their voices to God and said: 'Lord, thou art he that didst make heaven and earth, the sea and all things that are in them; who . . . by the mouth of our father David, thy servant, hast said: Why did the Gentiles rage, and the people meditate vain things? The kings of the earth stood up: and the princes assembled together against the Lord and His Christ?*[68] *For of a truth there assembled together in this city against thy holy child Jesus, whom thou hast anointed, Herod and Pilate, and the people of Israel, to do what thy hand and counsel decreed to be done.'* "[69]   If, then, what the Holy Spirit prophesied by the mouth of David should in no way be understood in another sense than the apostles understood it, if Herod and Pilate and the people of Israel did what God's hand and counsel had foreordained to happen, what difficulty is there in the text of our admirable author?   He says: "It lies within the power of the wicked to commit sin, but it does not lie in their power to control the particular effects of their sin, but in the power of God who governs darkness and light and so disposes things that in their very revolt against God's will the wicked fulfil nothing else but the designs of that will."   It is easy for the wicked to conceive an evil design, and it is beyond doubt that God's power so keeps their evil will within certain limits that they are unable to get what they covet without God's permission.   No one ever so little instructed in religious doctrine but knows that God's wisdom and justice make use even of the evil works they do with an evil intention to achieve His own designs and decrees,[70] when he sees that the most merciful will of God the Father who *did not spare even His own Son, but delivered Him up for us all,*[71] was carried out by the wicked will of the traitor Judas and of the Jews, and when he reads in the Gospel that when Pilate said to Jesus: *Speakest thou not to me? Knowest thou not that I have power to crucify thee, and I have power to release thee?*[72] our Lord answered: *Thou shouldst not have any power against me, unless it were given thee from above.*[73]

Accordingly, God governs light and darkness. Darkness is not without guilt because God makes use of it for a good purpose and disposes that even the works of darkness should result in the good of the sons of light, allowing the wickedness of men bent on doing them harm to the exact extent that He knows it will be helpful to chastise or to test His saints. And so, even when they go against God's will, they yet fulfil that very will.

Follows then an extract from Book 2.[74]

EXCERPT 8

"Will anyone make bold to say that God did not foreknow to whom He would give to believe and whom He would give to His Son that He should not lose any one of them?"[75] But if He did foreknow this, then certainly He also foreknew by what gifts He would deign to work our salvation. That exactly and nothing else is the predestination of the saints, namely, the foreknowledge and the preparation of the gifts by which He saves infallibly all those who are saved. As to the others, where else are they left, by a just decree of God, than among the mass of the reprobate among whom were left the men of Tyre and Sidon, who could have believed if they had been given to witness the miracles of Christ,[76] but because they were not given to come to the faith, they were not given either the means that would have led them to the faith."[77]

Answer

Those who refuse to admit this show clearly that they think that faith is not a gift of God, that grace does not precede but follows free will, that God's grace is given in answer to our merits. For if they agree to say that grace is a gift of God to man, and that man receives it only because of his faith which itself he did not receive as a gift, then faith contains a merit and what is given for it is rendered as a reward, not granted as a gift. Those who hold this view must logically say that the predestined for eternal life are they whom God foreknew would come to the faith of their own free will, that the predestination of the saints is only a recompense, that it is not God who produces faith in those who are predestined according to the decree of Him who works all things, that finally men cannot have any merits of their own if it is God that works in them everything.[78] Of a truth, those who hold such opinions have not received the faith, or have lost the faith they had received and follow the proud error of the Pelagians: they glory in themselves, not in the Lord who *worketh all in all*,[79] that is, of course, all good things, not the evil ones; and if all good things, then certainly faith also, *without which no one can please God*[80] and which is the foundation of all virtues. But what sort of foundation is it if, though it is God who constructs the building and *unless the Lord build the house, they labor in vain that build it*,[81] they yet refuse to say that the foundation is part of the building, or they wish to start themselves the building which the Lord should raise further? For then the Son of God is not for them the beginning of salvation, nor will they be established on the very cornerstone, Christ Jesus, nor do the words apply to them, *The sure foundation of God standeth firm;*[82] for they construct their entire system of election on shifting sand and fleeting dust.

Let us, then, follow true wisdom and godliness and confess that God in His unchanging prescience has foreknown to whom He would give to believe or whom He would give to His Son that He might lose no one of them,[83] and that, if He foreknew this, He also foreknew by what gifts He would deign to work our salvation; that the predestination of the saints is nothing else but the foreknowledge and the preparation of God's grace by which He saves them without fail. As to all the others who are not saved nor rescued by grace from the universal fall of the human race, let us acknowledge that it is by a just decree of God that they are not delivered. And let us learn from the misfortune of the reprobate, of whose damnation we have no right to complain, what is the guilt we ourselves have been forgiven.[84] For *there is no iniquity with God,*[85] nor does anyone under so just a judge ever perish without guilt. For as Augustine, our eminent doctor of grace, says in another of his works: "God renders evil for evil because He is just, and good for evil because He is good, and good for good because He is both just and good; but evil for good He never returns, because He is not unjust. He renders evil for evil, that is, punishment for guilt; good for evil, that is, grace for guilt; good for good, that is, grace for grace."[86] When we know that some are reprobate, we should not hesitate to attribute their reprobation to their own fault, though, of course, God could have saved them in His mercy had He been pleased to do so. When we see that others are saved, we should not make bold to say that they were worthy of salvation, since of course God could have condemned them

in justice had He so chosen.   But the reason why He does
not save all or saves some in preference to others, there is no
need for us to inquire, nor is it possible for us to find out.
Without considering the reason of that discrimination, it
should be enough for us to know that mercy does not do away
with justice, nor justice with mercy, in Him who condemns
no one except in justice and saves no one except through
mercy.[87]

As for the people of Tyre and Sidon, what else can we say
than that they were not given to have the faith?   The Lord,
Truth Itself, says of them that they would have believed if
they had been given to see the miracles that had been
wrought in other towns which remained in unbelief.[88]   Why
they were refused that gift, let our cavilers say if they can;
let them explain why the Lord worked miracles before people
who would not profit by them and did not work them before
others who would have profited.   We on our part, though
we cannot fathom the reason of God's action nor the depth of
His decree, yet know for certain that what He has said is true
and what He has done is right, that not only the people of
Tyre and Sidon but those also of Corozain and Bethsaida[89]
could have been converted and have come from unbelief to
faith had God been pleased to work this change in their
hearts.   No one can suspect of falsehood what Truth itself
says: *No man can come to me, unless it be given him by my
Father.*[90]   And: *To you it is given to know the mysteries of
the kingdom of heaven, but to them it is not given.*[91]   And:
*No one knoweth the Father but the Son and he to whom it
shall please the Son to reveal Him.*[92]   And: *As the Father
raiseth from the dead . . . so the Son also giveth life to
whom He will.*[93]   And: *No man can say "the Lord Jesus"
but by the Holy Ghost.*[94]

Instructed by these texts of Holy Scripture, let us give thanks to God, who has granted us the spirit of faith and virtue, of continence and charity, of wisdom and understanding, of counsel and fortitude, of knowledge and godliness, and of His fear. Had not He who *worketh all in all*[95] given us these, we should not have any of them, we should be sitting in darkness and in the shadow of death together with them who knew not God or *when they knew Him, have not glorified Him as God or given thanks,* but ascribing that knowledge to their own wisdom, became fools; *their hearts darkened, they became vain in their thoughts.*[96] Yet, even in that miserable state we should not be justified in complaining of this punishment nor in giving excuses for this ignorance, nor should we find any remedy for it in our fallen nature.

Let us now examine the following extract.

EXCERPT 9

"According to your letter, some object that an admonition to the congregation of the faithful would fail to arouse them to action if one were to address them in the following terms: By a decree of God's will it was settled in the divine predestination that some of you came over from unbelief to faith, having been given the docility to submit to the faith, and that by the gift of perseverance you remain constant in the faith. Those of you who continue to live and to find pleasure in sin, if you did not forsake your sins so far, it is because the help of God's merciful grace did not withdraw you from them as yet. However, those of you who have not yet been called, if you are predestined by God's grace to be among the elect, you will receive the same grace, which will make you desire what is good and place you among the elect. Those of you who now live in submission to the faith, if you are predestined to be of the reprobate, the help of grace which gives you strength to obey God's law will be taken from you and you will cease to live in obedience."[97]

Answer

I am amazed that your Christian sense was unable to make you distinguish the objections of Augustine's slanderers from the teaching of that defender of grace: you attribute the words of those who disparage his teaching to the very man who is refuting them! For some people objected against the teaching of our Catholic doctor in a manner as wicked as it is futile: if one explains the doctrine on divine grace, they said, so as to make people believe that they cannot have faith or submissiveness or the other virtues and perseverance in them except through a gift of God, then one is logically led to preach to the people in terms similar to those quoted above and by such scandalous speech to withdraw from their free wills every incentive for virtue.[98] That is why the holy doctor, having come to know this objection from the letter of those whom he answers, says: "According to your letter, some object"; and further: "When they say this." You could have noticed from these words that it is not he who says what follows them, but they of whom he said: "According to your letter, some object," and: "When they say this." Just as St. Paul says: *As some affirm that we say, let us do evil that there may come good.*[99]

When you read further in his book what he writes to answer those charges more fully, you can see more clearly still how he never spoke in such a strain and how much he disapproved of that parody of instruction. He changes, corrects, improves the method of preaching on predestination so as to make the sermon bearable to the audience. He tones down what is true, suppresses what is false, and after a long development adds: "As to what follows immediately on those words, I wonder whether anyone among the congregation of the faithful who is still weak in the faith could without being scandalized bear to be told: 'Those of you who now live in submission to the faith, if you are predestined to be of the reprobate, the help of grace which gives you strength to obey God's law will be taken from you and you will cease to live in obedience.' To speak in that strain, is it anything else but to curse people or somehow to prophesy evil?"[100]   And after that, when showing how to preach to the people on these truths, he expresses what is his own idea in these words: "The way of preaching on predestination which we have just explained is, when one has to preach to the people, still incomplete, I think.   One should still add something like this: You, then, must hope you will obtain from *the Father of lights, from whom every best gift and every perfect gift comes down,*[101] perseverance in obeying His law, and ask Him this in your daily prayers; and meanwhile trust that you are not excluded from the number of the predestined who are His people, because it is He Himself who gives you the grace to make this prayer. God forbid that you should despair of your salvation, for you are commanded to place your hope in Him, not in yourselves. *Cursed be the man that trusteth in man.*[102] And: *It is good to confide in the Lord, rather than to have confidence in man;*[103] for blessed are they all who trust in Him. Firm in that hope, *Serve ye the Lord with fear, and rejoice unto Him with trembling.*[104] For as long as this earthly life lasts which is a continuous trial, no one can be sure of eternal life, which God who is faithful promised from all eternity to the sons of the promise. But the Father to whom we pray every day, *Lead us not into temptation,*[105] will grant us to persevere faithful in His service till our last breath."[106]

Do you please see now what a difference there is between this manner of preaching and the parody concocted by our malicious objectors, who tried to twist, by their farfetched and tricky phrases, what Augustine had said in a correct manner? Rightly does our doctor say in this connection: "A physician who is a fraud or a muff prescribes even the right medicine in a manner that renders it either useless or harmful."[107] And again he writes of a similar travesty of preaching: "This may be perfectly true, certainly, but it is most improper, most unsuitable, most uncongruous. Though stating nothing that is false, this sort of sermon does not present its topic in the proper way, as is suited to the weakness of fallen men."[108] No need, then, to account for a discourse which we have shown is not of Augustine but of other people and which he disapproved of definitely, keeping to what is true and rejecting what is false. For though he never spoke to the Christian people in such a foolish manner and abhorred the clumsy elucubrations of his detractors, yet he always maintained with piety and firmness alike that it is necessary to preach to the Church both about predestination which is the preparation of grace and about grace which is the effect of predestination, and also about the prescience of God who foreknew from all eternity on whom He would bestow the gifts of His grace. Whosoever opposes the preaching of this doctrine is an open supporter of the Pelagian heresy.[109]

As to your last extract,[110] that should have been joined to the eighth, in which the people of Tyre and Sidon are mentioned. In Augustine's book it also follows immediately on that text; no other topic comes between. Accordingly, the answer I gave to that excerpt should also be sufficient for this. Nothing in it is obscure for one who holds on to the truth of the teaching of the faith on predestination and divine grace, which is the source of all good works and of perseverance in virtue.

ON GRACE AND FREE WILL,
AGAINST CASSIAN THE LECTURER[1]

CHAPTER 1

1. Some people make bold to say that Bishop Augustine, of saintly memory, did not defend the doctrine on divine grace, our Christian hallmark, in the right way; and constantly and without restraint they attack and slander the books he wrote against the Pelagian heresy.[2] Perhaps we should scorn the malevolent clamors they raise within the Church, as we scorn the endless barking of the heretics without.[3] But while they are of the fold, they favor the wolves who have been cast out of the Lord's fold, and they are of such standing that both their position in the Church and their talents command consideration. Because they put on an appearance of piety which their inner conviction belies, they attract a number of the uneducated and confuse the minds of people who are unable to discern error from truth. Thus, they effectually bring the Church to a dangerous situation: by asserting that our doctors defended the doctrine on grace in the wrong way, they create the opinion that the condemnation of the enemies of grace was unjust. We should, therefore, not overlook this evil, which started from hidden and tiny seeds and is growing every day, spreading far and wide. We must endeavor, with the help of the Lord, to disclose the hypocrisy of these deceitful slanderers. The very magnitude of their attack, directed in one doctor against all pontiffs and especially those of the Apostolic See,[4] inclines the unlearned and incautious to consider them as men of outstanding learning. Having through their assurance won respect for them-

selves, they unfortunately do harm by making people believe
their lies too readily. For because of the esteem in which
they are held, people think it could not be dulness of mind or
rashness of judgment that led them to voice so loud a protest;
people rather think they must have worked very cleverly and
very hard to penetrate the teaching of so subtle a doctor and,
after a stricter scrutiny and a more attentive examination, to
detect things which before had been overlooked because of
unsuspecting sympathy and uncritical benevolence.

2. Why, then, this new zeal for a strict scrutiny? Why
that severity, that supercilious and somber look in the crafty
inquisitor bent on evaluating every idea, weighing every
phrase, counting every syllable? Whence his assumption
that he is doing a great thing if he can fasten on a Catholic
doctor the label of heresy? As though he were attacking
some unknown book hitherto hidden! Is he not rather tear-
ing to pieces by his biting attacks the very teaching that
shattered the system of the new heretics and burst the swollen
pride of the Pelagian heresy?

It is now twenty years and more[5] that the Catholic army
led by Augustine has been fighting and defeating the enemies
of God's grace. Defeating, I say, for it grants no respite to
the conquered; the unanimous verdict of all the bishops confirmed their overthrow.[6] Chased from their sees and excommunicated,[7] they indeed may complain that we are the happy
victors and sharpen their tongues against us—they who preferred their error to communion with the Church. But why
must those who are one body with us and with us share in
the grace of Christ call into question the very weapons that
defended our common faith? Why must they start anew a
war that was finished? Why weaken the bulwark of a safe
and lasting peace? Are they sorry for our victory, and do
they feel sympathy for the defeated? Are they so insolent

as to defend the heresy and out of sheer jealousy attack both our writers and our judges?[8] Those new censors apparently have a more exacting criterion of their own: Do they mean to hold none of the condemned errors and yet to reject some points of the truth we defended? Then, without impairing the peace won by the Catholic victory and with due regard for the irreformable council decrees, we are prepared to hear the advocates of a more correct doctrine and to consider their teachings, which, they say, are freed from all errors and drawn up with perfect precision. Let us, then, expound the findings of these new geniuses!

CHAPTER 2

1. We have no desire to conceal the learning of the learned or to give the impression that our quarrel is only with sayings of common people or of talkers richer in words than knowledge. For that reason we shall limit our inquiry to the statements of one who is admittedly more competent than any other in the knowledge of Holy Scripture.[9] Another reason for taking his statements as the object of our discussion is their very definiteness. For they exist in writing and their author himself had them published. We need not inquire after their authenticity; we need only explain their meaning.

In a book entitled *On the Protection of God*[10] a certain priest who surpasses all the inmates of his monastery in the art of discussion introduces an abbot discoursing on divine grace and free will. The writer clearly shows that he approves and makes his own the abbot's teaching. So, we need not deal with the abbot, who would perchance say these opinions are not his or explain what seems wrong in them, but with the writer, who deliberately proposes a teaching that cannot but be a tool in the hands of the enemies of God's grace.

2. True, in the beginning of the conference his teaching is not at variance with the true doctrine, and it would deserve just praises did it not later fall into error and stray from its initial correctness. For after proposing the comparison of the farmer as an example of one who lives in grace and faith, he says of him that his labor would be vain but for the constant help of God. Then he makes a statement that is perfectly Catholic: "From this it is clear that the beginning not only of good works but also of good thoughts comes from God; He it is who inspires in us the beginning of a saintly will and gives us the power and the means to carry out our good desires. For *Every best gift and every perfect gift is from above, coming down from the Father of lights.*[11] He it is who initiates in us whatever is good and carries it out and brings it to its completion. As St. Paul says: *And He that ministereth seed to the sower will both give you bread to eat and will multiply your seed and increase the growth of the fruits of your justice.*"[12] Lest someone should think the free will has nothing left to do, he with good reason proves that God's gifts do not take away but rather strengthen free will, unless it chooses to go back to its sins and to turn away from God's help. He says: "But it is up to us humbly to follow grace, which draws us every day; else, as Scripture says, if we with stiff necks and uncircumcised ears[13] resist grace, we deserve to hear the words of Jeremias: *Shall not he that falleth rise again? Why, then, is this people in Jerusalem turned away with stubborn revolting? They have hardened their necks and would not return.*"[14] Again further, after saying that every effort for virtue is in need of God's grace, he adds these commendable words: "Just as we are unable to desire all these

things without a divine inspiration, so also can we in no way
carry them out without His help."[15]

3.   In chapter 7 he intends to show that the grace of
Christ is universal and does not pass by a single man; it does
not even forsake those who rebel and resist. He says: "The
divine protection follows us without intermittence. So great
is the loving-kindness of the Creator for His creatures that
His providence at all times not only accompanies them but
also leads the way."[16]   We note here that he says, God's
providence accompanies us, in the sense that generally He
does not forsake even those who forsake Him, or that He
follows up all those whom He first sets going. But he goes on
to say: "When God sees in us some beginning of a good will,
He gives it light and strength and directs it to salvation.
Thus He gives increase to what either He Himself planted or
what He saw had sprung from our own effort."[17]   Here he
can still say that he meant to speak of the origin of the good
will whose beginnings God Himself gives or inspires, because
we can understand that it is from hearts already illumined by
grace that these salutary efforts proceed; and so these good
efforts can be called man's own because he received only the
power to make them, and only their seeds must be attributed
to their Creator.[18]

4.   But in chapter 9 he still continues in these words:
"Therefore, it is not easy for human reason to see in what
manner the Lord gives to those who ask, is found by those
who seek, opens to those who knock; and again is found by
those who do not seek Him, shows Himself openly to those
who did not look for Him; how *All the day long He spreads
His hands to a people that believeth not and contradicteth;*[19]
how He calls people who resist and are far from Him, how He
draws them to salvation unwilling; how He withdraws from
people intent on sin the means of carrying out their design;

how in His kindness He stands in the way of those who rush
headlong into sin."[20] It is here that, apropos of a discrimination which we do not understand,[21] he introduces his proposition which says: Many there are who come to grace without
the help of grace and who have the desire of asking and seeking and knocking because of the alertness of their own free
wills; yet, the same free wills in other people are said to be so
blinded in their aversion from God that no sermon can call
them back unless they be drawn and guided by the power of
God. As though all of the many effects of divine grace in
the souls of men did not precisely mean that it makes them
willing from unwilling! Or as though anyone who has the
use of reason could come to the faith in any other way than
voluntarily! And so, it is no less absurd to say that someone
may strive to have a share in divine grace against his own
will than to assert that anyone comes to it without an impulse
of the Spirit of God.

5. Too soon, then, did our disputant lose sight of his first
proposition, too soon did he with fickle lightheadedness
depart from his own right opinion. He had stated the principle: "The beginning not only of good works but also of good
thoughts comes from God."[22] And lest this should be understood in the sense of an external teaching,[23] he was careful to
add: "God it is who inspires in us the beginning of a saintly
will and gives us the power and means to carry out our good
desires. For *Every best gift and every perfect gift is from
above, coming down from the Father of lights.*[24] He it is who
initiates in us whatever is good and carries it out and leads it
to completion."[25] Catholic doctor, why do you abandon the
doctrine you yourself professed? Why do you draw away
from the serene light of truth and lose yourself in the smoky
darkness of error? Why do you not attribute what you
marvel at in those who ask and seek and knock to the same

grace which they desire? You see their good efforts and holy dispositions, and you doubt they are God's gifts? The work of grace in them could remain hidden as long as interior faith was locked within the secret of their thoughts. But when you notice their humble prayer, their careful seeking, their repeated knocking, why do you not understand from the very nature of these facts that it is grace that caused them?

CHAPTER 3

1. You think you are bewaring sufficiently of the Pelagian errors if you grant us for a fraction only of the elect what should be held of all of them. But by so doing you fully agree neither with the heretics nor with the Catholics. The first held that in all good works of men the initiative belongs to the free will; we believe that the beginning even of good thoughts always comes from God. You have invented some hybrid third system, disagreeing with both parties, and so you neither find approval with our enemies nor keep in one mind with us. Moreover, how do you not see that, when you assert that men themselves take the initiative of their good works and because of that are given grace, you fall into an error that was condemned and willy-nilly appear to say that "the grace of God is given in answer to our merits"?[26] For you cannot say that the faith of those who ask and the devotion of those who seek and the perseverance of those who knock are not meritorious, especially since all these people are said to receive and to find and to enter. And in this matter it is vain or rather ungodly to admit that any merits would exist before grace; for then what the Lord said: *No man can come to me, except the Father, who hath sent me, draw him,*[27] would no longer be perfectly true. Our Lord would not have said this, if we were allowed to believe that someone can be converted

without a divine illumination or if man's will could of itself strive after God without God. God it is who draws to His Son those whom He calls; He does not compel them by force against their will, but He makes them willing from unwilling and by all sorts of ways overcomes the resistance of their unbelief. When the desire of submitting to God has been born in their hearts, those who hear Him rise up with the very will which first kept them down; they learn with the same mind which first was ignorant; they trust with the same heart which first felt diffident; they desire good with the same will which first was unwilling. For *The Lord will give goodness, and our earth shall yield her fruit.*[28]

But let us see what follows: "But who could easily understand how the whole of our salvation is attributed to the free will, of which Scripture says: *If you be willing and will hearken to me, you shall eat the good things of the land;*[29] and how yet *It is not of him that willeth or of him that runneth, but of God that showeth mercy?*[30] How also reconcile this: *God will render to every man according to his works,*[31] with *It is God who worketh in you both to will and to accomplish, according to His good will,*[32] or with *that not of yourselves, for it is the gift of God; not of works, that no man may glory?*"[33] And he goes on collecting texts from Scripture which appear mutually contradictory, in order to set face to face the gifts of grace and the efforts of human activity. Thus he can divide mankind into two classes: those whom the grace of God saves, and those whom the law and nature make just. The law can forbid what is evil, it cannot free from evil. It makes known the command, it does not give the willingness to submit, unless the very law which killeth through the command of the letter become life-giving through the spirit of grace.[34]

2. After these quotations he concludes as follows: "All

these texts show both the grace of God and the freedom of our wills; they show that sometimes man can conceive the desire of virtue of his own accord but that at all times he is in need of the help of the Lord."[35]   What has become of the correct proposition he first stated: "The beginning not only of good works but also of good thoughts comes from God, who starts in us what is good and carries it out and brings it to completion"?[36]   Look, although here you do say that the help of God is necessary for the good works which men have begun, yet you attribute to the unaided freedom of their wills, without the grace of God, the initiative of what is good and the desire of virtue.   And so you say that, though good and salutary endeavors cannot make progress unless helped by God, they can begin without a divine inspiration.

CHAPTER 4

1.   Further, the more clearly to determine what men derive from their free wills and what they receive from grace, you add: "For one does not enjoy good health by a mere wish nor is one freed from sickness by a mere desire."[37]   So you teach that men cannot indeed gain good health of themselves, but of themselves they can desire it; of their own accord they can come to the doctor, it is not the doctor who causes them to come.   As though the soul itself were not ill but, being healthy, looked only for a cure of the body!   But it is the whole man who by the soul and with the soul has fallen into an abyss of misery.   Until man receives from his Physician the very knowledge of his unhappy state, his soul delights in its misery, ever enamored of its errors and embracing falsehood for truth.   The beginning of its cure lies in its conceiving dissatisfaction with itself and hatred of its inherited weakness.   The next step is its desiring to get cured and knowing who it

is that can cure it. Though all these acts are previous to its
cure, yet it is He who will cure the soul that inspired them.
Else, since they cannot arise in the soul without producing
their effect, the soul would seem to have been cured by its
own merit and not by grace.[38]

2. You further add: "In order to see more clearly that at
times the beginning of the good will arises from the gifts of
nature bestowed by the liberality of the Creator—a beginning, however, that cannot reach the perfection of virtue
without the guidance of God's grace—we should listen to St.
Paul, who says: *For to will is present with me; but to accomplish that which is good, I find not.*"[39] According to this
statement, you were wrong when you said before: "The
beginning not only of good works but also of good thoughts
comes from God, who starts in us what is good and carries it
out and brings it to its completion."[40] But no, you were not.
Your first proposition was not wrong in any way. And you
should not have come with another, opposed statement. You
were right in declaring that our salvation originates in grace,
but now you assert that it comes from the gifts of nature and
from free will. True, the Apostle said: *For to will is present
with me; but to accomplish that which is good, I find not.*[41]
But he also said: *Not that we are sufficient to think anything
of ourselves, as of ourselves; but our sufficiency is from God.*[42]
And still: *For it is God who worketh in you, both to will and
to accomplish, according to His good will.*[43] St. Paul certainly does not contradict himself. He means to say that,
when we have received the gift of desiring what is good, we
are not at once able to do it but must ask and desire and knock
and be given to do it by Him who inspired the desire. For
these words, *For to will is present with me; but to accomplish
that which is good, I find not,*[44] are the words of one who was
called and given grace already; of one who is delighted with

the law of God according to the inward man, but sees another law in his members fighting against the law of his mind and captivating him in the law of sin;[45] of one who, although he has been taught to will the right thing, yet does not find in himself the strength to do what he desires—not until, by virtue of a good will he has been given, he deserves to obtain the strength he is looking for, the strength to practice the virtues.

Chapter 5

1.   After this you accumulate many texts to prove that free will is now strong, now weak.   You seem to say that there are some people who achieve by their own strength what others cannot do without the help of God, or that man is given a command for another purpose than to make him look for divine help.   And you draw the conclusion: "These sayings are somehow mixed and confused if we do not make a distinction.   Hence there arises the problem, which of the two depends on the other, namely, whether God shows us His mercy because we offered Him the beginning of a good will, or rather because God showed us mercy we are given the beginning of a good will.   There are many people who hold only the one or the other of these alternatives and, making it say more than it should, get entangled in various and mutually opposed errors."[46]   But see, you think you have disentangled the confusion, you have solved the riddle.   You say there are two mutually opposed errors in which they get entangled who do not know what to attribute to free will and what to grace.   In the first you put those who say God shows us mercy because we of ourselves offered Him the beginning of a good will; you have in mind, no doubt, the followers of the Pelagian doctrine, who say that grace is given in answer to

our merits.[47] In the other you place those who say that the beginning of a good will comes from God's mercy; you have in mind those who have defeated the enemies of grace. But if it is an error to attribute to man the beginning of a good will without the help of grace, and if it is also an error to confess that the will is prepared by the Lord, what then must we say to avoid both?

2. You say: "If we keep both alternatives, we avoid error."[48] But thus you lead us into two errors, and what you conceive and condemn as two falsehoods when taken separately, you legitimate when taken together. On that rule and principle you can preach that both they are mistaken who say one should deceive at all times and those who say one should never do so, but that in order to avoid both kinds of sin one should follow both rules: one need not always avoid falsehood, nor always neglect to tell the truth.[49] This opinion of yours is altogether mistaken. Two evils put together cannot make one good thing, nor can two vices produce one virtue, nor two falsehoods make one truth. Things of the same quality do not decrease but rather increase that quality when put together. Accordingly, it is not right to blame those who hold that the beginning of a good will is produced by the inspiration of God's grace for the very same reason by which you refute those who think that free will is self-sufficient for that beginning and is not in need of the help of grace. For the Church has condemned one of these two statements and upheld the other. The alliance between the two which your new system advocates does not reconcile them in any way; it unduly presents the Catholic position as wrong and the Pelagian one as correct.

3. "Many," you say, "hold only one or the other of these alternatives and, making it say more than it should, get entangled in various and mutually opposed errors."[50] You

wish, therefore, to condemn the Catholics together with the heretics, the victors together with the vanquished, and to brand as heretics the very men who cast heresy out of the Church. For according to your censure, when you say that God's grace is not in all men the principle of a holy will to believe but only in some (as though you did great honor to divine grace by granting this much!), Pope Innocent, most worthy of the See of Peter, erred when he said, speaking of those who pride themselves on their free wills: "What else can we believe to be right in the opinions of men who think that they owe their goodness to themselves?"[51] Or again, when writing of the fall of the first man, he states: "In times past, when Adam was put to the test in the use of his free will, he used this gift inconsiderately and fell into the abyss of sin. He could find no way to raise himself again. Forever deluded by his own freedom, he would have remained crushed down by his fall had not Christ come and raised him up by His grace."[52] The Oriental bishops also erred who, when sitting in judgment over Pelagius, compelled him outwardly at least to appear as a Catholic and to anathematize those who say that grace is given in answer to our merits.[53] The African Councils also erred when they stated in their decrees that both the knowledge of our duty and the desire of doing it are gifts of God.[54] And so, when charity edifies, knowledge cannot puff up;[55] just as it is written of God: *He that teacheth man knowledge,*[56] so is it also written: *Charity is of God.*[57] The two hundred and fourteen bishops[58] erred who, in the letter prefacing their decrees, addressed St. Zosimus, Pontiff of the Apostolic See, in these words: "We have decreed that the judgment passed upon Pelagius and Celestius by Pope Innocent from the See of St. Peter should stand till they profess openly that the grace of God given us through our Lord Jesus Christ helps us in every one of our actions, not only to know but also to do what is right. Without that grace we are unable to obtain or think or say or do anything that is really holy and salutary."[59] Even the Holy See of St. Peter erred when through the mouth of Pope Zosimus it spoke to the whole world: "We on our part, by a divine inspiration— for every good gift must be referred to its Author—committed the whole question to the conscience of our brethren and fellow bishops."[60] And the African bishops who answered Pope Zosimus also erred when they praised him for the soundness of his decision and wrote: "As to what you wrote in the letter you sent to all the provinces, namely, 'We on our part by a divine inspiration—for every good gift must be referred to its Author—committed the whole question to the conscience of our brethren and fellow bishops,' we understood this to signify that you, as it were, with the naked sword of truth quickly struck down the men who exalt the freedom of man's will to the detriment of God's grace. For what else did you ever do with greater freedom than to commit the whole question to the conscience of our humble selves? And yet, in your faith and wisdom you understood that you had done so by a divine inspiration: you said so in truth and trust. Your reason for saying so was of course that *the will is prepared by the Lord*,[61] and that He Himself with fatherly inspirations moves the hearts of His sons to do what is good. For *whosoever are led by the Spirit of God, they are the sons of God*.[62] And so, we are convinced that our free wills are not set aside, and yet we have no doubt that in each and every good action of our human wills His grace is the more powerful agent."[63]

Do you see how your principles are shattered by these irreformable decrees, and how the miserable patchwork full of cracks which you insert into the edifice of the faith has tumbled down as did the walls of Jericho at the sounding of the priests' trumpets?[64]

CHAPTER 6

For, at the time of the controversy between Catholics and Pelagians about the origin of the good will and the beginnings of faith and charity, the dispute was settled and ended with our decisive and clean victory. We should, then, no longer speak of the altogether wrong alliance which you propose between the two doctrines. The enemy army was defeated, the war is over; we have conquered through the help of Him who *has shown might in His arm, has scattered the proud in the deceit of their hearts, has put down the mighty from their seat and has exalted the humble, has filled the hungry with good things and sent the rich away empty;*[65] of Him who, *performing mercy to our fathers, remembered His holy testament, the oath, which He swore to Abraham our father that He would grant us: that being delivered from the hand of our enemies, we may serve Him without fear in holiness and justice before Him all our days;*[66] of Him from whom *we have received, not the spirit of the world, but the Spirit that is of God, that we may know the things that are given us from God.*[67] Why do you endeavor to gather broken weapons from the quibbles of the Pelagian argumentations that were shattered? Why do you stir the ashes of a dead doctrine and so try to rekindle the flame in a dying smoke? The grace of God does not endanger free will nor take away its volition when it produces in the will a good desire.[68] For if our wills were no longer ours when they are perfected and ruled and guided and animated by grace, then we should have to say that the sons of God *who are led by the Spirit of God*[69] are deprived of their freedom; that they to whom is given *the spirit of wisdom and understanding, counsel and fortitude, knowledge and piety and fear of the Lord,*[70] lose the power of their rational souls and no longer deserve the praises due to free service. Certainly, in men who think that they are not in need of being remade by grace, the inherited disease of sin has turned to madness: they refuse the remedy, they shout and rage and resist; but, if they happen to be of the sons of the promise,[71] they will calm down and get cured.

Chapter 7

1. Let us see now what other proofs are offered by our modest disputant, who, in order to dispel one vice by another and to correct one error by another, by a new art of his own combined mutually contrary statements. To make this concoction of his acceptable to unsuspecting people, he sought to color his mixture with some examples. He said: "If we say that we have the initiative of our good will, where was that initiative in Paul the persecutor or in Matthew the tax collector? They were drawn to salvation, while they were intent, the first on shedding blood and torturing innocent people, the other on doing violence and robbing. If, on the other hand, we were to say that the grace of God at all times originates the good will, what shall we say of the faith of Zacchaeus? What of the devotion of the crucified thief? They by their own desire forced their way into the heavenly kingdom and did not wait for a special and express call."[72]

2. From the different ways in which virtue begins in different men, our disputant attempts to prove that some people are able to do of their own free will, without the help of God, what others cannot do without God's assistance. This should be understood, he means, from the fact that some are slow to

answer the divine call, while others consent more readily. As though when a hardened unbeliever suddenly submits to God and accepts the gospel which he opposed for a long time, then it is the right hand of the Most High that works the change in this man;[73] but when a willing listener gives his consent after a quiet exhortation or just a few words without hesitation or distrust, then the merit of his conversion would have to be attributed to his free will alone! Would, then, the powerful grace of God draw to the Son those only whom it has first censured loudly or laid low by punishment or struck with terror, and not exert any of its power on the minds of men who run after the promises of the Redeemer with living hope and keen desire? But the eternal Truth says: *No man comes to me except the Father who hath sent me draw him.*[74] If, then, no one comes to the Son unless he be drawn, then all men who in any way whatever come to Him were drawn by the Father. Men are drawn to God by the contemplation of creatures and of the beautiful order of the entire creation. For *the invisible things of Him, from the creation of the world, are clearly seen, being understood by the things that are made.*[75] They are drawn by hearing the account of past events, their hearts set aflame by listening to those who *declare the praises of the Lord, and His powers, and His wonders, which He hath done.*[76] They are drawn by fear, for *The fear of the Lord is the beginning of wisdom.*[77] They are drawn by joy, because *I rejoiced at the things that were said to me: We shall go into the house of the Lord.*[78] They are drawn by desire, for *my soul longeth and fainteth for the courts of the Lord.*[79] They are drawn by delight, for *How sweet are thy words to my palate! More than honey to my mouth!*[80] And who could grasp and express the inner affections by which the visit of divine grace brings souls to pursue what they fled, love what they hated, hunger for what they loathed, and in a sudden and marvelous transformation what was closed is opened, what was burdensome becomes light, what was bitter, sweet, what was obscure, clear? *But all these things one and the same Spirit worketh, dividing to everyone according as He will.*[81] For *God, who commanded the light to shine out of darkness, hath shined in our hearts, to give light of knowledge of the glory of God, in the face of Christ Jesus,*[82] that is, for the revelation of His Son, who is in the glory of the Father.

3.   He, then, who illumined the heart of Matthew when a publican, and of Paul when he was persecuting the Church, is the same who sent light into the hearts of Zacchaeus and the thief crucified with the Lord.   Unless, perhaps, you say that the words of our Lord were ineffective when He deigned to address Zacchaeus, who *sought to see Jesus, who He was,* and said: *Zacchaeus, make haste and come down; for this day I must abide in your house;*[83] and that He did not prepare his soul for His coming when He chose the hospitality of his house.   Lastly, when the Pharisees murmured against our Lord because He had gone to stay with a public sinner, and when Zacchaeus, moved already to repentance and giving away half of his possessions to the poor, promised to restore fourfold his dishonest gains, our Lord said: *This day is salvation come to this house, because he also is a son of Abraham.*[84] And so as not to leave hidden what was the cause of his salvation, He added: *For the Son of man is come to seek and to save that which was lost.*[85]   Thus, while learning that Zacchaeus was saved, we also come to know for certain that he had first been sought out by the Saviour.

In the case of the justification of the thief, even if we did not perceive any indication that grace was at work in him, are we not given to understand that he also, like all the faithful, had been drawn by grace, when the Lord says: *All things are delivered unto me by my Father,*[86] and *I, when I shall be lifted up, will draw all things to myself?*[87]   Moreover, the thief's own confession shows that in *all things* he also was included and that he also was entrusted or drawn to Christ. He who before had been blaspheming Jesus Christ was suddenly converted and said: *Lord, remember me when thou hast come into thy kingdom.*[88]   From where arose in this man this new confession so different from his former speech? Let St. Paul tell us: *No man speaking by the Spirit of God saith anathema to Jesus. And no man can say the Lord Jesus but by the Holy Ghost.*[89]   We should have no doubt, therefore, that in the free behavior of one and the same man, his former blasphemies sprang from his own nature and his faith from the Holy Spirit.   In vain, then, did our dialectician try to explain by that new theory of his the inscrutable diversity of one and the same grace and to convince us that among the justified one section come to Christ at the sole prompting of their own wills, another section are drawn in spite of their reluctance and compelled against their wills.   It is God *who worketh all in all,*[90] whether He pleases to draw some one way and some in another; but no one comes to Him unless drawn in some manner.

CHAPTER 8

1.   He further quotes examples from sacred history to prove that we must attribute to grace the observance of the commandments and the perfection of virtue.[91]   We also admit this most readily.   He recalls the examples of Balaam, whom God caused to pronounce a blessing on Israel when he was intent on pronouncing a curse;[92] of Abimelech, whom He prevented from sinning against Rebecca;[93] of Joseph, sold by his brothers, whose evil design God turned unto good.[94]

Then he comes back to the proof of his theory, and though he says he keeps both free will and grace, yet from one section of mankind he as far as depends on him takes away free will and in another he admits it. He says: "These two, namely, grace and free will, seem to be opposed to each other; in reality, they go together; that we must admit both, we conclude from the very nature of a devout life. Were we to deny man either of the two, we should appear to abandon the faith of the Church."[95]

2. The faith of the Church is, according to St. Paul's preaching: *No man can say the Lord Jesus but by the Holy Ghost.*[96] The faith of the Church is: *What hast thou that thou hast not received? And if thou hast received, why dost thou glory, as if thou hadst not received it?*[97] The faith of the Church is: *By the grace of God I am what I am, and His grace in me hath not been void, but I have labored more abundantly than all they; yet, not I but the grace of God with me;*[98] and: *Having obtained mercy, to be faithful.*[99] The faith of the Church is: *But we have this treasure in earthen vessels, that the excellency may be of the power of God and not of us.*[100] The faith of the Church is: *By grace you are saved through faith, and that not of yourselves, for it is the gift of God.*[101] The faith of the Church is: *And in nothing be ye terrified by the adversaries, which to them is a cause of perdition, but to you of salvation, and this is from God; for to you it is given for Christ, not only to believe in Him, but also to suffer for Him.*[102] The faith of the Church is: *With fear and trembling work out your salvation. For it is God who worketh in you both to will and to accomplish according to His good will.*[103] The faith of the Church is: *Not that we are sufficient to think anything of ourselves, but our sufficiency is from God.*[104] The Lord Himself sanctions this rule of faith when He says: *No man can come to me,*

unless it be given him by my Father;[105] and: *All that the Father giveth me shall come to me;*[106] and: *Without me you can do nothing;*[107] and: *You have not chosen me, but I have chosen you;*[108] and: *No one knoweth the Son but the Father, neither doth anyone know the Father but the Son and he to whom it shall please the Son to reveal Him;*[109] and: *As the Father raiseth up from the dead and giveth life, so the Son also giveth life to whom He will;*[110] and: *Blessed art thou, Simon Bar-Jona, because flesh and blood hath not revealed it to thee, but my Father who is in heaven.*[111]

3. According to this Catholic faith, grace deprives no one of his free will, because the effect of grace on the wills of men is not to suppress their freedom but to make them good from evil and believing from unbelieving, to change their congenital darkness into light in the Lord,[112] to revive what was dead, raise up what lay prostrate, find what was lost. We believe that the grace of the Saviour effects this in all men without a single exception, in all who *are delivered from the power of darkness and translated into the kingdom of the Son of the love of God.*[113] For we also say and teach what Cassian stated correctly but did not adhere to faithfully: "The beginning not only of good works but also of good thoughts comes from God; He it is who inspires in us the beginning of a saintly will and gives us the power and the chance to carry out our good desires. For *Every best gift and every perfect gift is from above, coming down from the Father of lights.*[114] He it is who initiates in us whatever is good and carries it out and brings it to completion."[115] If he had kept firmly to this opinion, he would not stray from the faith of the Church, nor would he be both opposed to free will and ungrateful for the grace of God. When he says it is grace that was operative in Paul and Matthew, and free will in Zacchaeus and the good thief, he fails to see that he did away with free will in the first and with grace in the second.

CHAPTER 9

1. He goes further: "For when God sees us turn to a desire of virtue, He comes to us, guides and strengthens us. For *At the voice of thy cry, as soon as He shall hear, He will answer thee;*[116] and He Himself says: *Call upon me in the day of trouble; I will deliver thee, and thou shalt glorify me.*"[117] Who fails to see that this teaching attributes to free will a merit which precedes grace, and says that grace is servant to free will, renders what is due, and does not confer a gift? This statement was condemned in the synod of the bishops of Palestine and anathematized by Pelagius himself.[118] For we profess and believe that when a man conceives a good desire and wishes to withdraw from sin and error, it is the grace of God that causes this. For *With the Lord shall the steps of men be directed, and he shall like well his way;*[119] and *Every way of man seemeth right to himself, but the Lord weigheth the hearts;*[120] and *The steps of man are guided by the Lord, but who is the man that can understand his own way?*[121] And as the Apostle says: *For you have not received the spirit of bondage again in fear, but you have received the spirit of adoption of sons, whereby we cry: Abba, Father.*[122]

2. After this he goes on to say: "We must not believe that God created man in such a state that he would never desire nor do what is good. Else we should have to say that He did not give man free will, if He enabled him only to wish and to do what is evil but not to wish and to do what is good. And what becomes of the word the Lord said after the first man's transgression: *Behold, Adam is become like one of us, know-*

ing good and evil?[123]   For we should not fancy that before his
sin Adam had no knowledge whatever of what is good; else
we should have to say that he was fashioned like an animal
without reason and intelligence; and this is rather absurd
and altogether incompatible with the Catholic faith.   Nay
rather, according to the saying of the wise Solomon, *God made
man right,*[124] that is, so that he should only and always live by
the knowledge of what is good.   But they themselves *have
entangled themselves with an infinity of questions.*[125]   For
they became, as was said, *knowing good and evil.*[126]   And so,
after his sin Adam acquired the knowledge of evil, which he
did not have before, but he did not lose the knowledge of
what is good, which he had been given."[127]

   3.   It is not right to doubt that the first man, in whom the
nature of all men was created, was created by God in righteousness and without any blemish; that he had received a free
will by which, if he himself did not forsake God and His
help, he was able to persevere in the happy condition in
which he was created, because he willed it so; and that as a
reward of his free perseverance he could reach a state of
happiness in which he would neither wish nor be able to fall
into evil.[128]   But of his own free will, by which he remained
virtuous as long as he wished, he strayed from the commandment of God, nor did he fear the punishment of death with
which he had been threatened; he turned away from God, to
follow the devil; he rebelled against God who guarded him, to
submit to his enemy who gave him death.   "Adam then was,
and we all were in him; Adam perished, and we all perished
in him."[129]   This saying of St. Ambrose is true, as is no less
true what Truth Itself said: *For the Son of man is come to
seek and save that which was lost.*[130]   For in the universal
disaster of the Fall, human nature lost neither its substance
nor its free will, but the splendor and beauty of the virtues of

which it was stripped when deceived by the envy of the devil. Having lost then the means of attaining to everlasting and inamissible incorruption of body and soul, what else was left to our nature but what pertains to this temporal life, which is only a life of punishment and misery? For that reason the children of Adam must be reborn in Christ, lest anyone remain in the natural state, which is a fallen state. Were the descendants of Adam to practice by nature the virtues which Adam possessed before his sin, then they would not be *by nature children of wrath*,[131] they would not *be darkness*,[132] nor *under the power of darkness*;[133] in a word, they would not be in need of the grace of the Saviour, because, having the very gifts for whose loss our first parents deserved to be driven from Paradise, their natural goodness would not remain idle nor would they be deprived of their just reward. But now that no one can escape from eternal death without the sacrament of regeneration, does not the uniqueness of the remedy show clearly the very depth of evil in which the nature of all mankind has sunk because of the sin of the one in whom all have sinned[134] and lost all that he lost? He first lost faith, he lost temperance, he lost charity; he was stripped of wisdom and understanding; he was without counsel or fortitude; by aspiring after higher things against the will of God, he fell from the knowledge of truth and from loving obedience to God; not even fear was left him, by which he could have kept back from the forbidden thing for fear of the punishment, when he would not refrain from it for love of justice. When, then, the first man of his own free will, that is, out of a natural desire to do what he pleased, grew weary of the gifts he had received for use and ceased to appreciate the endowments of his happy state, he made the insane resolve to make the experience of sin: he drank the poison of all vices and steeped the whole of human nature in his own sinful in-

temperance. That is why now, until man is cured of that
deadly poison by eating the flesh of the Son of God and drink-
ing His blood,[135] his memory is weak, his judgment erring,
his step staggering; nor is he at all capable of choosing and
desiring the good gifts which he cast off of his own free will.
The case is different for the Fall and for its restoration: man
could fall without being driven on by God, he cannot rise up
again unless God raises him.

4.   Accordingly, it was not correct to say: "We should not
think that God created man in such a state that he would
never desire nor do what is good."[136] As though we said that
God created this weakness in men and not rather that man
incurred it as a punishment of sin. He, therefore, who thinks
that to admit that free will was blinded logically leads to
attributing this blindness to the Author of nature, intends to
suggest that free will is as sound in the children of Adam as it
was in Adam himself before his fall. We think this is inconsistent with the Catholic faith. For what is it that was
injured by sin if not free will, from which sin took its origin?
Unless, perchance, you say that only a penalty passes over
from Adam to his posterity, not a guilt. But this is absolutely
false, and perhaps for that reason you do not say so. For it is
all too blasphemous to conceive the justice of God in such a
manner as though He would condemn the innocent and the
guilty alike. Obviously, then, there must be guilt where
there is punishment; those who share in the punishment must
also have shared in the sin. And so, human misery does not
stem from the act of the Creator, it is the punishment decreed
by the divine Judge.[137]

5.   For what Cassian further says to prove the soundness
of our free wills is absurd and goes against the common teaching of all our writers. He said: "And what becomes of the
word the Lord said after the first man's transgression: *Behold,*

Adam is become like one of us, knowing good and evil?"[138]
As though the devil's promise had come true, and Adam by
transgressing God's commandment had grown in likeness
with God! As though God's word meant that it was He who
had bestowed on Adam that greater likeness, when rather
that word signifies what Adam failed to obtain when he followed the path of pride and so lost the Godlikeness he possessed by coveting a likeness he had not been given! No less
sophistical is the conclusion our author draws from this
reasoning when he says: "Adam, then, after his sin acquired
the knowledge of evil, which he did not have before, but he
did not lose the knowledge of what is good, which he had
been given."[139]   Adam had the knowledge of what is good
while he faithfully kept the good and holy commandment of
God; he remained in the state of justice while he kept the
likeness with his Creator and did not neglect His law. But
after he sold himself, the image and temple of his Creator, to
the seducer, he lost the knowledge of what is good, because
he lost a good conscience. Then iniquity drove out justice,
pride destroyed humility, greed shattered temperance, unbelief robbed him of faith, slavery took away his freedom.
No remainder of virtue could stay in a nature where such a
host of vices had made irruption. For *No one can serve two
masters;*[140] and *Whoever committeth sin is the servant of
sin;*[141] and *By whom a man is overcome, of the same also he is
the slave.*[142] But no one is a slave without keeping some freedom, just as no one is free without some sort of servitude;
as St. Paul says: *For when you were servants of sin, you were
free men to justice; what fruit had you then in those things of
which you are now ashamed? For the end of them is death.
But now being made free from sin, and become servants of
God, you have your fruit unto sanctification, and the end life
everlasting.*[143]   He, then, who is a slave of the devil is free

from the claims of God; but he who is freed from sin and becomes a servant of God is free from the claims of the devil. Hence, it is clear that man could have an evil freedom through his own fault, but he could not be given freedom for virtue without the help of his Saviour.

CHAPTER 10

1.   But our doctor, to keep us from believing that the misfortune of the first man is passed on to his posterity,[144] attempts to prove from the example of the Gentiles how sound natural judgment is in all men. He adds: "Lastly, that mankind did not lose after the transgression of Adam the knowledge of what is good, is stated clearly in the words of St. Paul: *For when the Gentiles, who have not the law, do by nature those things that are of the law, those having not the law are a law unto themselves; who show the work of the law written in their hearts, their conscience bearing witness to them, and their thoughts between themselves accusing or also defending one another, in the day when God shall judge the secrets of all men.*[145]

2.   If the Gentiles of whom St. Paul speaks are those who are called to the faith from the uncircumcision, and though *they were far off, are made nigh,*[146] who believed in Him who now shows them mercy when formerly He did not,[147] in Him who, justifying *circumcision by faith and uncircumcision through faith,*[148] established the two peoples of the Jews and the Gentiles in Himself and, breaking down the wall of enmity,[149] made peace between them in one new Man, *concluding all under sin, that the promise by the faith of Jesus Christ be given to them that believe;*[150] if, I say, St. Paul speaks of the Gentiles in whose hearts God with His finger, that is, with the Holy Spirit, writes the new covenant that they may fulfil the entire law and the works of charity by nature, namely, by a reformed and renewed nature:[151] then, what argument can the new and proud doctrine draw from these texts, since we must attribute the reconciliation of these enemies of God to no other cause than the grace of the Mediator? *For all have sinned and do need the glory of God, being freely justified by His grace.*[152] Grace, therefore, is the glory of God, it is not merited by him who is liberated. For *who hath first given to Him, and recompense shall be made him?*[153] Men who are dead can do no good works, nor can infidels do the works of justice. Their salvation is entirely gratuitous, and for that reason it is the glory of God, that he who glories may glory in Him whose glory he was in need of.

3. But if (according to the meaning our disputant prefers) these texts refer to the Gentiles who, having no share in the grace of Christ, of their own judgment made regulations after the likeness of the precepts of the law,[154] because they understood that there was no other way to uphold morality in cities and union among peoples except by conferring rewards on the virtuous and punishments on malefactors, according to the words of the Wisdom of God: *I came out of the mouth of the Most High, and I have held first place among every race; I have sought rest in Jacob and have found it,*[155] then could one doubt that this wisdom is still with mankind for the benefit of this temporal life, a remnant left from the nature God had created? For if the native power of the rational soul were not even capable of ruling the things of the earth, it would mean that its nature is not only vitiated but extinct. Yet, though human nature may boast of the best arts and of all branches of human learning, it cannot be made just of itself, because of itself it uses its good gifts wrongly, and without the worship of the true God it cannot in that use keep free from impiety and uncleanness. What it considers

as its defense is its condemnation.[156]   When St. Paul declares
that *from the works of the law no flesh shall be justified,*[157]
and when *in Christ neither circumcision availeth anything,
nor uncircumcision, but the new creature,*[158] how does our
author say that the unbelieving free will of infidels is endowed with divine gifts by nature and can be justified by
these powers of its own?   How does he declare that the unaided knowledge of sinful nature is apt to make a new man
of the smitten old man?   As though that knowledge, whether
acquired by what remains of our natural gifts or found in the
study of the sciences of the law, could by itself make us love
and do what we know to be our duty; or as though there
could be any good act of our wills that is not aroused by an
inspiration of the charity which is poured forth in us by the
Holy Spirit![159]   For *Without faith it is impossible to please
God;*[160] and *All that is not of faith is sin;*[161] and *In Christ
Jesus neither circumcision availeth anything, nor uncircumcision, but faith that worketh by charity.*[162]

Chapter 11

1.   The author thereafter quotes many texts to prove that
those whom the prophets rebuke for being deaf and blind[163]
could by the power of their nature open their ears to listen
and their eyes to see.   As though the Lord did not say of these
same people: *And I will give them another heart, and I will
give them a new spirit; and I will take away the stony heart
out of their flesh, and will give them a heart of flesh, that
they may walk in my commandments, and keep my judgments, and do them.*[164]   At the end he reasons: "Finally, to
point out to his listeners that they are able to do what is good,
the Lord rebuked them and said: *And why even of yourselves do you not judge that which is just?*[165]   He would not

have said this had He not known that they are able by their natural reason to see what is right."[166] Now he attributes to free will not only the knowledge of what is good but also the power to do it; as though the Lord could require of men understanding of their duty and fulfilment of good works only on the supposition that they are able to produce these by their own natural powers without any help of God! Actually, those commands are given to man to teach him, from the very precept which imposes on him what he had been given, that he has lost the gift through his own fault; that it is not right to say that God's command is unjust only because man is unable to render what he owes; that he should from the letter that killeth have recourse to the spirit that quickeneth,[167] and seek in grace a power which he does not find in nature. If he does so, it is a great mercy of God; if he neglects to do so, it is a just punishment of his sin.

2. Then, to crown this discussion, he lays down a general principle in these words: "We must beware, then, referring all merits of the saints to God in such manner as to ascribe to human nature nothing but what is evil and disorderly."[168] Could a disciple of Pelagius or of Celestius say anything more clearly and more explicitly in keeping with their heresy? These heretics say that "grace is given in answer to our merits";[169] they also say that "grace is not given us for every individual good act."[170] Our man expresses this twofold blasphemy in one sentence when he says: "We must beware referring all merits of the saints to God in such manner as to ascribe to human nature nothing but what is evil and disorderly." He means to say, then, that there are many merits of men which are their own and are no gifts of divine grace, merits that have a claim to some heavenly gifts which must go to increase the rich gifts of nature. He means to say that we do not receive grace for every individual good act and need

not therefore pray for help in every good work. Hence, it follows that we must believe that it is not the gifts of God which are the principle of merit, since a man whom God would always help for every one of his actions would have no merit;[171] or if we say there is some merit even with the gifts God grants, yet it should be clear that one could have gained it even by one's own power. The reason, then, why we must be helped by God for some good works is that grace should make easier what we were able already to do by nature.[172] There you have in a few brief words not only two but a whole string of statements against the faith which, if you were to scrutinize them closely, you would find are not different from another series, that of the condemned heresy.[173]

Chapter 12

1. But lest one think that we act on suspicion and pry into the hidden intentions of the author beyond what his words say, let us see whether his further text adds anything new to what we know already. In the beginning of his tract he had said: "The beginning not only of our good actions but also of our good thoughts comes from God. He it is who inspires in us the beginning of a saintly will and gives us the power and the means to carry out our good desires."[174] But now, with the intention of showing that pious thoughts and holy counsels can spring from natural wisdom without any divine inspiration, he quotes the words of Solomon: *And David my father would have built a house to the name of the Lord, the God of Israel. And the Lord said to David my father: Whereas thou hast thought in thy heart to build a house to my name, thou hast done well in having this same thing in mind. Nevertheless, thou shalt not build me a house.*[175] Then, to show the meaning of this text, our author

reasons: "What shall we say of this thought and this intention of David's: that it was good and came from God, or that
it was evil and came from himself? If it was good and came
from God, why did He who inspired it not allow it to be
carried out? And if it was evil and came from man, why did
the Lord praise it? It remains, therefore, that we should
believe both that it was good and that it came from man.
And in the same manner we must also judge of our own
thoughts of every day. For it is not possible that David was
the only man to whom it was given to conceive good thoughts
by himself and that it is not given to us ever to be able by
nature to understand or to conceive what is good."[176]

2. From this text and this reasoning it is not proved in
any way that pious thoughts spring from the unaided free
will and not from a divine inspiration. For one should not
say that David's intention, which was certainly good, did not
come from God for the sole reason that the Lord did not want
that it should be he who built Him a temple but his son.[177]
We must examine, therefore, from what spirit this good desire
of David's sprang. It came from the spirit which made him
say: *If I shall enter into the tabernacle of my house; if I shall
go up into the bed wherein I lie; if I shall give sleep to my
eyes, or slumber to my eyelids, or rest to my temples: until I
find out a place for the Lord, a tabernacle for the God of
Jacob.*[178] When the prophet David expressed this desire, he
well knew that the true and perfect temple was to be built by
Him who, being the Son of God, became also the Son of
David; who, when seeing the temple erected by Solomon,
said: *Destroy this temple, and in three days I will raise it up.
But He spoke of the temple of His body.*[179] It was, therefore,
in order to prefigure the temple that was prepared in Christ
and the Church, that for the construction of the first temple
not David but the son of David was chosen. The son of man,

that is, of David, represents Him who is Son of God and man. The material temple prefigures the indestructible tabernacle. It is for the sake of this prefiguration that God approved of David's intention but entrusted its execution to his son, who was better fit to prefigure the Son of David. And so it was God who both inspired David with this intention and entrusted its execution to Solomon.[180]

3. To make this clearer from examples, let us look for other cases in which God did not want the execution of the good intentions which men conceived through His inspiration. Our Lord commanded the apostles: *Going, therefore, teach ye all nations, baptizing them in the name of the Father, and of the Son, and of the Holy Ghost, teaching them to observe all things whatsoever I have commanded you.*[181] When the apostles heard this, they beyond doubt heard more than the mere material sounds of the words which struck the ears of their bodies; in their hearts, by the power of the living word, an unquenchable flame of charity was kindled which inspired them with a burning desire of preaching the gospel of Christ to all nations. Yet, when later they were forbidden to preach the word of the gospel in Asia, when at their attempt to go into Bithynia they were not allowed to do so by the Spirit of Jesus,[182] shall we say that God had not inspired their desire of converting to the faith those people also whom God in His hidden judgment did not yet want to hear the gospel preached? Or that the Church, when praying every day for her enemies, that is, for those who have not yet accepted divine faith, is not guided by the Spirit of God? Who would say so except one who himself neglects these prayers, or does not believe that faith is a gift of God? Yet, the Church does not obtain for all what she asks for all. Nor is there any injustice in God, who often omits to grant to men what He inspired them to ask.

4. Accordingly, of a good will, that is, of attachment to God's will, we must not say that it is not man's, and yet say that man conceives it by a divine inspiration. For since *none is good but God alone*,[183] what sort of good can it be that does not come from the Author who alone is good? It is true, human nature, whose Creator is God, kept even after the Fall its substance, form, life, intelligence, reason, and the other good gifts of body and soul; even the wicked and vicious are not without these. But by these powers nature does not attain to what is truly good; they can give decency to this temporal life but are unable to lead to eternal life.[184] For it is well known how all the philosophers of Greece, the orators of Rome, the savants of the entire world, with all their keen study and their excellent minds, with all their labor, achieved nothing else in their search for the supreme Good than that *they became vain in their thoughts, and their foolish heart was darkened*,[185] because they took their own wisdom for guide in their search for truth. When, then, someone, ashamed of following these wretched vanities and those deceitful illusions, comes to understand that what he took for light and life is nothing but darkness and death, then his conversion does not come from himself, though it does not happen without his co-operation. Nor is it of his own strength that he succeeds in attaining to this beginning of salvation. It is the hidden and powerful grace of God that wrought this change. This grace, sweeping aside the embers of worldly opinions and dead works, rekindles the dead log of his heart and sets it aflame with the desire of the truth; it does not bring man into subjection against his will but makes him desirous of that subjection; it does not draw him without his knowledge but shows him and leads the way. For his free will, which still exists, created as it was by God together with his human nature, does not of itself withdraw from the vain

desires to which he turned when he neglected the law of God; it is the Creator that works this change. And so, the whole cure of fallen man is effected neither without his co-operation nor by anyone else than by his Physician.[186] For we are His new creature and new handiwork, *created in Christ Jesus in good works, which God hath prepared that we should walk in them.*[187]

CHAPTER 13

1. Let us see now what our author is really after. "We may not doubt," he says, "that every soul of its nature possesses the seeds of the virtues that were planted there by a favor of the Creator. But unless they be stirred to life by God's assistance, they will never grow and reach perfection, because, according to St. Paul, *Neither he that planteth is anything nor he that watereth, but God that giveth the increase.*[188] But it is clearly said in the book called the *Shepherd* that man can freely choose what he pleases.[189] There we read that each one of us has two angels, one good and one bad, who never leave him; but that it lies in man's own choice which of the two he will follow. And in that sense man always keeps his free will: he can either neglect or find his delight in the grace of God."[190]

If it is certain that "every soul of its nature possesses the seeds of the virtues planted there by a favor of the Creator," then we must say that Adam alone sinned and no one else sinned in his sin; that we were not conceived in iniquities nor did our mothers bring us forth in sins;[191] that we were not by nature children of wrath,[192] nor were we under the power of darkness;[193] rather, since by nature we possessed the virtues, we were born sons of peace and light. God forbid that a teaching so false and so dangerous ever make its way into the hearts of the faithful! Virtue and vice cannot live together. For St. Paul says: *What participation hath justice with injustice? Or what fellowship hath light with darkness?*[194] The virtue par excellence is God Himself, for whom it is one and the same thing to possess virtue and to be virtue. When we become partakers of this virtue, then Christ, who is *the power of God and the wisdom of God,*[195] dwells in us; and with Him dwell in us faith, hope, charity, continence, understanding, counsel, fortitude, and the other virtues. But when we draw away from the supreme Good, all the opposite vices spring up in us from our own nature. For when beauty withdraws, what else takes its place but ugliness? When wisdom departs, what remains but foolishness? When justice ceases to reign, what will rule but injustice?

2. Therefore, the seeds of the virtues planted in the soul by a favor of the Creator were thrown out by the sin of the first man. No one can recover them unless He who gave them the first time restores them again. For human nature can be remade by its Maker, it can receive again the good gifts it once possessed, it can through the Mediator of God and men, the man Christ Jesus,[196] recover the gifts which it lost by using those which it kept. It still kept a rational soul, which is not itself virtue but a dwelling place for virtue. By sharing in wisdom and justice and mercy, we become, not wisdom and justice and mercy, but wise and just and merciful. And although our rational soul is full of vices and through sin the unclean spirit took possession of the temple of God, yet those virtues can be restored to the rational soul by Him who *casts out the Prince of the World,*[197] who *binds the strong man and seizes his vessels,*[198] who puts to flight the spirit of this world and gives the Spirit that is from God *that we may know the things that are given us from God.*[199] But he who has not the Spirit of Christ, he is none of His.[200]

3. I think our author was deceived by a semblance of truth and led astray by the glitter of false virtues. He believes that the virtues which man cannot have unless God give them are found also in the souls of unbelievers, because actually a number of them do practice justice, temperance, chastity, kindness; and they possess these virtues neither to no purpose nor without reward: they gain from them much honor and glory for the present life.[201] But because in their good actions they do not serve God but the devil, though they may reap from them a temporal reward of human praise, they remain far from the true virtues that lead to eternal happiness. And so it is clear that there can be no true virtues in the souls of infidels, but all their works are unclean and stained, because their wisdom is not spiritual but animal, not heavenly but earthly, not Christian but devilish, not from the Father of lights but from the Prince of Darkness, since the gifts which they could obtain from no one but from God they offer in homage to the devil, who was the first to turn away from God.[202]

4. When, then, our author says that by nature, without any intervention of grace, every soul possesses the seeds of the virtues, what else does he mean except that from those seeds spring some sprouts of merit which precede the grace of God? But to give the impression that he attributes something to the grace of God, he says: "But unless they be stirred to life by God's assistance, they will never grow and reach perfection."[203] By this assistance of God he intends nothing else but exhortation and instruction,[204] while it is the soul, rich with the seeds of the virtues, that makes use of the power it possesses; it is in need of help only to reach the heights of the virtues, of which it is aware it has of itself the beginnings. Consequently, according to him, the human soul will become a temple of God but without having for its foundation the one

than which no man can lay another, which is Christ Jesus.[205]
For when is this foundation begun if not when faith arises in
the heart of one who hears the preaching of the gospel? If
faith was there by nature, then there was no question of a
beginning but of a superstructure. And it was wrong to call
unbeliever one who had the faith before he believed. The
same can be said of the beginnings of the other virtues: grace
must only increase them, since they exist already; it need not
give them as though they were not there.

But very different is what the texts of Holy Scripture teach!
There we read that *the beginning of wisdom is the fear of the
Lord;*[206] and we also read that this fear is a gift of God.[207]
The fear of God, the text says, *hath set itself above all things.
Blessed is the man to whom it is given to have the fear of
God.*[208] If, then, the fear of God is the beginning of wisdom,
what virtue can one have without wisdom, which takes its
beginning in the gift of fear?[209] The Apostle St. Peter says:
*Grace to you and peace be accomplished in the knowledge of
God, and of Christ Jesus our Lord, who hath given us all
things of His divine power which appertain to life and godliness.*[210] Does he say "who has stirred to life the seeds of the
virtues which we found planted in us by nature"? No, he
says: *who hath given us all things which appertain to life and
godliness.* When he says this, of which virtue does he mean
to say that the beginning is in nature and has not been given
by Him who gave them all? That is why St. Paul also says:
*For what hast thou that thou hast not received? And if thou
hast received, why dost thou glory as if thou hadst not
received?*[211]

5. Therefore, all that pertains to a life of godliness we
receive not from nature, which fell in Adam, but from grace,
which heals nature.[212] Nor should we think that the beginnings of the virtues lie in our natural gifts, because we see

many praiseworthy qualities also among the natural gifts of infidels. Those praiseworthy actions do indeed originate in nature, but they cannot be true virtues, because their authors are far from God, who created their nature.[213]   For only what is in the light is lit up, and what is without light is dark night. For *the wisdom of this world is foolishness with God.*[214] Thus, what looks like virtue is vice, just as what looks like wisdom is foolishness. And when will it come to pass that people who boast of these natural seeds of the virtues, so exalted by our author, bow down with these virtues of theirs and expect their increase from the practice of a doctrine which says: *If any man among you seem to be wise, let him become a fool that he may be wise,*[215] and: *Seeing that in the wisdom of God the world by wisdom knew not God, it pleased God, by the foolishness of our preaching, to save them that believe?*[216]   What could those people, so proud of their knowledge and wisdom, consider more foolish and more ridiculous than this? Only the Spirit of God can bend their proud arrogance and by the power of His grace shatter the reasonings in which like mad dogs they bark against the truth which they do not know. Then only will the field of their hearts be well ploughed and ready to receive the seed of the word and be able to produce fruits worthy of the eternal granaries.

6.   Our author also quoted a text, of no value, from the book of the *Shepherd* for the purpose of proving that every man, placed between the influences of the good and the bad angel, is so left to his natural reason and his own discretion that he need no more expect help from God than fear danger from the devil.[217]   He then adds his own comment and principle: "And in that sense man always keeps his free will: he can either neglect or find his delight in the grace of God."[218]   In this sentence, already the phrase "man always

keeps his free will" is not true for a section of mankind. Many thousands of infants, who are taken into the kingdom of God or excluded from it, either receive or are deprived of God's grace without any act of their free wills.[219] And a number of insane people, deprived of every use of reason, are through the sacrament of regeneration freed from the fetters of eternal death. But let us take it that he meant his proposition properly to refer to those only who have the use of their free wills. Is that freedom so free that of itself it feels as much delight in and love for the grace of God as distaste and indifference for the same grace?[220] If so, then there was no need of any breeze from the warm south to thaw the thick ice of its ancient unbelief: the benumbed and sluggish soul would get warm again of itself. When the Lord says: *I came to cast fire on earth*,[221] shall we believe that no spark of His divine fire touches a cold heart, but that its dead ashes burst into the flames of charity of themselves? Have those lovers of grace[222] felt nothing similar to what the disciples felt who said: *Was not our heart burning within us while we were with Him on the way, and He opened to us the Scriptures?*[223] Or nothing similar to the experience of Lydia, the purple seller from the town of Thyatira, who, we are told, among the women to whom St. Paul was preaching, was the only one to believe and *whose heart, it is said, the Lord opened to attend to those things which were said by Paul?*[224] So great, according to our author, is the soundness and power of free will that men can acquire even charity, which is the highest of all the virtues, not through a favor of God but of their own doing.[225] What, then, in the soul remains to be remade by its Maker? Or by which gift of grace can He beautify a soul which possesses already of itself the virtues that must render His gifts fruitful? But the Apostle, who declares that without charity neither working of miracles nor knowledge nor faith nor prophecy nor distribution of one's wealth nor even endurance of the most cruel torments can bring any profit,[226] does not leave us in the dark about the origin of charity. He says: *Because the charity of God is poured forth in our hearts by the Holy Ghost, who is given us;*[227] and elsewhere: *Peace be to the brethren, and charity with faith, from God the Father and the Lord Jesus Christ.*[228]   Let the Apostle St. John also teach us how we come to share in this excellent gift: *Dearly beloved,* he says, *let us love one another, for charity is of God.*[229]   And lest we fancy that he calls love a gift of God, only because God planted its seed in the very creation of man's nature, he adds a little further: *Not as though we had loved God, but because God hath first loved us;*[230] and again: *Let us love God, because God hath first loved us.*[231]   Let men, then, confess their destitution and grant that what must be said of any good gift whatever must still more be said of the virtue without which all other virtues avail nothing: *What hast thou that thou hast not received?   And if thou hast received, why dost thou glory, as if thou hadst not received?*[232]

CHAPTER 14

1.   After this, when he has attributed to man unaided by grace as many good works as man could possibly do with the help of grace, our author adds a few ambiguous and confused sentences to show the natural power of free will.   He alleges the works which a man does with the strength received from grace as a proof of what he says is man's natural endowment. As though when someone has performed a good work with the help of God, this implied that he began it of his own free will.[233]   But let us pass over these things as tolerable, since we also say that free will with the help of grace conceives a

desire of what is good and a beginning of faith, in order that
it may, with the gifts which it has received without any
previous merit, merit what God has promised as the reward
of good works; but at all times man has to ask the strength of
doing good from Him who said: *Without me you can do
nothing.*[234]   Making, then, no further mention of these
points, let us examine what he said of the sufferings of the
holy man Job. "We read that God in His justice followed
that principle in behalf of Job, His most valiant and much-
tried athlete, when the devil asked to fight him in single combat. Had Job engaged the devil not by his own strength but
by the protecting grace of God alone, and had he borne the
many hard trials and losses demanded by his cruel enemy not
by virtue of his own patience but only through the help of
God, how then would not the devil rightfully have come back
with his former slanderous speech against Job: *Does Job
worship God in vain? Hast thou not made a fence for him
and his house and all his substance round about? But stretch
forth thy hand a little*—that is, allow him to fight against me
with his own strength—*and see if he blesseth thee not in thy
face.*[235] Since, then, this enemy, so inclined to slander, did
not after his fight dare to repeat a complaint of that sort, he
confesses by his silence that he was defeated by the strength
not of God but of Job himself. Though we must also say that
Job was not left altogether without the help of divine grace,
since God allowed the tempter no more power than He knew
Job was strong enough to withstand. He did not, however,
shield him from the devil's attack in such manner as not to
leave any room for his own human effort; He only saw to it
that his violent enemy did not deprive him of reason or smite
his intellect to overcome him in an unequal and unjust
combat."[236]

2.   Who would believe that Catholics can say such things

among Catholics? Yet, we can read in writing what before was said again and again in private conversations. Is, then, the mind's vision so darkened in all, and has the spirit of knowledge and piety so abandoned all sons of the Church, that such brazen lies dare obtrude themselves on the readers? Great man, wise teacher, truthful master, let us hear again the Catholic proposition by which at the outset of your tract you caught our attention and won our hearts. You then spoke as a true Christian and professed the faith of the Church. "The beginning not only of good works but also of good thoughts comes from God: He it is who inspires in us the beginning of a saintly will and gives us the power and the means to carry out our good desires. For *Every best gift and every perfect gift is from above, coming down from the Father of lights.*[237] He it is who initiates in us whatever is good and carries it out and leads it to completion."[238] With this sound and correct statement you have shattered the whole machinery of the remnants of Pelagianism.[239] Why do you now change your teaching? Why do you now rebuild what you had pulled down, attack what you formerly defended? Why do you leave the impregnable fortress of truth and step by step run down into the precipice of the Pelagian heresy? You had said that the beginnings of holy thoughts, of pious desires, of good works do not come from us, but that it is God who by His inspirations and the help of His grace produces in us whatever is good and leads it to progress and completion.[240] A little later you began to place the efforts of free will on a par with the gifts of grace, and you sought to show that man can have of himself the beginnings of the good things which first you attributed to God. You said: "Man can sometimes by his own activity conceive the desire of virtue, but always is he in need of the help of the Lord";[241] and again: "Even from the good gifts of nature, which were bestowed by the Creator's liberality, comes at times the beginning of a good will, a beginning, however, which cannot reach the perfection of virtue without the guidance of God."[242] And after that, to show that there are some people in whom grace anticipates their good will, while for others a preceding merit is the reason why they receive grace, you said: "It is uncertain which of the two depends on the other, that is, whether God shows us His mercy because we offered Him the beginning of a good will, or whether rather because God showed us mercy we are given the beginning of a good will."[243] Not to leave these two points undecided, you took the trouble to confirm them with examples which you thought quite apt for the purpose: the first by the example of Paul's and Matthew's forced conversion, the other by that of Zacchaeus' and the good thief's spontaneous faith.[244] The desire of these two, you said, was so passionate that "they did not wait for a special and express call to force their way into the kingdom of heaven."[245] Then, carried away by your own thought, you wished to show that our interior man is unimpaired, and you maintained that "Adam did indeed acquire the knowledge of evil which he did not have before, but did not lose the knowledge of what is good which he had been given."[246] And desirous to prove this from the example of infidels, you went so far as to say boldly: "We must beware lest we refer all the merits of the saints to God in such manner as to ascribe to human nature only what is evil and disorderly."[247] And lest we should believe that our nature lost in Adam's sin any of the virtues, you declared that the souls of all men are by nature as hale as was that of the first man before he sinned. In fact, you said: "We may not doubt that every soul of its nature possesses the seeds of the virtues that were planted there by a favor of the Creator."[248] When, then, one considers all these statements of yours, it is evident how far you have strayed from your first sound principle. In it, against your inner conviction,[249] you loudly declared what must be attributed to grace, with the intention of finding favor with Catholic readers, who, reassured by the orthodox appearance of your initial confession, would as easily admit your later statements as they approved of your first teaching.

Chapter 15

1. Up to now, to avoid the impression that you were straying from your first proposition, you somehow referred the beginning of virtue and of merit to grace, instead of ascribing it to free will, to the extent at least of admitting that the same good desires which spring from the unaided will cannot without the help of God make any progress or reach their perfection.[250] But now you remove God and His help further and further from man, and you attribute to free will so much power as to say that a man was not only able to bear with fortitude and calm the loss of his many possessions and the painful destruction of all his family and all his dear ones, but also to endure unspeakable torments in his own body by the sole strength of his unaided will. And lest anyone be mistaken about your intention, you propose the example of the holy man Job, who, according to you, without the help of God fought the attacks of the devil, treating him with unheard-of cruelty.[251] You try to prove this by the following argument: the cruel enemy confessed that he was defeated not by the power of God but by that of Job, since he did not say that in the thick of that last fight it was the grace of God that opposed him.[252] As though the holy man needed to be surrounded by the protection of heaven to bear the loss of his goods and children, but was not in need of any help in the midst of the torments in his body and soul! If, then, in the

victories of the saints there is nothing more memorable or more glorious than a strength of soul like that of Job unbroken by so many deadly torments which the devil inflicted on each and every one of his limbs, and if, as you assert, this strength was supported only by human virtue, to what height of fame and merit will not free will be able to rise when it can apply itself to virtue in peace and undisturbed? For you say that Job's free will gained the victory in his combat by its own powers.

2. I ask you, therefore, do you think that this holy man, when tried by the torments we read of in Holy Scripture, had within himself the Holy Spirit? If you say he had, then it is certain that God, whom he did not forsake, did help him.[253] But if you say the Holy Spirit had forsaken him, you err, as appears from the prophetic words of Job himself: *For I know that my Redeemer liveth, and in the last day I shall rise out of the earth. And I shall be clothed again with my skin, and in my flesh I shall see my God. Whom I myself shall see, and my eyes shall behold, and not another; this is my hope that is laid up in my bosom.*[254] If it is right to understand this text as a prophecy concerning the incarnation of our Lord Jesus Christ and the resurrection of Him who is *the first fruits of them that sleep,*[255] and concerning the hope of the redemption which in Him is laid up for all the saints, then it is manifest that the grace of God did not forsake one who was His temple, and that the Lord did already in this saint of His what later He promised He would do in His apostles and martyrs when He said: *But when they shall deliver you up, take no thought how or what to speak, for it shall be given you in that hour what to speak. For it is not you who speak, but the Spirit of the Father that speaketh in you.*[256] And did holy Job not show his trust in God's help when in answer to his clumsy comforters he said: *He that is mocked by his*

friends as I, shall call upon God, and He will hear him?[257]
Or was he unaware that he had received the virtue he possessed from Him of whom he said: *With Him is wisdom and
strength, He hath counsel and understanding;*[258] and: *In
whose hand is the soul of every living thing and the spirit of
all flesh of man;*[259] and again: *I expect until my change come.
Thou shalt call me, and I will answer thee; to the work of thy
hands thou shalt reach out thy right hand. Thou indeed hast
numbered my steps, but spare my sins; thou hast sealed up
my offenses, as it were in a bag, but thou hast cured my
iniquity?*[260] The Lord, then, had not forsaken a man whom
He took care to heal, nor had He withdrawn His help from
one to whom He applies remedies for purification and whom
He thus made purer and more glorious.

3. This patience in suffering of which Job gives such a
splendid example we find illustrated in other men. The Lord
it is who had trained David, who said: *For though I should
walk in the midst of the shadow of death, I will fear no evils,
for thou art with me;*[261] and: *But the salvation of the just is
from the Lord, and He is their protector in the time of
trouble.*[262] The Lord it is who had formed St. Paul, who
attributed to Christ both faith in Him and suffering for His
sake, when He said: *Being justified, therefore, by faith, let
us have peace with God through our Lord Jesus Christ, by
whom also we have access through faith into this grace
wherein we stand, and glory in the hope of the glory of the
sons of God. And not only so, but we glory also in tribulations, knowing that tribulation worketh patience, and patience trial, and trial hope, and hope confoundeth not;
because the charity of God is poured forth in our hearts by
the Holy Ghost, who is given to us;*[263] and: *Who, then, shall
separate us from the love of Christ? Shall tribulations, or
distress, or famine, or nakedness, or danger, or persecution,*

or the sword? (As it is written) "For thy sake are we put to death all the day long. We are accounted as sheep for the slaughter." But in all these things we overcome because of Him that hath loved us.[264]   St. Peter and in him the whole Church learned from the mouth of Truth Itself where the spring is from which comes this strength and patience in suffering, when our Lord told him: Behold, Satan hath desired to have you, that he may sift you as wheat. But I have prayed for thee, that thy faith fail not.[265]   Whosoever, therefore, remains firm in his trials should have no doubt that his strength comes from Him to whom all the faithful cry out from their hearts every day: Lead us not into temptation, but deliver us from evil;[266] since The Lord preserveth the souls of His saints, He will deliver them out of the hand of the sinner.[267]

4.   When you still said: "We must also say that Job was not altogether left without the help of divine grace, since God allowed the tempter no more power than He knew Job was strong enough to withstand,"[268] would it not be more correct to say, instead of: "no more power than He knew Job was strong enough to withstand," rather: "no more power than He knew He had given Job strength to withstand"?   By correcting that one word, you would have toned down your idea and expressed it more soberly; instead of attributing Job's wonderful fortitude in trial to human strength only, you would have ascribed it to both God's help and his free will. But you were afraid of lowering the glory of human nature if you were to confess that its strength is a gift of God.   For that reason you did not want us to believe that God was Job's helper in his struggle and victory, but only a spectator.   In this manner a reader whom you will have been able to convince that in this hard combat Job was victorious by the natural strength of his free will, will not dare doubt that in

less difficult circumstances man's good will is much more master of its doings; and so he will fall into the snare of the condemned heresy which stated that we are given the grace of justification only for the purpose of being able to do more easily what we are commanded to do of our own free will; which supposes that, even if we were not given that grace, we should still be able to fulfil the commandments of God without it, though not so easily.[269]   But since the Catholic bishops judged that this doctrine deserves condemnation, we also should appeal to the same authoritative text as they did when they said: "For the Lord was speaking of keeping the commandments when, instead of saying: 'Without me you can do it only with great difficulty,' He said: *Without me you can do nothing.*"[270]

Chapter 16

1.   To all these propositions of yours, which you consider properly proved and which, you feel sure, are agreed to by your readers, you add that God is wont to test our faith by now and then offering more help than we strictly need,[271] so that it may become manifest how steadfast is the faith of those who believe.   You attempt to prove this by quoting the example of the centurion who asked of our Lord that He should cure his servant and who, when Jesus offered to come to his house, answered: *I am not worthy that thou shouldst enter under my roof; but only say the word, and my servant shall be healed.*[272]   Our Lord admired and praised his answer so much as to declare He had *not found so great faith in Israel.*[273] And you conclude in a few words which contain almost the whole of the Pelagian heresy: "The centurion would have deserved no praise nor gained any merit if Christ singled him out only because of something which He Himself had given

him."[274] If that is true, then it is an error of Scripture to say: *No one can be continent, except God gave it.*[275] It is an error of St. Paul to say, when speaking of the same virtue: *For I would that all men were even as myself; but everyone hath his proper gift from God, one after this manner, and another after that.*[276] It was an error of another apostle to teach: *But if any of you want wisdom, let him ask of God, and it shall be given him.*[277] Nor did another apostle speak the truth when he said: *Every best gift and every perfect gift is from above, coming down from the Father of lights.*[278] Nor John the Baptist, who said: *A man cannot receive anything, unless it be given him from heaven.*[279] Must we say that all the virtues must indeed be reckoned among the gifts of God, but that man deserves praise only for those which he possesses of his own, and gains merit only for what is no gift of God? This would mean that, according to this principle of yours, those to whom it was given not only to believe in Christ but also to suffer for Him[280] lost all praise and merit; that those who glory not in themselves but in the Lord[281] have no true glory. But we do better to listen to the prophet who says: *Cursed be the man that trusteth in man, and maketh flesh his arm, and whose heart departeth from the Lord,*[282] and to the other prophet who said: *I will love thee, O Lord, my strength;*[283] and: *In the Lord shall my soul be praised;*[284] and: *The Lord is my strength and praise.*[285] From these texts we know for certain that neither glory nor merit comes to those who do not possess the virtues, which no one can have unless the Lord give them.[286]

2. You thought that from the Scripture texts in which faith is praised one can deduce that it is not among the gifts of God, as though a text which praises faith meant to say that it is not a gift of God. Now, St. Paul praises the faith of the Romans and gives thanks to God for this virtue of theirs in

these words: *First I give thanks to my God, through Jesus Christ, for you all, because your faith is spoken of in the whole world.*[287]   To the Corinthians also he writes in a similar vein: *I give thanks to my God always for you, for the grace of God that is given you in Christ Jesus, that in all things you are made rich in Him, in all utterance and in all knowledge.*[288]   Did he, then, by giving thanks to God, mean to say that the believers deserve no praise for their faith? Did he, by praising the believers, mean to deny who is the author of their merit?   Let us listen still to what he thought of the faith of the Ephesians; he wrote to them: *Wherefore, I also, hearing of your faith that is in the Lord Jesus, and your love towards all the saints, cease not to give thanks for you, making commemoration of you in my prayers, that the God of our Lord Jesus Christ, the Father of glory, may give unto you the spirit of wisdom and of revelation in the knowledge of Him, the eyes of your heart enlightened.*[289]   So, they had the faith; they also did works of charity, which could not but deserve praise and merit.   Yet, for these very virtues St. Paul does not cease to give thanks to God, knowing that they are gifts that came from the Father of lights; and he adds that he asks from the same Father to grant also the spirit of wisdom and understanding to those whom He gave already the faith that worketh in charity.   So the Ephesians may come to know that they have received the virtues which they have from Him from whom they are told to expect those which they have not yet.   In a similar manner he gives thanks to God for the Philippians, nor does he mean to say that they have no merit and credit when he writes: *I give thanks to my God in every remembrance of you, always in all my prayers making supplication for you all with joy, for your communication in the gospel of Christ from the first day till now, being confident of*

*this very thing, that He who hath begun a good work in you
will perfect it unto the day of Christ Jesus.*²⁹⁰   Of which
human desert and merit do these words say that the source is
not in God?   Which particle of virtue or piety do they except,
as if it had not flowed from the source of grace, when they
attribute to the Lord, from first to last, both the inception and
the completion of good works?   To the Lord the prophet
addresses his song, speaking of the saints: *They shall walk,
O Lord, in the light of thy countenance, and in thy name
they shall rejoice all the day, and in thy justice they shall be
exalted.   For thou art the glory of their strength.*²⁹¹

Chapter 17

It is certainly worth considering how much with this teaching of yours you favor the Pelagians, who say that grace is
given in answer to our merit.²⁹²   Yet, so as to take cover under
the mantle of the Catholic faith, you treat their opinion as
opposed to the faith when you write: "Let no one think that
we have written all this in order to show that the whole of our
salvation is at the command of our faith, according to the
unholy opinion of those who attribute the whole of our salvation to free will and declare that God distributes His grace
according to each one's merit."²⁹³   I am amazed that you do
not see, or fancy that others do not see, that you condemn
yourself by your own words.   For by saying that "the centurion whose faith the Lord praised would not have deserved
any praise or merit if our Lord singled him out only because
of something which He Himself had given him,"²⁹⁴ you
declare that the centurion's faith came not from a gift of God
but from himself, and that accordingly grace did not con-
tribute to the beginning of that faith; you say that this very

faith of his was the reason of this praise and of his merit, neither of which he would deserve if the virtue for which they are given were itself bestowed by the Lord. In vain, then, do you afterwards, in order to avoid falling into the condemned heresy, deny that the whole of our salvation is at the command of our faith, when there can be no salvation whatever except through faith; for *The just man liveth by faith.*[295] And Truth Itself said: *Amen, amen, I say unto you, that he who heareth my word and believeth Him that sent me, hath life everlasting, and cometh not into judgment, but is passed from death to life;*[296] and: *This is the will of my Father that sent me: that everyone who seeth the Son and believeth in Him may have life everlasting, and I will raise him up on the last day;*[297] and again: *Now this is eternal life: that they may know thee, the only true God, and Jesus Christ, whom thou hast sent.*[298] Since, then, it is certain that the eternal life of the blessed is the reward of their faith, and of this faith you say that it deserves merit and praise because, according to your pet opinion, it must be reckoned among the achievements of free will rather than among the gifts of God, how will you shield yourself from the blow you strike at yourself when you declare, on the one hand, that they err in the faith who say that grace is distributed to men according to their merit, and on the other hand, maintain that they who accept the faith by a gift of grace can certainly not deserve either praise or merit for their faith? Whichever way you try to escape, you are beaten by your own arms, caught in your own words. For if merit does not precede grace, and if faith cannot be without merit, then faith does not precede grace; then it is perfectly true to say that man receives from grace whatever is a source of merit, since he cannot gain any merit before having received grace.[299]

CHAPTER 18

1. In order to cover up the incoherence and contradiction between your different propositions, you endeavor to combine what cannot go together, and with a new sort of audacity you split up the unity of the members of the Body of Christ into two sections of believers: one to whom pertains what you said in the beginning of your conference: "The beginning not only of good works but also of good thoughts comes from God; He it is who initiates what is good, and carries it out, and leads it to completion";[300] another to whom applies the other principle, in which you said that "the centurion would have deserved neither merit nor praise had our Lord singled out in him only what was His own gift."[301] And though you build up the whole of your dissertation to establish these two principles, which cannot be combined in any way, yet now you state your intention still more definitely and explicitly when you say: "From all these examples taken from the texts of the Gospel we can perceive very clearly that God works the salvation of mankind in countless different ways, by means that elude our investigation; the zeal of some people who are already desirous of and thirst after what is good He rouses to greater ardor; others, who are unwilling, He compels even against their will; at times He helps us to accomplish the good works of which He sees in us the holy desire, at other times He also inspires in us the very beginning of the holy desire; He gives us either the beginning of our good work or perseverance in it. That is why in our prayers we call the Lord not only our protector and Saviour, but also our help and refuge. For when He calls us first and draws us towards salvation without our knowing or desiring it, He acts as protector and Saviour; but when according to the ordinary way of His

providence He helps our efforts and welcomes and strengthens us, He is called our helper and refuge."[302]

2.   Thus, according to this distinction of yours, there will
be, you say, a new discrimination within the one Church: our
Lord Jesus Christ—of whom Holy Scripture says: *And thou
shalt call His name Jesus; for He shall save His people from
their sins;*[303] and also: *For there is no other name under
heaven given to men whereby we must be saved;*[304]—is not
the Saviour of all Christians but of some only, and of others
He is only the refuge.   He saves those only whom God compels to accept grace against their own desire and will, but He
is the refuge of those who anticipated the divine call by the
fervor of their free action.   To the former He grants a
gratuitous gift, to the latter He renders a just reward.   The
first deserve no praise or merit, since they have no other good
gifts than what they have received; the others are crowned
with glory and receive a rich reward, because they turned to
God by their own strength and offered Him what they had
not received.   And so, Jesus Christ would have found some
already liberated, and others He would have liberated.   Nor
would His word concern all men when He said: *You have
not chosen me, but I have chosen you,*[305] if there are some
whom He did not choose but by whom He was chosen.   Nor
would this other saying of His apply to all: *No man can come
to me, unless it be given him by my Father,*[306] if there are
some who could come to the Son without it being given them
by the Father.   Nor does it pertain to all what the Evangelist
said: *That was the true light, which enlighteneth every man
that cometh into this world,*[307] if there are some who either
came into this world without being darkness or began of
themselves to be light, so as not to be in need of the true
Light.   Nor is it of all the adopted sons of God that we must
understand the words of the Apostle: *who hath delivered us*

from the power of darkness and hath translated us into the kingdom of His love,[308] if some by themselves break their fetters and, casting off the yoke of the ancient slavery with an alertness born of their own free wills, run over from the slavery of the devil into the kingdom of God. If both these doctrines must be preached within the one Church in such a way that neither of them excludes the other but both must yield to each other mutually, then it may come to pass that we accept what the Pelagians hold and that the Pelagians accept what we hold.[309] But then it would be less true to say that they become Catholics than that we (God forbid!) become Pelagians. For when contraries are thus mixed, it is the better elements that are destroyed, because when virtue opens the door to vice, then man falls away not from vice but from virtue.

3. Therefore, Christian hearts will in no way admit what you have been trying to convince them of, namely, that those who by the grace of God are what they are,[310] deserve no praise nor merit; that Christ, who came to save that which was lost,[311] saves only one section of the Christians, while for the other He is only a helper. Christian hearts refuse this distinction, because, being followers of the gospel and of the apostles, *not minding high things, but consenting to the humble,*[312] they feel a horror for such insane pride. For it is true to say of the entire Body of the Church and of each one of its members that what was dead has been brought back to life, what was in slavery redeemed, what was blind enlightened, what was lost sought, what had gone astray found. Nor may it be said, according to your novel division of the members of the Church, that Christ is the Saviour of some and a helper of others: He is both Saviour and helper of all the faithful the world over.[313] And it is wrong to say that they who are given the means to gain merit deserve no praise;

rather, they are all the happier for having fewer gifts of their own and more of the gifts of God. For we are little troubled by the foolish grievance of those proud people who assert that free will is set aside if we say that the beginning and the progress and final perseverance in virtue are all gifts from God. Rather, DIVINE GRACE HELPS BY STRENGTHENING THE HUMAN WILL.[314] Of our own free will we pray, yet *God sent His Spirit into our hearts, crying Abba, Father.*[315] Of our own free will we speak, and yet, if what we say is devout, it is not we who speak but the Spirit of our Father who speaks in us.[316] Of our own free will we work our salvation, and yet *it is God who worketh in us both to will and to accomplish.*[317] Of our own free will we love God and our neighbor, and yet *charity is from God,*[318] *poured forth in our hearts through the Holy Ghost, who is given us.*[319] The same we say of faith, of patience in suffering, of conjugal chastity, of virginal purity, and of all the virtues without exception: we profess that they would have no place in our hearts were they not given us, and that free will, which belongs to man's nature, always remains in nature, but its quality and condition are changed[320] through the Mediator of God and man, the man Christ Jesus, who turns our wills away from their evil object and turns them to willing what is good; then, roused by delight, cleansed by faith, raised by hope, inflamed by charity, they submit to a free servitude and renounce an enslaving freedom.

CHAPTER 19

From the propositions which we have examined thus far (leaving aside many other points), one can see clearly and without ambiguity what is the opinion about grace of those who disparage its most true defenders and who disturb the peace which the Church enjoyed after her victory by bringing up again from the school of the condemned heretics some petty points of discussion. Were we to examine in detail all that was reported to us, our present tract would grow beyond measure. What has been exposed here from their writings will easily give the pious reader to understand to what abyss these paths lead: these muddy rivers flow into a filthy gorge exhaling a deleterious fog. Yet, I think it necessary, before ending this book, to collect in a brief conspectus the statements which we have shown to disagree with the Catholic faith, so as to enable the readers more easily to recall from this summary what during the reading may have escaped their memory owing to the interruptions made by our answers.

FIRST PROPOSITION: "The beginning not only of good works but also of good thoughts comes from God; He it is who inspires in us the beginning of a saintly will and gives us the power and the means to carry out our good desires. For *Every best gift and every perfect gift is from above, coming down from the Father of lights.*[321] He it is who initiates in us whatever is good and carries it out and brings it to completion."[322]

We also heartily admit this proposition and declare that it is Catholic.

SECOND PROPOSITION: "The divine protection follows us without intermittence; so great is the loving-kindness of the Creator towards His creatures that His providence at all times not only accompanies them but also leads the way. It is from the experience of that kindness that the prophet speaks in these words: *My God, thy mercy shall prevent me.*[323] When God sees in us some beginning of a good will, He gives it light and strength and directs it to salvation; thus He gives increase to what either He himself planted or what He saw had sprung from our own effort."[324]

Here already he departs from the first proposition, and

what he first attributed entirely to grace, he now partly ascribes to free will.

THIRD PROPOSITION: "All these texts only state both the grace of God and the freedom of our wills; they show that sometimes man can conceive the desire of virtue of his own accord, but that at all times he is in need of the help of the Lord. For one does not enjoy good health by a mere wish, nor is one freed from sickness by a mere desire."[325]

As though our Physician did not also inspire in the sick the desire of good health.

FOURTH PROPOSITION: "In order to see more clearly that at times the beginning of the good will arises from the gifts of nature bestowed by the liberality of the Creator—a beginning, however, that cannot reach the perfection of virtue without the guidance of the Lord—we should listen to St. Paul, who says: *For to will is present with me; but to accomplish that which is good, I find not.*"[326]

As though the Apostle, who professes that it is God who enables him to have good thoughts, would have this good will by a natural inclination and not from a gift of grace.

FIFTH PROPOSITION: "These sayings are somehow mixed and confused if we do not make a distinction. Hence, there arises the problem which of the two depends on the other, namely, whether God shows us His mercy because we offered Him the beginning of a good will, or whether rather because God showed us mercy we are given the beginning of a good will. There are many people who hold only one or the other of these alternatives, and making it say more than it should, get entangled in various and mutually opposed errors. For if we say that we have the initiative of our good will, where was that initiative in Paul the persecutor or in Matthew the tax collector? They were drawn to salvation, while intent, the first on shedding blood and torturing innocent people, the second on doing violence and robbing. If, on the other hand, we were to say that the grace of God at all times originates the good will, what shall we say of the faith of Zacchaeus? What of the devotion of the crucified thief? They by their own desire forced their way into the heavenly kingdom and did not wait for a special and express call."[327]

The author asserts that both he who holds that the good will springs from grace and he who says that grace depends on the good will are in error; and yet, he concludes that we should accept both these opinions and quotes an illustration of the first in Paul and Matthew, and of the second in Zacchaeus and the good thief.

SIXTH PROPOSITION: "These two, namely, grace and free will, seem to be opposed to each other; in reality, they go together; that we must admit both, we conclude from the very nature of a devout life. Were we to deny either of the two, we should appear to abandon the faith of the Church."[328]

As though we had to admit both in the sense that in some men the will precedes grace and in others grace precedes the will, and not rather in the sense that in all men the will follows on grace. For if it is true, as they say, that free will is set aside if grace comes first, then it is equally true that grace is no longer grace if free will precedes.

SEVENTH PROPOSITION: "And so Adam after his sin acquired the knowledge of evil, which he did not have before, but he did not lose the knowledge of what is good, which he had been given."[329]

Both parts of the proposition are false: Adam had learned before from God's own warning of how great an evil he should beware; and he lost sight of the great gifts in which he had been established by God, when he lent a willing ear to the devil.   And just as it is the worst kind of knowledge of evil to be evil oneself, so also is it the worst kind of ignorance of what is good not to be good.

EIGHTH PROPOSITION: "We must beware of referring all merits of the saints to God in such manner as to ascribe to human nature nothing but what is evil."[330]

As though human nature, before it receives grace, were not in a state of condemnation, were not blinded and wounded; or as though the saints were not made just gratuitously, since their merit springs from the same source as their justice.

NINTH PROPOSITION: "We may not doubt that every soul of its nature possesses the seeds of the virtues that were planted there by a favor of the Creator.   But unless they be stirred to life by God's assistance, they will never grow and reach perfection."[331]

As though Adam by sinning had not lost any of his spiritual gifts, and as though man, if he is to have virtue, had not to receive it from God but had only to be exhorted to its practice and so to reach perfection more easily.

TENTH PROPOSITION: "We read that God in His justice followed that principle in behalf of Job, His most valiant and much-tried athlete, when the devil asked to fight him in single combat.   Had Job engaged the devil not by his own strength but by the protecting grace of God alone, and had he borne his many hard trials and losses demanded by his cruel enemy not by virtue of his own patience but only through the help of God, how then would not the devil rightfully have come back with his former slanderous speech against Job: *Does Job worship God in vain?   Hast thou not made a fence for him and his house and all his substance round about?   But stretch forth thy hand a little*—that is, allow him to fight against me with his own strength—*and see if he blesseth thee not in thy face.*[332] Since this enemy, so inclined to slander, did not after his fight dare to repeat this complaint, he confesses by his silence that he was defeated by the strength not of God but of Job himself. Though we must also say that Job was not left altogether without the help of divine grace, since God allowed the tempter no more power than He knew Job was strong enough to withstand."[333]

If God only knew what Job's strength was, He did not give it to him; He was only an onlooker, not a helper of Job's endurance. But then, when will the help of grace be necessary, if that great victory of his was the result of his human strength alone?

ELEVENTH PROPOSITION: In connection with the faith of the centurion: "Our Lord marveled at the centurion and praised him and singled him out above all the Israelites who had believed in Him, when saying: *Amen, I say to you, I have not found so great faith in Israel.*[334] For he would have deserved no praise nor gained any merit if our Lord singled him out only because of something which He Himself had given him."[335]

It is an ungodly thought to fancy that a man who received nothing from God is more blessed than one who received from Him all that he has.

TWELFTH PROPOSITION: "That is why in our prayers we call the Lord not only our protector but also our helper. For when He calls us first and draws us towards salvation without our knowing and desiring it, He acts as protector and Saviour; but when He helps our efforts and welcomes and strengthens us, as He is wont to do, He is called our helper and refuge."[336]

Only he can agree with this proposition who does not wish to have been saved by Christ.

Chapter 20

This, then, is what our author teaches in these propositions, this is what he writes and spreads in published tracts: when Adam sinned, his soul suffered no harm, and his free will by which he sinned remained unimpaired. The knowledge of what is good which he had been given he did not lose, nor could his descendants lose what he himself had not lost. Every soul possesses by nature the seeds of the virtues planted there by a favor of the Creator. With them any man is able, if he wishes, to anticipate the grace of God by the right use of his natural reason and so to merit His help in order more easily to attain perfection. For one who has only the gifts he was given and has none of his own is not worthy of any praise or merit. We must also beware lest we refer all the merits of the saints to God in such a manner as to seem to say that human nature cannot of itself do any good. Its natural powers are so uninjured and hale that it is able without the help of God to fight against the devil and to endure his every cruelty and even the most extreme torments. All men possess this ability by nature, but not all are willing to make use of their inborn virtues. But the goodness of the Creator towards all men is so great that He welcomes with praise those who come to Him of their own accord and draws others against their will when they resist; thus He is the helper of those who are willing and the Saviour of those who are unwilling. And since in the Church one section of the faithful are made just by grace, another by their own free wills, those whom nature thus raises have more glory than they whom grace liberated. Free will in the descendants of Adam is as able to do every good work as it was in Adam before he sinned.[337]

CHAPTER 21

1. These are the dogmas of the new teachers who, in order to corrupt the faith in Catholic minds, spread calumnies against the defenders of grace and with furious speeches assault the most outstanding among the doctors in ecclesiastical sciences of our time;[338] they hope they will be able to break down all the defenses of the Church's authority if they succeed, by repeated blows of the Pelagian battering-ram, in knocking down this strongest tower of pastoral vigilance. True, *the foundation of God standeth firm;*[339] but they, following in the footsteps of the Pelagians, serve the cause of the heretics. It serves them right if they catch the madness of those whose error they follow. And they say nothing else than what is known already from the grievances of the condemned heretics and the invectives of the insolent Julian.[340] Alike are the shoots that spring from one same seed; the fruits reveal what lay hidden in the roots.[341] There is no need of a new strategy against them nor of any special tactics, as if they were unknown enemies. Their war engines were already ruined, they themselves already defeated together with those who are the companions and leaders in their proud teaching, when Innocent of happy memory slew with the apostolic sword the heads of the execrable heresy,[342] when the synod of the Palestinian bishops forced Pelagius to pronounce himself his own condemnation with that of his followers,[343] when Pope Zosimus of happy memory added the authority of his own judgment to the decrees of the African councils and so placed the sword of Peter in the hands of all the bishops to cut off the heretics from our communion,[344] when Pope Boniface of saintly memory directed the Catholic zeal of pious emperors and countered the enemies of God's grace not only with apostolic but also with imperial decrees,[345] when the same Pope, himself of high learning, asked Bishop Augustine to write answers to the books of the Pelagians.[346]

2.   Pope Celestine of revered memory, upon whom the Lord had bestowed many gifts of His grace for the defense of the Catholic Church, saw well that there was no need of granting the condemned heretics a new trial; they needed only a salutary penance.[347]   When Celestius applied for a new hearing as though his case were still unsettled, he gave orders to ban him from the territory of Italy.   So convinced was he that the decisions of his predecessors and the decrees of the councils were to be kept inviolate that he in no way allowed a new trial of what had once been judged and condemned.   Nor was he less alert in taking care to free Britain from the same infection: he banned from that remote corner of the ocean some enemies of the grace of God[348] who took refuge there as in the land of their birth,[349] and while thus endeavoring to keep that island of the Roman Empire in the Catholic faith, he ordained Palladius to be bishop of the Irish and so drew this pagan nation to the Christian fold.[350]   Celestine, again, cleansed the Eastern Churches of a twofold scourge: to Cyril, Bishop of Alexandria and the most renowned defender of the Catholic faith, he lent the help of the apostolic sword to extirpate the Nestorian heresy, and so the Pelagians also, kin and comrades of the Nestorians in error, received a new blow.[351]   The same Pope intimated to those who in Gaul censured the writings of Augustine of saintly memory that they could no longer speak against this doctor; he welcomed the application of some consultants[352] and praised the holy teaching of Augustine's books, in opposition to those misguided censors; he gave an official pronouncement on the authority of these writings,[353] and declared openly

how much he was displeased with the novel rashness of people so insolent as to rise against ancient doctors and disturb the preaching of the truth by their uncontrolled slander. "We," he said, "have always kept Augustine of saintly memory in communion with Us because of his saintly life and his services to the Church. His name was never touched by any sinister suspicion. We rather recall him as a man of eminent learning whom Our predecessors too always reckoned among the greatest doctors. All, then, were unanimous in their favorable opinion of him; he was loved everywhere and honored by all."[354]

3. In the face of so loud and so high a praise contained in so venerable and so authoritative a declaration, does someone make so bold as to murmur a sinister interpretation and to throw a cloud of ambiguity over a pronouncement that cannot be clearer nor more sincere? On the plea that the Pope does not explicitly mention in his letter the titles of the books in question, he thinks that the papal approval and praise of St. Augustine does not cover them but only his earlier writings.[355] Let us grant him, let him have, what he suggests: the later books[356] of Augustine were not included in that praise if on the same points of doctrine they do not agree with his earlier writings; we may consider as of no value or not to the point what in his latest books is not in conformity with what he wrote earlier against the Pelagians. Not to mention the tracts on grace which Augustine published from the beginning of his episcopate, long before the enemies of grace made their appearance, let them read his three books to Marcellinus,[357] reconsider his letter to Paulinus, Bishop of Nola,[358] reread his letter to Sixtus, then priest and now Bishop of Rome,[359] go through his books to St. Pinianus,[360] to Valerius,[361] to the servants of God Timasius and James,[362] look over the first six books against Julian,[363] his book to St. Aure-

lius, Bishop of Carthage, on the events of Palestine,[364] his other book to Bishops Paulus and Eutropius against the questions of Pelagius and Celestius,[365] and his four volumes to Pope Boniface of happy memory.[366]   And if in all these books of his, and in many others which it would be too long to enumerate, they find the same spirit and teaching, the same manner of presentation, then let those slanderers confess that they object in vain that the Pope did not express a particular and distinct approval of Augustine's latest books, when his praise goes to the doctrine itself which these books have in common with all his other works.   When the Apostolic See approves books submitted to its judgment, by that very fact it approves such teaching as does not differ from that of the submitted books.   When it comprises both in its judgment, it does not make any distinction in the praise it bestows.   Let, then, those who raise objections against Augustine's recent books admit the teaching of his earlier ones and agree with what he wrote there in defense of Christian grace.   But this they refuse to do, because they know that all those earlier works are opposed to the Pelagians, and that they would not be able to find there anything which could serve their destructive criticism of his later volumes if they agree to say that the earlier books contain nothing but the truth.[367]

4.   Accordingly, the wicked errors of such men must be countered less by way of argument than by the weight of authority.   Thus, no limb of the body of the heresy crushed long ago should be allowed to come to life again.   As is well known, the Pelagian heresy is so cunning that, if it notices that after having made a show of self-amendment, some shoot of its own stem that favors it is being spared, it endeavors to restore itself fully from this small remnant.[368]   For when a part is not different in nature from the whole, it is no real submission to surrender nearly the whole, it is a fraud to retain

even a small part. But lest this should be achieved by these cunning hypocrites, we trust that the protection of our Lord will grant that what He accomplished through Popes Innocent, Zosimus, Boniface, and Celestine, He will also do in Pope Sixtus,[369] that the glory reserved to this shepherd in guarding the flock of the Lord may consist in routing the hidden wolves, as his predecessors routed the known ones, always mindful of the words which Augustine in his old age addressed him at the time when they were working together for the same cause: "There are some people who think they are still free to hold those rightfully condemned errors; there are others who quietly steal into people's homes and do not leave off spreading in secret what they are afraid of saying in public. There are others still who keep perfectly silent out of sheer fright, but who still treasure in their hearts what they dare no longer speak out, yet they can easily be recognized by the brethren from their past defense of the heresy. Consequently, the first should be curbed by severity, the second watched carefully, the last treated with leniency and instructed with great insistence; for, if there is no danger that they will corrupt others, they themselves should nevertheless not be left to perish."[370]

Chapter 22

I think I have proved sufficiently that the opponents of Augustine raise only groundless objections, that they fight against the truth and defend falsehood, that by starting a war within the Church with the weapons of the defeated enemies they rise up against the word of God and the decrees of men. Yet, as long as they are not cut off from the communion of the brethren, we should rather excuse their intention than give up hope of their amendment. Until the Lord be pleased to settle, through the instrumentality of the princes of the Church and the lawful ministers of His justice, the trouble aroused by the pride of a few and the ignorance of some others,[371] let us with the help of God endeavor with calm and humble patience to render love for hatred, to avoid disputes with the silly, to keep to the truth and not fight with the weapons of falsehood, and to beg of God at all times that in all our thoughts and desires, in all our words and actions, He may hold the first place who calls Himself the origin of all things. *For of Him, and by Him, and in Him are all things; to Him be glory forever. Amen.*[372]

ANSWERS TO THE OBJECTIONS
OF THE GAULS[1]

Bishop Augustine of saintly memory has for a number of years and in accordance with the apostolic tradition defended and taught certain doctrines in his writings against the Pelagians, those enemies of divine grace and exalters of free will. Recently some people have thought fit to attack these doctrines, either from lack of understanding or with the intention of preventing their understanding; they have drawn up a summary of what they know of them[2] for the people who follow their opinions. This catalogue of brief articles contains what they claim to have found objectionable in the writings of the above-mentioned author. By this means they hope to turn people away from the bishop whom they attack and to deter them from reading his books thus stigmatized. Therefore, lest people should blindly admit those slanderous views and come to believe that the writings of this Catholic doctor actually have the objectionable meaning which his calumniators wrongfully give them, I shall answer, one by one, each of the articles which they brand as unacceptable, in a few brief and precise words. I shall faithfully keep to the points of doctrine which the saintly man has expounded in his tracts.[3] My intention is to enable even a hurried reader to see the injustice of the slander they spread against this Catholic doctor and the guilty behavior of those who, at the instigation of others, are more inclined to blame than to study a writer of the highest renown.

PART 1: ANSWER TO EACH OF THE OBJECTIONS

ARTICLE 1

OBJECTION: By God's predestination men are compelled to sin and driven to death by a sort of fatal necessity.

ANSWER: No Christian who is a Catholic denies God's predestination.[4]   But fatalism many, even non-Christians, reject.   Sin, indeed, leads to death, but God compels no one to sin.   For *He hath commanded no man to do wicked*.[5]   And: *Thou hatest, Lord, all the workers of iniquity; thou wilt destroy all that speak a lie*.[6]   Accordingly, one who preaches fatalism under cover of predestination is no less worthy of disapproval[7] than one who censures predestination on the plea of fatalism.   Fatalism as a theory is groundless and born from falsehood.   But faith in predestination is based on many texts of Holy Scripture.[8]   And it is altogether wrong to attribute to predestination the evil deeds of men.   Their propensity to evil does not come from God's creation but from the sin of their first parent.   And no one is freed from the punishment of this sin except by the grace of our Lord Jesus Christ, which was prepared and predestined in God's eternal design before the creation of the world.[9]

ARTICLE 2

OBJECTION: The grace of baptism received by those who are not predestined to eternal life does not wipe away original sin.[10]

ANSWER: Every man who believes in the Father, the Son, and the Holy Ghost, and who is reborn in baptism, obtains remission both of his own sins which he committed by his own evil will and of original sin which he inherited from his parents. But one who denies that a man who after baptism falls back into unbelief or evil ways was cleansed from original sin, is no less in error than another who says that this sinner will not be punished with eternal death. For what else awaits a man who falls away from Christ and dies deprived of grace but eternal damnation? Yet, he does not fall back into the sins he was forgiven, nor will he be damned because of original sin, though he will be punished for his later sins with the same eternal death to which he was liable by the sins he had been forgiven. And since God's prescience was neither uncertain nor mistaken about the future actions of this man, He never elected nor predestined him, nor did He set apart from eternal damnation him who was to be a reprobate.[11]

ARTICLE 3

OBJECTION: To those who are not predestined to eternal life it is of no use to be reborn in Christ through baptism and to live a God-fearing and righteous life.[12] God allows them to live till they fall into mortal sin and perish eternally, and He does not take them out of this world till this happens.[13]

ANSWER: There is no doubt that a number of men fall away from holiness of life into impurity, from justice into iniquity, from faith into unbelief; and it is perfectly certain that those people do not come within the predestination of the sons of God and coheirs with Christ. If these sinners die an impenitent death, this does not mean that their damnation was necessary because they were not of the predestined.[14] Rather, the reason why they were not of the predestined is that God foreknew they would be impenitent through their own fault.[15] If God did not take them away from this world at the time when they had the faith and led a good life, this disposition of His providence comes from His decrees, which though hidden are never unjust.[16]   For who fails to know that, though all men are equally liable to die, yet the moment of death comes to them in very different ways—some babies die after an hour of life only, other people live to an age full of years—and that no one's soul leaves the body it animates either sooner or later than God wills?[17]   If a man in the course of a long life turned away from God, he made a bad use of a good gift of God.   For a long life is nothing else than a gift of God, and what is a gift of God cannot but be good, and what is good cannot be a cause of evil.   It is, therefore, a mistake to think that God by protracting life causes the ruin of those who use it to sin.   For to live long is no sin, but it is a sin to live a bad life, and this is possible even in a short life. Accordingly, as good works must be referred to God, who inspires the willingness to do them, so evil works must be attributed to those who commit them.[18]   It is not God who forsook them that they should forsake Him; it is they who forsook Him and then were forsaken.   Of their own free wills they changed from good to evil.   And though they were reborn from sinfulness and made just, yet they were not predestined by God, who foreknew that they would be impenitent.[19]

ARTICLE 4

OBJECTION: Not all men are called to grace.[20]

ANSWER: To say that all men, that is, all men to whom the gospel is announced, are not called to grace, is not a correct way of speaking, even though some of them do not obey the gospel call.   It can only be said that not all men are called if those also are included to whom the mystery of the cross of Christ and of our redemption in His blood has not yet been announced.[21] Suppose even that the whole world and every country have already heard the preaching of the gospel (that it will be so, an infallible prophecy has foretold[22]): there yet can be no doubt that from the time of our Lord's resurrection till today many have died without having known the gospel. Of these we may say that they were not called, since they never heard of the hope to which we are called.[23] And if anyone says that the universality of the call was always so public and so full that, from our Lord's ascension on, there was not a single year in which the preaching of the gospel failed to reach all men,[24] then he should explain how the Asiatics also shared in that call at the moment when, according to Holy Scripture, the apostles were forbidden by the Holy Spirit to preach the divine word in Asia;[25] or the people of Bithynia at the moment when the same apostles tried to go and preach to them and were not allowed to do so by the Spirit of Jesus.[26] He should explain what Truth Itself proclaims in these words: *This gospel of the kingdom shall be preached in the whole world, for a testimony to all nations; and then shall the end come.*[27] The certainty of this prophetic text would waver—and God forbid that anyone should say so!—if for four hundred years the gospel was spread in the entire world and yet our Lord's coming did not take place.[28] Finally, let him consider how even among the Christian nations so many thousands of infants die without baptism: he should explain how they too were called,[29] to whom no minister of the gospel could come to plant and water the seed of the word.[30]

ARTICLE 5

OBJECTION: Those who were called were not all called in the same manner: some were called to the faith, others to unbelief.[31]

ANSWER: If you mean by call nothing more than the preaching of the gospel, then it is untrue to say that the gospel is preached in different ways for different persons: there is only one God, one faith, one baptism, one promise of eternal life. But if you consider the effect of the ministry of him who plants and waters,[32] then God did one thing in those who heard only the sound of words with the ears of the body, and another in those whose interior understanding He opened for the truth and in whose hearts He laid the foundation of the faith and enkindled the fire of love.[33] But it is nonsensical to say that some were called to unbelief, as though the call were the cause of their unbelief and the preaching of the gospel turned them into infidels. True, as it is written, the preachers of the word of God are for some people *the odor of life unto life* and for others *the odor of death unto death.*[34] Yet, *the good odor of Christ unto God*[35] are they who *preach Christ crucified, unto the Jews indeed a stumbling block and unto the Gentiles foolishness, but unto them that are called, both Jews and Greeks, Christ the power of God and the wisdom of God.*[36] If, then, the preaching of Christ crucified was a stumbling block for the Jews and foolishness for the Gentiles, this was due to the free refusal of their human wills. And that the same preaching, for those who were called, both Jews and Greeks, was Christ the power of God and God's wisdom, was the effect of divine grace.[37]

ARTICLE 6

OBJECTION: Free will is nothing in man; it is God's predestination that is operative in all men, whether for good or for evil.[38]

ANSWER: It is wrong to say that free will is nothing or does not exist; but it is also wrong to deny that, before it is illumined by the light of faith, it moves about *in darkness and in the shadow of death*.[39] Before man is freed from the slavery of the devil by the grace of God, he lies in the depth of the abyss in which he threw himself headlong through his own free will. He then loves his weakness and, because he is unaware of his disease, he fancies he is in good health. The beginning of the cure of this sick man is that he realizes his sickness and is enabled to desire the help of the Physician who will cure him.[40] When, then, a man is justified, that is, from sinner made into a just man, he receives, without any previous merit of his own, a gift by which he is able to gain merits. And the goodness which the grace of God started in him must grow by his own free co-operation, though never without God's help, without which man can neither advance nor persevere in virtue.[41] But it is altogether silly to say that the predestination of God is operative in men both for good and for evil. This seems to imply that some sort of necessity drives men to both good and evil, when actually in good men their willingness comes from grace, while in the wicked their wills act without grace.[42]

ARTICLE 7

OBJECTION: God denies final perseverance to some of His sons who were reborn in Christ and endowed with faith, hope, and charity, because in His prescience and predestination they were not set apart from the mass of the reprobate.[43]

ANSWER: There are, alas, many examples to prove that of the Christians who were reborn in Christ some abandon the faith and the Christian manner of life and fall away from God, to end their wicked lives far away from God in a sinful state. But it is wickedness beyond measure to ascribe their ruin to God, as though He were the instigator and author of their eternal loss. He foresaw that they would fall through their own fault and for that reason did not by His predestination set them apart from the sons of perdition.[44] How could the election preordained in Christ comprise those who were to fall away from Him and so deserve to be struck by a just punishment? But since there is no doubt that final perseverance is a gift of God—which the very fact of their nonperseverance shows not to have been granted to them—there is no reason to blame God for not bestowing on them what He gave to others. We must humbly confess that He showed His mercy in giving what He gave, and His justice in withholding what He withheld.[45] Else we might come to fancy that, just as free will is by itself the cause of sin, in the same manner it is the cause of perseverance in virtue, when in fact sin is the work of man and perseverance the gift of God.[46]

ARTICLE 8

OBJECTION: God will not have all men to be saved and to come to the knowledge of the truth, but only the fixed number of the predestined.[47]

ANSWER: To assert that throughout the ages God's will concerning the salvation of the human race and its call to the knowledge of the truth is universal and equal for all, in the sense that it never passed over any single individual, is to trespass on the unfathomable depths of God's judgments.[48] For why is it that *in times past* God *suffered all nations to walk in their own ways,*[49] when He *chose Jacob unto Himself,*[50] and did not do *in like manner to every nation and did not make manifest to them His judgments?*[51] Why is it that *that which was no people* is now *the people of God,* and that *to those on whom He had no mercy He now is merciful?*[52] Why is it that *Israel hath not obtained what he sought, but*

the election hath obtained it and the rest have been blinded?[53]
The why of all this it is not possible for us to understand, and
it is dangerous inquisitiveness to try to know it.   Yet, no one
is allowed to be unaware that there is *no inquity with God.*[54]
Nor should one think that any man was made just, either
before the law or under the law, by another grace or another
faith than the grace and the faith of our Lord Jesus Christ,
who, according to the decree of God's will, came at the end of
times *to seek and to save that which was lost.*[55]   But one who
gives the wills and actions of men as the reason of God's
decrees and judgments, though he cannot find any of these in
the case of the adoption or rejection of infants,[56] one who says
that the dispositions of God's providence vary according to
the various ways of the free wills of men, declares that for him
God's judgments are comprehensible and His ways searchable.[57]   The mystery which the Apostle of the Gentiles did not
dare to consider, he thinks he has discovered and can explain.[58]   Worse error still: he means to teach that the grace
by which we are saved is either rendered for merit or ob-
structed by demerit.[59]

Let us, then, set aside the whirl of these obscure questions
and turn to the broad light of what God has revealed to us
about grace.   Let us say with the Apostle: *God will have all
men to be saved and to come to the knowledge of the truth.*[60]
Let us listen to the Lord's instruction to His apostles: *Going,
therefore, teach ye all nations, baptizing them in the name of
the Father and of the Son and of the Holy Ghost, teaching
them to observe all things whatsoever I have commanded
you.*[61]   Let us listen to God's promise to Abraham: *In thy
seed all the tribes of the earth shall be blessed.*[62]   If we are
sons of the promise, let us not *stagger by distrust*[63] but with
our father Abraham *give glory to God and believe absolutely
that whatsoever He has promised, He is able to perform.*[64]

Let us read David's prophecies: *All the ends of the earth shall remember and shall be converted to the Lord, and all the kindreds of the Gentiles shall adore in His sight.*[65]   Another: *And in Him shall all the tribes of the earth be blessed, all nations shall magnify Him.*[66]   Another: *All the nations thou hast made shall come and adore before thee, O Lord, and they shall glorify thy name.*[67]   These prophecies, being infallible, cannot fail to come true, and they are actually being fulfilled in the elect who are saved the world over, for *whatsoever* God *has promised, He is able also to perform.*[68]   That is exactly what we mean by God's acceptance of the whole human race, by the adoption of the sons of God, of that fulness of the Gentiles which was foreknown and predestined in Christ before the creation of the world.[69]   That is the Jerusalem which is being built up from the beginning till the end of times with living and picked stones,[70] a town built on the very *cornerstone,* Jesus Christ, *in whom all the building being framed together, groweth into a holy temple in the Lord.*[71] None of these stones is rejected, or chopped, or torn away. Truth Itself says: *All that the Father giveth to me shall come to me, and him that cometh to me I will not cast out.*[72]   Or again: *You do not believe, because you are not of my sheep. My sheep hear my voice.   And I know them, and they follow me.   And I gave them life everlasting, and they shall not perish forever.   And no man shall pluck them out of my hand.*[73]

It is true, therefore, that God takes care of all men and that there is no one to whom either the preaching of the gospel or the commandments of the law or the voice of nature does not transmit God's call.[74]   The unbelief of some we must ascribe to men themselves, and the faith of others we must proclaim to be a gift of God, without whose grace no one comes to grace.   With the two hundred and fourteen bishops[75] whose decree against the enemies of God's grace was accepted by the whole world, let us confess the truth and say in their own words: "The grace of God through the Lord Jesus Christ assists us in every one of our good actions, not only to know but also to do what is right, in such a manner that without grace we are unable to think, to say, or to do anything which is truly holy and salutary."[76]   Nor should we believe that all these gifts come from God only in the sense that, being the author of our nature, He gave them in our very creation.[77]   It is true that from the beginning He gave men the power of knowing and doing what is right, but we have all lost it in him in whom we have all sinned.[78]   Accordingly, we are in need of being renewed by another creation and another principle of life in Christ, in whom we are a new creation, a new handiwork,[79] and through whom, without any previous merit of our own and despite many a previous demerit, we are given to be transformed from the vessels of wrath we were into vessels of mercy.[80]

ARTICLE 9

OBJECTION: The Saviour was not crucified for the redemption of the entire world.[81]

ANSWER: There is not one among men whose nature was not taken by Christ our Lord, though He was born *in the likeness of sinful flesh*[82] only, while every other man is born in sinful flesh.   Thus, the Son of God, who was God Himself, becoming partaker of our mortal nature without partaking in its sin,[83] granted to sinful and mortal men the grace that those who by regeneration would share in His nativity would be freed from the bonds of sin and death.   Accordingly, just as it is not enough that Jesus Christ was born for men to be renewed, but they must be reborn in Him through the same Spirit from whom He was born, so also it is not enough that Christ our Lord was crucified for men to be redeemed, but they must die with Him and be buried with Him in baptism.[84]   If that were not so, then after our Saviour was born in the flesh of our own nature and crucified for us all, there would be no need for us to be reborn and to be *planted together in the likeness of His death.*[85]   But because no man attains to eternal life without the sacrament of baptism, one who is not crucified in Christ cannot be saved by the cross of Christ; and he who is not a member of the Body of Christ is not crucified in Christ.[86]   And he is not a member of the Body of Christ who does not put on Christ through water and the Holy Spirit.[87]   For Christ in the weakness of our flesh underwent the common lot of death, that we by virtue of His death be made partakers of His resurrection.

Accordingly, though it is right to say that the Saviour was crucified for the redemption of the entire world, because He truly took our human nature and because all men were lost in the first man, yet it may also be said that He was crucified only for those who were to profit by His death.[88]   For St. John the Evangelist says: *Jesus should die for the nation, and not only for the nation, but to gather together in one the children of God that were dispersed.*[89]   *He came unto His own, and His own received Him not.   But as many as received Him, He gave them power to be made sons of God, to them who are born, not of blood, nor of the will of the flesh, nor of the will of man, but of God.*[90]   Their condition, therefore, is different from that of men counted among those of whom he said: *The world knew Him not.*[91]   In that sense we may say: the Redeemer of the world shed His blood for the world, and the world refused to be redeemed, because *the darkness did not comprehend the light.*[92]   Yet, there was a darkness which did comprehend the light, that, namely, of which the Apostle says: *You were heretofore darkness, but now light in the Lord.*[93] The Lord Jesus Himself, who said He came *to seek and to save that which was lost,*[94] also says: *I did not come but to the sheep that are lost of the house of Israel.*[95] And St. Paul explains who are those sheep of the house of Israel: *For all are not Israelites that are of Israel, neither are all they that are the seed of Abraham children; but in Isaac shall thy seed be called.*[96] *That is to say, not they that are the children of the flesh are the children of God, but they that are the children of the promise are accounted for the seed.*[97] Among them are counted those to whom refers what we quoted above: *Jesus should die for the nation, and not only for the nation, but to gather in one the children of God that were dispersed.*[98] It is not only from among the Jews but also from the Gentiles that the sons of God, the sons of the promise, are gathered into the one Church by Him who *calleth those things that are not, as those that are,*[99] and who *gathereth together the dispersed of Israel,*[100] in order to fulfil the promise of God to Abraham, that in his seed all the tribes of the earth would be blessed.[101]

ARTICLE 10

OBJECTION: The Lord withholds from some men the message of the gospel, lest hearing it they be saved.[102]

ANSWER: If you can prove that from the time when the gospel began to be preached there has been no one who failed to hear the message of Christian grace, then it would be wrong to say that the message thus proved to have been announced to all was not announced to all.[103] But if in some way there are still men who have not heard the gospel message, then you cannot say that this happened without a hidden judgment of God, which it would be wrong to blame because it transcends your understanding.[104]

ARTICLE 11

OBJECTION: God by His own power drives men to sin.[105]

ANSWER: No Catholic ever said nor is there anyone who says that God by His own power drives to sin men who lead a pious and righteous life, or that God's power does violence to innocent men and forces them out of their resolve to live a virtuous life. Such things are no works of God but of the devil, who delights in the ruin of the saints. *The Lord lifteth up all that fall and setteth up all that are cast down;*[106] and: *He gives them repentance,* that they may *recover themselves from the snares of the devil, by whom they are held captive at his will.*[107] When we read of some that *God gave them up to their desires,*[108] or hardened or forsook them, we confess that they deserved this by their own grievous sins,[109] because they committed before such grave sins as to deserve to become to themselves their own punishment, their very chastisement increasing their guilt. And so we do not murmur against God's decree by which He forsakes those who deserve to be forsaken,[110] and we give thanks to His mercy for saving men who did not merit salvation.

ARTICLE 12

OBJECTION: Some of those who were called and who lead a pious and righteous life are deprived of the grace of obedience to God's law, in order that they should cease to obey Him.[111]

ANSWER: If it is true that God forces out of a God-fearing life a man who lives in obedience to His will, and that He causes to fall one who advances in His service, then we must say that He renders evil for good and that He is unjust in punishing what He Himself compels man to do.[112] Can you imagine or say anything more wicked or foolish? Yet, that is what they come to who in all things mix up God's prescience and His will.[113] Actually, God at all times wills only what is good, but He foreknows both what is good and what is evil. What is good He either does Himself or grants us to do, but what is evil He neither does Himself in any way nor does He inspire or drive man to do it. Consequently, God does not withdraw from any man the grace of living in obedience to His will because He did not predestine him, but rather He did not predestine him because He foresaw he would swerve from obedience.[114]

ARTICLE 13

OBJECTION: There are some men whom God did not create for eternal life but only for the greater welfare of the present world and for the utility of others.[115]

ANSWER: We know well that God created each and every man, and that of the whole human race some will be reprobate with the devil, others will reign with Christ. But the Creator is not to be blamed because He created those also who will fail to attain to eternal life, for He is the author of nature but not of the sin which nature has contracted. Who is so dull as not to understand that the creation of the reprobate also serves for the beauty and variety of the present world, when he sees how the endeavors and exertions of unbelievers make for the convenience of this present life by the invention

of the arts, the building of towns, by legislation, by the fede-
ration of the nations?[116]   And if someone asks whether divine
Providence draws some good from wicked men whom heresy
keeps away from the true religion also for the benefit of the
faithful and the growth of the Church,[117] then let him first of
all turn his eyes to the cross of Christ and see how the merci-
full will of God that His only Son should die for our redemption was fulfilled by the heinous crime of the Jews.[118]   Let
him consider the glorious fortitude of the apostles, who,
facing the fury of their persecutors, with one voice called on
God: *For of a truth there assembled together in this city
against thy holy Child Jesus, whom thou hast anointed,
Herod and Pontius Pilate, with the Gentiles and the people
of the Jews, to do what thy hand and thy counsel decreed to
be done.*[119]   Let him, finally, consider the glorious victories of
countless martyrs on whom the fierce cruelty of unbelievers
bestowed the blessed palm of victory.[120]   Let him listen to St.
Paul exhorting the Church to persevere in holy religion: *In
nothing be ye terrified by the adversaries: which to them is a
cause of perdition, but to you of salvation.   And this from
God.   For unto you it is given for Christ, not only to believe
in Him, but also to suffer for Him.*[121]   Even as regards the
errors which God allows to arise in the Church, we should
understand how His goodness turns them to our good, not of
course by fostering them but by fostering through them the
zeal of His sons for the search and preservation of the truth.
That is what the Apostle says: *There must also be heresies,
that they also who are approved may be made manifest among
you.*[122]   When a Christian looks at the darkness that enwraps
the unbelievers and at the light that shines on the faithful, is
he not aroused by that very contrast to greater fervor in his
thanksgivings to God?   Can he not learn from the eternal loss

of the reprobate into what misery he himself would rush headlong of his own free will, did not the grace of God through our Lord Jesus Christ come to his assistance?

ARTICLE 14

OBJECTION: If some do not believe in the message of the gospel, they do so owing to God's predestination: His decree is such that those who do not accept the faith do so owing to His disposition.[123]

ANSWER: The unbelief of those who do not believe in the message of the gospel is in no way produced by God's predestination. God is the author of good, not of evil. And so the object of His predestination always is what is good, whether He renders justice or bestows grace.[124] For *All the ways of the Lord are mercy and truth.*[125] Accordingly, the unbelief of unbelievers should not be referred to God's disposition but to His prescience.[126] The infallibility of this prescience, which could not err about their future unbelief, does not entail that they refused to believe of necessity. But as to faith and works of charity and final perseverance, because these are bestowed on man through God's grace, one must acknowledge that both they and their reward have been predestined, on the authority of St. Paul, who says: *By grace are you saved through faith: and that not of yourselves, for it is the gift of God; not of works, that no man may glory. For we are His workmanship, created in Christ Jesus in good works, which God hath prepared that we should walk in them.*[127] It is, therefore, as erroneous to attribute the unbelief of the godless to God's disposition as it is not to confess that God is the author of the faith and the righteousness of the faithful.[128] One who lost what he had received does not recover it from the same hand that made him lose it; he recovers it from the Giver from whom he had received what he lost.[129]

ARTICLE 15

OBJECTION: Prescience and predestination are one and the same thing.[130]

ANSWER: If you make no distinction whatever between God's prescience and His predestination, then you endeavor to attribute to God with regard to evil what must be ascribed to Him with regard to what is good.[131] But since what is good must be ascribed to God as to its author and helper, and what is evil to the wilful wickedness of the rational creature, it is beyond doubt that God both foreknew and predestined at one and the same moment the good that would be done and of which He would be the author, or the just punishment which He would render to evil merits; but He only foreknew and did not predestine those actions of which He would not be the author in any way. And so prescience can exist without predestination, but predestination cannot exist without prescience.

PART 2: QUALIFICATION OF EACH OF THE ARTICLES

Though I believe I have, with the help of God, given a clear and complete answer to all the objections that were made against us, be they grievances arising from ignorance or sophisms prompted by bad faith, yet let us add a summary expression of our convictions in brief statements. Simple and brief sayings should show still better that we do not seek to wrap our judgment on each of the above articles in ambiguous verbiage, but that we reject absolutely and decidedly what is wrong in them and do not withhold our assent from what is reasonable.

QUALIFICATION OF ARTICLE 1: Whosoever says that the predestination of God drives men to sin and to death by a sort of fatal necessity is not a Catholic.[132]

God's predestination does not in any way cause men to be wicked, nor is it in any way the cause of sin.

QUALIFICATION OF ARTICLE 2: Likewise, he who says that in those who are not predestined the grace of baptism does not wipe away original sin is not a Catholic.[133]

The sacrament of baptism, which takes away all sins without exception, is a true baptism also in those who are not to persevere in the truth and who for that reason were not predestined for eternal life.

QUALIFICATION OF ARTICLE 3: Likewise, he who says that to those who are not predestined to eternal life it is of no use to be reborn in Christ through baptism and to live a God-fearing and righteous life, but that God allows them to live till they fall into sin and does not take them out of this world till this happens, as though the eternal loss of such men were to be attributed to God's decree, is not a Catholic.[134]

For it is not true that God protracts a man's lifetime in order that by living longer he might fall into sin and in his old age fall away from the faith. Rather, a long life is to be reckoned as one of God's gifts, and man should have made use of it to become better, not worse.

QUALIFICATION OF ARTICLE 4: Likewise, he who says that not all men are called to grace is above reproach if he speaks of those only to whom Christ has not been announced.

We know, indeed, that the gospel is meant to reach all parts of the world, but we do not think it has already been preached in all countries. Nor can the call of grace be said to have reached where no men are as yet reborn into the fold of Mother Church.[135]

QUALIFICATION OF ARTICLE 5: Likewise, he who says that those who are called were not all called in the same manner, but some were called to the faith, others to unbelief, as though the call of grace were for anyone the cause of unbelief, is wrong.[136]

A man's faith, it is true, is both a gift of God and a fruit of his free will, but unbelief comes solely from the will of man.

QUALIFICATION OF ARTICLE 6: Likewise, he who says that free will is nothing in man but that it is the predestination of God which is operative in all men whether for good or for evil, is not a Catholic.[137]

God's grace does not suppress free will but strengthens it. Grace calls and leads free will back from error to the right way, so that from evil that it was through its own freedom it is set right by the action of the Spirit of God. And then, predestination always regards only what is good. As for sin, which was committed by the will of man, God knew that it was either to be forgiven in praise of His mercy or to be punished in praise of His justice.

QUALIFICATION OF ARTICLE 7: Likewise, he who says that God denies final perseverance to some of His sons who were reborn in Christ and endowed with faith, hope, and charity, because in His prescience and predestination they were not set apart from the mass of the reprobate: if he means to say that God did not wish that these men should persevere in the good gifts He bestowed on them and that He Himself is the cause of their turning away from Him, then he harbors thoughts against God's justice.[138]

God's omnipotence could, it is true, have given the strength to stay faithful to those who were to sin; yet, His grace did not forsake them before they themselves forsook Him. It is because God foresaw that they would do so through their own fault that He did not include them among the elect that were predestined.

QUALIFICATION OF ARTICLE 8: Likewise, he who says that God will not have all men to be saved but only the fixed number of the predestined, speaks more harshly than we should speak of the depth of the unsearchable grace of God.[139]

God, *who will have all men to be saved and to come to the knowledge of the truth,*[140] fulfils this free decree of His in those whom He foreknew and predestined, predestined and called, called and justified, justified and glorified.[141] In so doing, He does not lose anyone that belongs to that fulness of the nations and to that completeness of the race of Israel for whom the eternal kingdom was prepared in Christ before the creation of the world. Out of the entire world the whole world of the elect is chosen; out of the totality of men the totality of the elect are adopted.[142] Nor can the unbelief and disobedience of many annul the promise God made to Abraham: *In thy seed shall all the nations of the earth be blessed.*[143] *Whatsoever God has promised, He is able to perform.*[144] And so the elect are saved because God willed them to be saved, and the reprobate are lost because they deserve to be lost.

QUALIFICATION OF ARTICLE 9: Likewise, he who says that the Saviour was not crucified for the redemption of the entire world does not take into account the power of the mystery of the cross, but considers only the portion of mankind who have no faith.[145]

For it is certain that the blood of our Lord Jesus Christ is the price for the redemption of the entire world. But they do not share in the application of this price who either cherishing their captivity refused to be liberated or having been liberated returned to their captivity. The word of the Lord did not fail to be accomplished, nor was the redemption of the world frustrated of its effect. For though the world considered in the *vessels of wrath* did not know God, yet the same world considered in the *vessels of mercy* knew God.[146] God liberated the second, without any previous merit on their part, *from the power of darkness and translated them into the kingdom of the Son of His love.*[147]

QUALIFICATION OF ARTICLE 10: Likewise, he who says that the Lord withholds from some men the message of the gospel, lest hearing it they be saved, can escape the odium of the objection by invoking the authority of the Saviour Himself.[148]

He did not want to work miracles among people who, He said, would have believed had they seen them.[149] He forbade His apostles to preach the gospel to some nations,[150] and He still allows other nations to live untouched by His grace. Yet, we actually know with a firm faith that the Church shall spread to all parts of the world and that the world shall not end before the gospel has been announced in all regions of the earth,[151] and *every tongue shall confess that the Lord Jesus Christ is in the glory of God the Father.*[152]

QUALIFICATION OF ARTICLE 11: Likewise, he who says that God by His own power drives men to sin deserves severe reproof.[153]

We may not believe that God, who is the author of justice and goodness, whose every decree and command is directed against sin, would compel any man to commit sin or hurl anyone from innocence into crime. If some men are so obstinate in their sin as to resist all means of amendment, then it is not God who increases their wickedness: they grow more vicious by themselves, because by their previous sins they deserved to be forsaken by God and delivered to themselves and to their deceivers, so that sin itself becomes the very punishment of their sin.

QUALIFICATION OF ARTICLE 12: Likewise, he who says that some of those who were called and who lead a pious and righteous life are deprived of the grace of obedience to God's law in order that they may cease to obey, is very wrong in his idea of God's goodness and justice, by presenting God as forcing the God-fearing into ungodliness and withdrawing innocence from good men.[154]

God is rather both giver and keeper of godliness and innocence. And so, one who cleaves to God is led by the Spirit of God,[155] but one who turns away from God ceases to obey through his own fault.

QUALIFICATION OF ARTICLE 13: Likewise, he who says that there are some men whom God did not create for eternal life but only for the greater welfare of the present world and for the utility of others, would speak more correctly if he said that it is not to no purpose that God, who is the Creator of all men, creates those also who He foreknows will fail to attain to eternal life.[156]

For in wicked men also nature itself is a good thing, whose author is God, and His justice is also worthy of praise when He condemns the ungodly. But one is beyond reproof if one says that the creation of these men serves for the glory of this world and that they who by their wickedness will be harmful to themselves are born to be helpful to others. For however great the number of ungodly men, it does not take away the beauty of the world, nor is it without use for the kingdom of God, because from them also children are born who will be reborn in Christ,[157] and bearing with them in charity the people of God grow in glory and learn to imitate the goodness and patience of Him *who raineth upon the just and the unjust and maketh His sun to rise upon the good and the bad.*[158]

QUALIFICATION OF ARTICLE 14: Likewise, he who says that if some do not believe in the message of the gospel they do so owing to God's predestination, and that His decree is such that those who do not accept the faith do so owing to His disposition, is not a Catholic.[159]

For just as faith that *worketh by charity*[160] is a gift of God, so unbelief is not an ordinance of God. God knows how to render punishments for sins without sharing in the causality of those sins, and it is not reasonable to conclude, from the fact that He did not remit sins, that He committed them. Accordingly, a predestined man lives by the faith he was given, a reprobate perishes in the unbelief that is his own free doing.

QUALIFICATION OF ARTICLE 15: Likewise, he who says that prescience and predestination are one and the same thing may certainly unite the two with regard to our good works.[161] For since these are gifts of God, when we say that they were foreknown, they cannot but have been predestined, and when we say they were predestined, they cannot but have been foreknown.

But with regard to evil works, we must refer these solely to God's prescience. For as He both foreknew and predestined what He Himself does and what He grants us to do, so also He only foreknows and does not predestine what He Himself neither did nor commanded us to do.

ANSWERS TO THE VINCENTIAN ARTICLES

Some people, forgetful of Christian fraternal charity, are so bent on damaging our reputation in every way as to fail to notice that they are destroying their own by their manifest eagerness to harm us. They compose a tissue of horrible lies, a list of articles of their own invention, of most inept and blasphemous statements.[1] They circulate them and force them upon many readers both in public and in private, assuring their listeners that the errors of this devilish catalogue express exactly our opinions. It would be easy to show that their gossip is slanderous, meant to create bad blood against us: it would be sufficient for us to sign the anathema of those errors.[2] But the ill will of those people who regard as their loss whatever enhances our reputation would make them look with suspicion upon so brief an answer. Accordingly, in order to forestall any squabble, we have thought it necessary and fit, for the sake either of placating our adversaries or of enlightening those who heard of their slander, to explain in a complete and lucid manner, as far as we are able with the help of the Lord, what we really think of those shocking propositions. We shall, therefore, state the sixteen articles which they impute to us and after each of them say what is our real conviction and what is the faith we defend against the Pelagians by the authority of the Apostolic See.[3] Thus, anyone who is willing to spend ever so little time and care in reading this explanation will see clearly that there is in our mind no trace whatever of those ungodly and blasphemous opinions; and seeing how we condemn those impious statements by our profession of faith, he will feel that the punishment for them ought to fall on their inventors.

ARTICLE 1

OBJECTION: Our Lord Jesus Christ did not suffer for the salvation and redemption of all men.[4]

ANSWER: The truly effectual and unique remedy for the wound of original sin, by which the common nature of all men was vitiated in Adam and condemned to death and which is the source of the three forms of concupiscence, is the death of the Son of God, our Lord Jesus Christ, who being free from all necessity to die and the only sinless one, died for sinful men, who are condemned to die. Considering, then, on the one hand the greatness and value of the price paid for us, and on the other the common lot of the whole human race, one must say that the blood of Christ is the redemption of the entire world. But they who pass through this world without coming to the faith and without having been reborn in baptism, remain untouched by the redemption.[5] Accordingly, since our Lord in very truth took upon Himself the one nature and condition which is common to all men, it is right to say that all have been redeemed, and that nevertheless not all are actually liberated from the slavery of sin. It is beyond doubt that the redemption is actually applied only to those from whom the Prince of the World has been cast out,[6] those who are no longer vessels of the devil but members of Christ. His death did not act on the whole human race in such a manner that even those who would never have been reborn in baptism would share in the redemption, but so that the mystery accomplished once for all in the person of Christ should be renewed in each and every man by the sacrament of baptism which he is to receive once also. The beverage of immortality prepared from our weakness and God's power is apt to restore health to all men, but it cannot cure anyone unless he drink it.

ARTICLE 2

OBJECTION: God does not wish to save all men, even though all should wish to be saved.[7]

ANSWER: When Truth Itself says: *If you, being evil, know how to give good things to your children, how much more will your Father who is in heaven give good things to them that ask Him?*[8] how could it be that God, who saves even those of whom it cannot be said that they wish to be saved, does not wish to save some others, even though they wish to be saved? There must be some reasons hidden from us but well known to Him of whom it cannot be said that He had to do anything in another manner than He actually did.[9] Leaving aside, then, the reasons for a division which God's wisdom keeps hidden in the mystery of His justice, we must believe sincerely and profess loudly that God *will have all men to be saved.*[10] For the Apostle who said this commands with great insistence what is now the observance in all churches, that prayers be offered to God for all men.[11] If many of those for whom we pray are lost, it is only through their own fault. If many are saved, it is through a gift of their Saviour. When a sinner incurs eternal damnation, it is through an effect of God's blameless justice; but if a sinner is made just, it is by an ineffable gift of God's grace.

ARTICLE 3

OBJECTION: God creates the greater part of mankind for eternal reprobation.[12]

ANSWER: God, indeed, is the creator of all men, but no man was created for the purpose of reprobation. The cause of a man's birth is one thing, and another that of his perdition. The birth of men is a gift of the Creator, their loss is what the first sinner deserved. For in Adam, in whom the nature of all men was first made, *all men have sinned:*[13] they are held guilty by the same sentence that was pronounced against him. Nor can they be freed from this condemnation, even if they committed no personal sins, unless they be reborn through the Holy Spirit in the sacrament of Christ's death and resurrection.[14] It is, therefore, a sign of both ungodliness and little understanding if one fails to distinguish between the vice of nature and the author of nature, to whom is altogether foreign what is evil in each and every man. For He creates men that they should be men, nor does He withhold His action needed for the multiplication of the generations that succeed each other, knowing well that He will, according to the design of His good pleasure, remake in many of them the nature which He made and punish in others the sin of which He is not the author. For *as by the disobedience of one man many were made sinners, so also by the obedience of one many shall be made just.*[15]

ARTICLE 4

OBJECTION: The greater part of mankind were created by God not to do His will but that of the devil.[16]

ANSWER: It is foolish and contrary to reason to say that it is intended by God's will that His will be not done; that God, who condemned the devil and his servants, wants men to be his slaves. But the Pelagians, who deny that Adam's sin passes over to all men,[17] think they can raise this objection against Catholics. In fact, if original sin does not vitiate man from his very birth, then it follows that infants are not under the power of the devil, and they who never turned away from their Creator are not in need of being delivered from the power of darkness.[18] But we who profess that all men fell in Adam (*for the Son of man is come to seek and to save that which was lost*),[19] though we do say that every man who was not redeemed is a slave of the devil, yet are far from saying that anyone was created for the purpose of doing the will of the devil.[20] For the sin of men was unable to upset the order of creation decreed by God from all eternity, and it is right that a sinful creature should undergo the penal slavery of the devil, to whom he wilfully sold himself when turning away from his true Lord.[21] That slavery is not a disposition of God but an effect of His justice: the deception of the devil, who misled man, became for man, who allowed himself to be deceived by sinfully giving credence to him, the punishment of his sin. No one is freed from this punishment except through the Mediator of God and men, the man Christ Jesus,[22] whose gratuitous grace is both withheld from many because of their evil merits and preceded in no one by good merits.[23]

ARTICLE 5

OBJECTION: God is the author of our sins: by making man's will evil, He fashions a nature which of its own inclination cannot but sin.[24]

ANSWER: This groundless objection emanates from the same school which affirms that human nature is free from Adam's sin and remained unharmed.[25] And because we say that all men are born in sin and liable to damnation, and that they would be reprobate if they were not reborn in Christ, they pretend that we make the creator of their nature also the author of their sin. We reject this conclusion as altogether foreign to our idea. We rather confess that God, who is supremely just and good, is the creator of human nature and of our interior and exterior faculties in such manner that whatever belongs to nature is entirely His gift and whatever is against nature does not come from Him in any way.[26] Now, sin is against nature, and from sin proceeds death and all that goes with death. Man contracted these evils when he renounced the faith and obedience he owed to God and was induced by the devil to prefer his false promises to God's law;[27] by vitiating the very stem of the human race, the devil made of all its offspring his slaves. Accordingly, *if anyone be in Christ a new creature,*[28] he is made free from the slavery of the devil and becomes a servant of God, free from his deformity and remolded *according to the image of Him who created him.*[29] But if one is not reborn in Christ, he remains in Adam, in whom all die, and has no part with Christ, in whom all are made alive.[30]

Consequently, God is not the author of any sin, but He is the creator of our nature. Our nature had it in its power to sin; it sinned freely and by its sin freely subjected itself to the devil. It is not by its natural bent but because of its enslaved condition that it is subjected to the devil, until it *dies to sin and lives to God,*[31] a change-over which it cannot make without the help of grace. The freedom which our nature lost by its free action it cannot recover except through Christ the Saviour. *For there is no other name under heaven given to men whereby we must be saved.*[32]

ARTICLE 6

OBJECTION: God fashions in man a free will akin to that of the devils, which of its own impulse cannot will but evil.[33]

ANSWER: It is true that *the whole world,* as St. John says, *is seated in wickedness,*[34] that the wickedness of many men is similar to that of the devils, of such as those to whom our Lord said: *Generation of vipers, how can you speak good things, whereas you are evil?*[35] And: *You are born of your father the devil, and the desires of your father you will do.*[36] But the difference between evil men and devils is this, that even for very bad men there is always a means of forgiveness if God has mercy on them, while for devils He has for all eternity excluded any grace of conversion. And so, just as it is not God who gave the sinful angels the resolve *not to stay in the truth,*[37] so also it is not He who inspired men with the desire to follow the devil. A liar *speaketh of his own,*[38] and he will not get rid of his lie unless the truth set him free.

ARTICLE 7

OBJECTION: It is the will of God that a great number of Christians have neither the desire nor the possibility of being saved.[39]

ANSWER: If you mean to speak of those who have abandoned the practice of a Christian life and of the faith and gone over irretrievably to impious errors and evil ways, then there is no doubt that men so disposed do not wish to be saved. But one should not think in any way that it is God's will that these men fall into this desperate condition.[40] Rather, *The Lord lifteth up all that fall and setteth up all that are cast down.*[41] For no man can be raised up except through His grace, no one can be steadfast in virtue except through His grace. Accordingly, it is God's will that men maintain their good dispositions. He forsakes no one who did not first forsake Him,[42] and He often converts many who did forsake Him.

ARTICLE 8

OBJECTION: God does not wish all Catholics to persevere in the faith but wants a great number of them to apostatize.[43]

ANSWER: This blasphemous statement does not differ from

the previous one. We may refer to the answer we gave to
that difficulty, since the two objections are identical.

ARTICLE 9

OBJECTION: God wants a great number of the faithful to
fall away from their resolve of living a saintly life.[44]

ANSWER: The folly of this proposition is the same as that
of the two preceding ones. It is amazing that our objector
should repeat three times what it was enough to say once. As
it is, he only wanted to add to the number of his calumnies,
though he could find no new themes.

ARTICLE 10

OBJECTION: Adulteries and seductions of consecrated virgins take place because God predestines those people to fall.[45]

ANSWER: It is a horrible and abominable thought to believe
that God is the author of any evil desire or any evil action.
His predestination never swerves from His goodness nor
from His justice.[46] For *All the ways of the Lord are mercy
and truth*.[47] God, who is all-holiness, cannot be the cause of
adulteries of married women or of seductions of consecrated
virgins; He can only condemn these. He cannot preordain
but only punish them. When men commit these evil deeds,
they are slaves of their evil desires and passions, which they
contracted with the stain of the sin of Adam. But when they
turn away from evil and do good, then *with the Lord shall
the steps of man be directed, and he shall like well His way*.[48]
That is why the Apostle says: *Now we pray God that you
may not do evil; not that we may appear approved, but that
you may do that which is good*.[49] And so God's predestination did neither arouse nor suggest nor instigate the sin of

those who fall, or the wickedness of the wicked, or the evil desires of sinners. But we cannot deny that He did predestine His own judgment, by which He is to render everyone according to his deeds whether good or evil,[50] a judgment that would not take place if it were by God's will that men commit sin. But it will take place before the eyes of all mankind, and every man whom God in His all-knowing judgment will have placed on His left[51] will be condemned because he did not do God's will but his own.

ARTICLE 11

OBJECTION: When fathers defile their own daughters, or mothers their own sons, when slaves murder their masters, all this happens because God has predestined it to happen.[52]

ANSWER: If one were to accuse the devil of being the instigator of these enormities, I think he could in a way free himself from this slander and show that the authors of those crimes committed them of their own free wills; for though he delights in the frenzy of sinners, yet he could prove to them that he did not compel them by force to commit these sins.[53] What folly, then, and what insanity it is to dare say that one should attribute to God's counsel what cannot even be ascribed fully to the devil; for though the devil may foster the temptations to these shameful deeds of sinners, yet he may not be regarded as the cause of their evil desires. God, then, did not predestine any such things to happen. There is not one man on earth leading an evil and shameful life whom God destined for this manner of life. But He knew well that some man's life would be such, and He foresaw what would be His own judgment of him. And so we can ascribe to His predestination nothing else than what pertains to the just judgment He pronounces on sinners according to their deserts[54] or to the gifts of His grace which He grants without merit.

ARTICLE 12

OBJECTION: By the predestination of God, sons of God become sons of the devil,[55] the temples of the Holy Spirit[56] temples of demons, and the members of Christ members of a harlot.[57]

ANSWER: Though the predestination of God is always uncertain and hidden from us as long as we live among the perils of this life,[58] yet it remains unchanged for Him who has already accomplished what for us is still to come.[59]   This predestination does not make blind what it enlightened nor destroy what it built nor uproot what it planted.   For *the gifts and the calling of God are without repentance.*[60]   And: *The sure foundation of God standeth firm, having this seal; the Lord knoweth who are His.*[61]   God's predestination, therefore, in no way causes some sons of God to become sons of the devil, or the temples of the Holy Spirit temples of demons, or the members of Christ members of a harlot.   The reverse rather is true: it is predestination that makes of sons of the devil sons of God, of temples of demons temples of the Holy Spirit, of members of a harlot members of Christ.   He *binds the strong man* and *robs his goods,*[62] *delivering them from the power of darkness*[63] and transferring them from a dishonorable condition to true glory.   Those of whom it is said: *They went out from us but they were not of us.   For if they had been of us, they would no doubt have remained with us,*[64] went away of their own choosing, they fell through their own fault.   And because God foresaw that they would fall, they were not predestined.   They would have been of the predestined, should they have come back to God and persevered in holiness and truth. And so we conclude that the predestination of God is for many the reason of their perseverance in grace and for none is it the reason of their fall.

ARTICLE 13

OBJECTION: All those faithful and saints who are predestined for eternal death, when they return to their vomit,[65] seem indeed to do so through their own fault, but their fault itself is caused by divine predestination, which secretly withdraws from them their good dispositions.[66]

ANSWER: It is always the same spirit of blasphemy that persists, and this last impiety is not different from the preceding calumnies. Therefore, it is rejected altogether by right reason and condemned without hesitation by sound doctrine. It is true that to all those who fell away from the faith into unbelief or from holiness of life into vice and who were not cleansed of their sins by a true conversion, nothing but eternal death is owing. But it is criminal to ascribe to God the cause of their ruin.[67] For though in His eternal prescience He always knew what He would render to each one for his merits, yet we may not conclude from the infallibility of His knowledge that He places anyone in the necessity of sinning or inspires in him the desire of sinning. If anyone lapses from justice and piety, it is through his own fault that he throws himself into the abyss of sin, it is by his own passion that he is carried away, by his own opinion that he is deceived. In all this the Father does not do anything nor does the Son[68] nor the Holy Spirit. In a happening of this kind the divine will is in no way involved. We recognize His action in the many whom He keeps back on the border of the precipice, but we also know that He causes no one's fall.

ARTICLE 14

OBJECTION: The great number among the Christians who now are Catholic, faithful, just, holy, and who are predestined to fall and be eternally lost, will not obtain the grace of perseverance, even if they beg God for it, because the divine predestination which preordained, prepared, predisposed them to fall into sin is an immutable decree.[69]

ANSWER: There exists in God no predestination whatever which would destine men to transgress the law or abandon holy religion or break the commandments or give up the faith or commit any sin whatsoever.[70]   And it is impossible that He by whose help men rise from evils of that sort should make them fall into the same evils. If men live in holiness, advance in virtue, and persevere in their good endeavors, this manifestly is a gift of God, without whom no one can bear any fruit of good works.[71]   But when they stray from the path of virtue and turn to vice and sin, it is not in any way God who sends the temptation to sin, nor does He forsake anyone who will turn away from Him before He Himself is forsaken;[72] He often causes man not to forsake Him, or even when he did turn away from Him causes him to come back. But the reason why He keeps one man in the faith and does not keep another is a mystery which we cannot understand and which we should not investigate. It should suffice us to know that perseverance in grace comes from Him and falling into sin does not.[73]

ARTICLE 15

OBJECTION: All those of the faithful and saints who are predestined for eternal death are after their sin so guided by

God that they neither can nor desire to be saved through penance.[74]

ANSWER: To speak in this manner is neither truthful nor wise. For just as those who fell away from the faith and from holiness of life did so of their own choosing, so also is it of their own choosing that they fail to rise again, and it is freely that they undergo the slavery of the passions they gave way to. But if any lament their slavery and, accusing themselves, with a change of heart have recourse to God's mercy, then they do not do so without an inspiration of God's grace.[75] For *This is the change of the right hand of the Most High,*[76] who gives the grace of repentance to countless sinners, that *they may recover themselves from the snares of the devil, by whom they were held captive at his will.*[77] But to no one does God preclude the way to repentance nor does He deprive him of the power to do what is good. It is the man himself who turns away from God that stripped himself of the desire and the power of doing what is good. Therefore, it does not follow, as our objectors fancy, that God deprived of the means of returning to their senses those whom He did not give the grace of repentance, and that He struck down those whom He did not raise up from their fall. It is one thing to lead an innocent man into sin, which is far from God, and another not to grant pardon to a sinner, which is what the sinner deserves.[78]

ARTICLE 16

OBJECTION: The great number of the faithful and the saints who are predestined for eternal death, when they say in the Lord's Prayer *thy will be done,*[79] do nothing else than pray for their own ruin, that is, they ask that they may sin and be lost eternally, because the will of God in their behalf is that they should perish in eternal death.[80]

ANSWER: The Truth does not say that it is the will of God that the faithful and the saints should fall away from the faith and from innocence of life and perish in eternal death. On the contrary, the Truth says: *This is the will of the Father who sent me: that of all that He hath given me, I should lose nothing, but should raise it up again in the last day.*[81] The Son, therefore, does not lose any of those whom the Father has given Him. For He Himself says: *All that the Father giveth to me shall come to me, and him that cometh to me I shall not cast out.*[82] If, in consequence of the universality of the call and of the abundance of God's goodness, there are just men who will not persevere, and live together with other just men who will, when the first fall away from holy religion, they do so not through any action of God but of their own choosing. God does not push them to fall nor cast them out that they should forsake Him. Yet, He foreknew their sin and their defection by His infallible prescience.[83]

Accordingly, when they say in the Lord's Prayer *thy will be done,* they do not ask to their own harm for something which God does not cause in any way, namely, that they should fall into sin and perish forever. For it is their own wickedness and their own freedom that will accomplish this. But one thing they do indeed ask to their own harm which is undoubtedly in keeping with God's will,[84] namely, that *when the Son of Man shall come in His majesty and shall sit upon the seat of His majesty, all nations shall be gathered together before Him, and He shall separate them from one another, some on His right hand, others on His left; and those on His right hand shall hear Him say: Come, ye blessed of my Father, possess you the kingdom prepared for you from the foundation of the world;*[85] and those on His left hand shall hear: *Depart from me, ye cursed, into everlasting fire, which my Father hath prepared for the devil and his angels.*[86] So, men who refuse to do the will of God and yet pray that God's will be done, are heard with regard to what will happen through God's will, namely, that being followers of the devil they should be condemned with the devil.[87] For having spurned the will of God inviting them to His service, they will experience the will of God punishing their infidelity.

OFFICIAL PRONOUNCEMENTS OF THE APOSTOLIC SEE ON DIVINE GRACE AND FREE WILL[1]

There are some people who pride themselves on being Catholics,[2] yet hang on to the condemned opinions of heretics[3] whether in bad faith or from inexperience. They are so presumptuous as to oppose our most religious writers. Though unhesitatingly condemning Pelagius and Celestius, they yet speak against our doctors[4] and say that these have overstepped the due limits. They profess to follow and to admit only the doctrine sanctioned and taught against the enemies of God's grace[5] by the Holy See of the Apostle St. Peter through the ministry of its bishops. Therefore, a careful investigation was required of the pronouncements made by the rulers of the Roman Church concerning the heresy[6] which arose in their day and concerning the doctrine which they declared should be held about the grace of God, against the dangerous extollers of free will. We should add to this also some pronouncements of the African councils which the bishops of Rome approved and made their own. Accordingly, for the better instruction of the waverers, we now publish the declarations of the holy Fathers in a brief catalogue.[7] Anyone who is not overcritical will be able to see from it that the outcome of all that was written on grace lies in this summary of official pronouncements which we collect here, and that he can no longer have any reason to oppose the doctrine on grace if he holds the faith of Catholics and says:

ARTICLE 1

By the sin of Adam all men lost their natural ability for good and their innocence.[8] No one can rise from the depths of this fall of his own free will unless he be raised by the grace of God's mercy. Thus, Pope Innocent of happy memory stated and wrote in his letter[9] to the Council of Carthage:[10] "When Adam was tested in his free will,[11] he used this gift inconsiderately and fell down into the abyss of sin. He could find no way of raising himself out of it. Forever deceived by his own freedom, he would have remained crushed down[12] by this fall, had not Christ come and raised him up by His grace. By a new birth Christ washed away in baptism his every past stain."

ARTICLE 2

No one has any goodness of himself unless he be given a share in the goodness of Him who alone is good. A pronouncement of the same Pontiff[13] in the same letter says so in the following words: "Could we henceforth[14] consider as correct the opinion of men who think that they owe their goodness to themselves, who neglect to take into account Him whose grace they receive every day, who feel confident that they can attain as much without His help?[15]

ARTICLE 3

No one is able, even after receiving new life in the grace of baptism, to overcome the snares of the devil and to master the desires of the flesh unless he be given with God's daily help to persevere in a good life.[16] The teaching of the same Pontiff in the same letter[17] confirms the truth of this statement in these words: "God had indeed redeemed man from his past sins, yet He knew that he could fall back into sin. Hence, for the purpose of his restoration, He kept in reserve many means of amending him after new sins and He offers him daily remedies. Unless we trust and rely on these, we shall be unable to overcome the dangers of human faults. For there is no other alternative: we either overcome with God's help, or without His help we are overcome."

Article 4

No one makes a proper use of his free will unless he be helped by Christ. The same doctor, in the letter[18] he sent to the Council of Mileve,[19] says this in the following words: "Note finally, O wicked teaching of wicked minds, that freedom itself so deceived the first man that, using its power of control too freely, he allowed himself to be thrown down into sin by pride. And he could not have been raised up from this fall, had not the coming of Christ restored the happy state of his original freedom[20] by providing the regeneration of baptism."

Article 5

To God must be given the glory of all endeavor and work and merit of the saints. No one can be pleasing to God except by making use of the gifts of God. To this conclusion we are led by the authoritative pronouncement of Pope Zosimus[21] of saintly memory, who wrote to the bishops of the entire world in these words: "We on our part, by a divine inspiration—for every good gift must be referred to its Author —committed the whole question to the conscience of our brethren and cobishops."[23] The African bishops received this statement, radiant with evident sincerity and truthfulness, with such veneration as to answer the same Pontiff:[24] "As to what you wrote in the letter you sent to all the provinces, namely, 'We on our part, by a divine inspiration, etc.,' we understood this to signify that you, as it were, with the naked sword of truth quickly struck down the men who exalt the freedom of man's will to the detriment of God's grace. For what else did you ever do with greater freedom than to commit the whole question to the conscience of our humble selves? And in your faith and wisdom you understood that you had done so by a divine inspiration: you said so in truth and trust. Your reason for saying so was, of course, that *the will is prepared by the Lord*,[25] and that He Himself with fatherly inspirations moves the hearts of His sons to do what is good. For *whosoever are led by the Spirit of God, they are the sons of God*.[26] And so we are convinced that our free wills are not set aside, and yet we have no doubt that in each and every good action of our human wills His grace is the more powerful agent."

ARTICLE 6

God acts in the hearts of men and in their free wills in such manner that holy thoughts, pious counsels, and every good movement of our wills spring from God; we can do good only when helped by Him without whom we can do nothing.[27] Such is the faith the same doctor Zosimus taught us when he wrote to the bishops of the whole world[28] about the assistance of divine grace: "Is there any moment," he said, "when we are not in need of its help? So, in every action or resolve or plan or move we must pray God, our helper and protector. It would be pride were human nature to ascribe anything to itself, when the Apostle proclaims loudly: *Our wrestling is not against flesh and blood, but against principalities and powers of this air, against the spirits of wickedness in the high places.*[29]   And again he says: *Unhappy man that I am, who shall deliver me from the body of this death? The grace of God by Jesus Christ our Lord.*[30]   And again: *By the grace of God I am what I am. And His grace in me hath not been void, but I have labored more than all they. Yet not I, but the grace of God with me.*"[31]

Article 7

We also admit, as though they were the very decrees of the Apostolic See, the decisions of the Synod of Carthage;[32] and first, the decree laid down in its third article: "Whosoever says that the grace of God by which we are justified through Jesus Christ our Lord is apt only to forgive sins already committed, and not also to help us so as not to commit sins, let him be anathema."[33]

And again in its fourth article: "Whosoever says that the grace of God through Jesus Christ helps us not to commit sins in this sense only, that it shows the way to a correct understanding of the commandments, so that we may know what we ought to seek and what to avoid, but not in the sense that grace gives us the love and the power to do what we know to be our duty, let him be anathema.[34]   For when the Apostle says: *Knowledge puffeth up, but charity edifieth,*[35] it would be very wrong to believe that we receive grace for what puffs up and not for what edifies. Both the knowledge of our duty and the love of doing it are gifts of God. And so, when charity edifies, knowledge cannot puff up. Just as it is written of God: *He that teacheth men knowledge,*[36] it is also written: *Charity is of God.*"[37]

Likewise in the fifth article: "Whosoever says that we are

given justifying grace only for the purpose of facility in ful-
filling with the help of grace what we are commanded to do
by our free wills, as though even if we were not given grace,
we still could, though only with difficulty, keep the commandments of God, let him be anathema.[38]   For it is of keeping the commandments that our Lord spoke when He said, not
'without me you can do with difficulty,' but *Without me you
can do nothing.*"[39]

Article 8

These are the inviolable decrees of the Holy and Apostolic
See by which our holy Fathers slew the pride of the baneful
heresy[40] and taught us to ascribe to the grace of Christ both
the beginning of our good dispositions and the growth of our
praiseworthy efforts and our final perseverance in them.   Let
us next look also at the sacred prayers[41] which in keeping with
the apostolic tradition our priests offer after one norm the
world over in every Catholic church.   Let the rule of prayer
lay down the rule of faith.[42]   When the pastors of the Christian people discharge their mandate and mission, they plead
the cause of the human race with the divine mercy and, in
union with the supplications of the entire Church, beg and
pray that faith may be given to unbelievers, idolaters freed
from the errors of their ungodliness, Jews relieved of their
mind's veil and shown the light of truth, schismatics given
the spirit of a new charity, sinners granted salutary penance,
finally catechumens led to the sacrament of regeneration and
admitted into the court of divine mercy.[43]   And that all this
is no pure formality and no vain prayer to the Lord, the facts
themselves prove.   God deigns to draw to Himself out of
errors of all kinds many men whom *delivered from the power
of darkness He translates into the kingdom of the Son of His*

love,[44] and whom He transforms from *vessels of wrath* into *vessels of mercy.*[45]   And the Church is so convinced that this is exclusively due to God's action that she offers perpetual thanksgivings to God as to its author[46] and sings His praises for the light and grace bestowed on these people.

ARTICLE 9

The ceremonies which Holy Church follows uniformly the world over for the administration of baptism we should not consider as a meaningless display.   When either infants or youths come to the sacrament of regeneration, they do not go to the fountain of life before the unclean spirit was expelled from them by the exorcisms and the ritual insufflations of the clergy.[47]   This rite is meant to show how *the Prince of this World is cast out,*[48] how *the strong is first bound*[49] and then *his goods are robbed,*[50] transferred into the ownership of the Conqueror who *led captivity captive and gave gifts to men.*[51]

These laws of the Church and these proofs from divine revelation so strengthen us in our faith that we profess with the help of God that He is the author of every good desire, every good action, every good effort, every virtuous move by which from the beginning of faith we draw near to God.   We are convinced that all human merit is forestalled by the grace of God,[52] who moves us to will and to accomplish[53] what is good.   This help and this gift of God, certainly, do not take away free will but rather set it free,[54] and change it from darkness to light, from evil to righteousness, from sickness to health, from ignorance to wisdom.   God's goodness for all men is so great that He wishes His own gifts to become our merits and will give eternal rewards for what are His own bounties.[55]   He, in fact, effects it in us that we come to will and to do what He wants; He does not allow that His gifts, granted us for use and not for disregard, should remain idle in us, so that we in turn should be co-operators with the grace of God.[56]   And if we notice that weariness on our part steals into our endeavor, then let us urgently have recourse to Him *who healeth all our diseases and who redeemeth our life from destruction,*[57] to Him to whom we pray daily: *Lead us not into temptation, but deliver us from evil.*[58]

Article 10

As to the more profound and more difficult points[59] in the topical problems of our day which were treated at length by the opponents of the heretics,[60] we neither mean to scorn them nor need we expound them here.   For a profession of faith in the doctrine on the grace of God, from whose action and mercy nothing whatever may be withdrawn, we consider amply sufficient what the writings of the Apostolic See, as given above in these articles, have taught us.[61]   We cannot consider as in any way in keeping with the Catholic faith whatever is contrary to these propositions.[62]

NOTES

LIST OF ABBREVIATIONS

ACW Ancient Christian Writers, ed. J. Quasten (J. C. Plumpe†) and W. J. Burghardt. Westminster (Md.) and London 1946–.
ATA L'Année théologique augustinienne. Paris 1952–54.
BLE Bulletin de littérature ecclésiastique. Toulouse 1899–.
CSEL Corpus scriptorum ecclesiasticorum latinorum. Vienna 1866–.
DHG Dictionnaire d'histoire et de géographie ecclésiastiques, ed. A. Baudrillart, R. Aubert, and E. van Cauwenbergh. Paris 1912–.
DTC Dictionnaire de théologie catholique, ed. A. Vacant, E. Mangenot, and E. Amann. Paris 1903–50.
EC Enciclopedia cattolica, ed. P. Paschini and others. Rome 1948–54.
ES Enchiridion symbolorum, ed. H. Denzinger and K. Rahner. 30th ed. Freiburg 1955.
Mansi Sacrorum conciliorum nova et amplissima collectio, ed. J. D. Mansi. Florence 1759–98. Reprint and continuation: Paris and Leipzig 1901–27.
ML Patrologia latina, ed. J. P. Migne. Paris 1844–55.
MSR Mélanges de science religieuse. Lille, 1944–.
NRT Nouvelle revue théologique. Tournai, 1879–.
RB Revue bénédictine. Maredsous 1884–.
RHE Revue d'histoire ecclésiastique. Louvain, 1900–.
RSPT Revue des sciences philosophiques et théologiques. Paris 1907–.
RSR Recherches de science religieuse. Paris 1910–.
RTAM Recherches de théologie ancienne et médiévale. Louvain 1929–.
TU Texte und Untersuchungen. Leipzig and Berlin 1882–.
ZKT Zeitschrift für katholische Theologie. Innsbruck 1877–.

INTRODUCTION

[1] Cf. P. De Letter, St. *Prosper of Aquitaine, The Call of All Nations* (ACW 14; Westminster, Md. 1952) 7–9. To the evidence and authorities there noted may be added J. J. Young, *Studies on the Style of the De vocatione omnium gentium Ascribed to Prosper of Aquitaine* (Washington, D.C. 1952): "The vocabulary is not conclusive for or against Prosperian authorship. . . . The study of the clausulae on the other hand furnishes strong evidence that the author of the *De vocatione omnium gentium* was the author of the *Contra collatorem*—Prosper of Aquitaine" (179). On St. Prosper and his works, cf. L. Valentin, *Saint Prosper d'Aquitaine. Etude sur la littérature latine ecclésiastique au cinquième siècle en Gaule* (Paris-Toulouse 1900); M. Cappuyns, "Le premier représentant de l'augustinisme médiéval, Prosper d'Aquitaine," RTAM 1 (1929) 309–37 (references to this will be indicated hereafter as: Cappuyns, "Premier représentant"); G. Bardy, "Prosper d'Aquitaine," DTC 13 (1936) 846–50; L. Pelland, *S. Prosperi Aquitani doctrina de praedestinatione et voluntate Dei salvifica* (Montreal 1936); G. de Plinval, "Prosper d'Aquitaine, interprète de saint Augustin," *Recherches augustiniennes* 1 (1958) 339–55.

[2] On Semi-Pelagianism cf. ACW 14.4–6 and bibliography *ibid.* 158–60; E. Amann, "Semi-pélagiens," DTC 14 (1941) 1796–1850. For the origin of the name, cf. M. Jacquin, "A quelle date parut le terme 'semi-pélagien'?" RSPT 1 (1907) 506–8.

[3] On Cassian cf. L. Cristiani, *Jean Cassien* (2 vols. Paris 1946); O. Chadwick, *John Cassian. A Study in Primitive Monasticism* (Cambridge 1950).

[4] *Epist. ad Rufin.*: "quidam nostrorum" (ML 51.79A); *Epist. ad August.*: "Multi ergo servorum Christi qui in Massiliensi urbe consistunt. . . ." (CSEL 57.455; ML 51.67B); cf. Cappuyns, "Premier représentant" 310 n. 4.

[5] Cf. Valentin, *op. cit.* 140–51; G. Morin, "Saint Prosper de Reggio," RB 12 (1895) 241–57.

[6] Cf. Cappuyns, "Premier représentant" 326; ACW 14.9.

[7] ML 51.535–608. The *Chronicon* stops at the year 455.

[8] For the chronology of these works and various opinions about it, cf. ACW 14.164f.

[9] In the long list of these anti-Pelagian writings, dating from 412 to 426 (and continued till the last year of Augustine's life), his books *Contra*

Iulianum and his letter to Sixtus were the main occasion for difficulties among his followers. Cf. M. Jacquin, "La question de la prédestination aux Ve et VIe siècles," RHE 7 (1906) 272f.

[10] Cf. *Contra Iul.* 6.19.59: ". . . non ex operibus vel praeteritis, vel praesentibus, vel futuris. Alioquin gratia iam non est gratia" (ML 44.858).

[11] Cf. *Epist. 194 ad Sixt.* 2, 5 (ML 33.875f.).

[12] The occasion was the letter *ad Sixtum* (n. 11 above); cf. Amann, *art. cit.* 1800f. On this prelude to Semi-Pelagianism, cf. ACW 14.3f., and Amann, *art. cit.* 1798–1802. Before this a similar difficulty about the *initium fidei* was answered by Augustine in his *Epist. 217 ad Vital.* (ML 33.878–89); cf. Amann, *art. cit.* 1798f. Augustine's reply to the Hadrumetan monks came with the two tracts of 426/27, *De gratia et libero arbitrio* (ML 44.881–912) and *De correptione et gratia* (ML 44.915–46).

[13] ML 51.77–90; cf. Jacquin, *art. cit.* 270–73; Cappuyns, "Premier représentant" 311–13.

[14] The reasons for dating the *Epist. ad Rufin.* before the *Epist. ad August.* are mainly two: in the second Augustine's *De corr. et grat.* is mentioned, while in the first it is not; the assured tone of the *Epist. ad Rufin.* is in sharp contrast with the anxious request for more light and explanation made to Augustine in the letter addressed to him. Cf. Cappuyns, "Premier représentant" 311 and 313f. Its probable date is 426/27.

[15] Prosper later (about 430) rewrote in verse the theme of his letter to Rufinus in his *Carmen de ingratis* (ML 51.91–148), in which he develops more extensively the logical connection between the position of the Massilians, who ascribe the *initium fidei* to man's initiative, thus annulling the gratuity of grace, and the heresy of the Pelagians; e.g. 126–46. Cf. Jacquin, *art. cit.* 274; Amann, *art. cit.* 1816f.; Cappuyns, "Premier représentant" 316f.; ACW 14.159 n. 14.

[16] Edition in CSEL 57 (1911) 457–68, by Goldbacher; ML 51.67–74, or 33.1002–7. Cf. Amann, *art. cit.* 1809f.; Cappuyns, "Premier représentant" 313–16.

[17] ML 44.915–46.

[18] CSEL 57.468–81; ML 33.1007–12. For a recent comparative study of the two letters, cf. J. Chéné, "Le semipélagianisme du midi de la Gaule d'après les lettres de Prosper d'Aquitaine et d'Hilaire à saint Augustin," RSR 43 (1955) 321–41.

[19] In his letter Prosper did not speak about perseverance and its dependence on grace, another point of Augustine's doctrine rejected by the Semi-Pelagians; Hilary, however, did; cf. Chéné, *art. cit.* 335–38.

20 ML 44.759–992; 45.993–1034.

21 Cf. Amann, *art. cit.* 1812–14.

22 The phrase is H. Marrou's, *Saint Augustin et l'augustinisme* (Paris 1956) 150: "Prosper d'Aquitaine . . . avec toute l'ingénieuse et inlassable activité d'un 'press-agent.' "

23 ML 51.187–202.

24 Cf. also *Retractationes* 1.9 (ML 32.595ff.).

25 The tenth extract is not quoted by Prosper. According to his indications, it follows in Augustine's text on extract 8. It must, therefore, have begun with the words "Ex quo apparet habere quosdam in ipso ingenio . . ." (*De dono persev.* 14), as the "editores Lovanienses" remark.

26 Cf. the Pope's letter: "Filii nostri *praesentes* Prosper et Hilarius" (ML 50.528).

27 ML 50.528–30. Its date is 431/32; cf. Cappuyns, "Premier représentant" 319 n. 26.

28 Cf. H. Koch, *Vincenz von Lerins und Gennadius* (TU 31.2; 1907) 51.

29 *Conlatio* 13, *De protectione Dei*, ed. M. Petschenig (CSEL 13 [1888] 361–96; cf. ML 48.897–954).

30 The title of the anonymous work is *Tractatus Peregrini pro catholicae fidei antiquitate et universalitate adversus profanas omnium haereticorum novitates* (ML 50.637–86). Among the "novitates" Augustine's teaching on grace and predestination is meant to be included. Thus, Pope Celestine's warning, "desinat incessere novitas vetustatem," was twisted to attack Augustine, reversing the very intention of its author.

31 ML 53.583–672; cf. Amann, "Praedestinatus," DTC 12 (1935) 2775–80; Cappuyns, "Premier représentant" 320.

32 The text of the pamphlets was preserved in Prosper's answer; cf. nn. 39 and 44 below. Cf. Amann, "Semi-pélagianisme," DTC 14.1823–25.

33 Cf. Prosper's letter to Rufinus: "inter multas collationes asseruere" (4).

34 This is no doubt the reason why Prosper does not treat of predestination in the *Contra collat.*: his opponent did not mention it. On this point Cappuyns' surprise ("Premier représentant" 321f.) seems to be unjustified.

35 *De gratia et libero arbitrio liber contra collatorem* (ML 51.214–76).

36 Cf., in this sense, Amann, *art. cit.* 1826.

37 The main reason for this anteriority, according to Cappuyns, "Premier représentant" 321 n. 34, is that the *Contra collat.* reflects a less critical situation for the Augustinians than the *Responsa*. Valentin and Jacquin, however, invert the chronological order.

38 For this reason, and because Prosper's answer is more developed, the

Objections of the Gauls is considered as anterior to those of Vincent; cf. Cappuyns, *loc. cit.*

[39] *Pro Augustino responsiones ad capitula obiectionum Gallorum calumniantium* (ML 51.157–70).

[40] There are, in fact, different interpretations of Prosper's teaching on the salvific will; Jacquin, for example, *art. cit.* 282–84, says there is no universalism; Cappuyns, "Premier représentant" 323, suggests there is.

[41] Cf. Jacquin, *art. cit.* 278–88.

[42] Cf. Cappuyns, "Premier représentant" 324–26; Jacquin, *art. cit.* 290.

[43] Cf. Jacquin, *art. cit.* 290.

[44] *Pro Augustino responsiones ad capitula obiectionum Vincentianarum* (ML 51.177–86).

[45] As apparent from his *Chronicon;* cf. Cappuyns, "Premier représentant" 326 n. 47.

[46] *Capitula seu praeteritorum sedis apostolicae episcoporum auctoritates de gratia Dei* (ML 51.205–12). On Prosper's authorship cf. M. Cappuyns, "L'Origine des capitula pseudo-célestiniens contre le semipélagianisme," RB 41 (1929) 156–70. The capitula are also in ES 129–42.

[47] Cf. Cappuyns, "Premier représentant" 328.

[48] This approval, however, was perhaps less unqualified than may have been traditionally believed; cf. F. Floëri, "Le pape Zosime et la doctrine augustinienne du péché originel," *Augustinus magister* (3 vols. Paris 1954–55) 2.753–62; 3.261–63.

[49] These two points of doctrine were mentioned and defined explicitly in the documents that concluded the second phase of the Semi-Pelagian controversies, namely, in the Council of Orange; cf. ES 176ff. The chapters annexed to the canons of this Council (*ibid.* 182–98) are taken from Prosper's *Sententiae,* on which cf. the following note.

[50] We simply mention here Prosper's compilatory works on Augustine, which bring nothing personal, yet continue in a way his defense of Augustine. They are three: *Expositio in psalmos* (of uncertain date, between 435 and 449; cf. Cappuyns, "Premier représentant" 327 n. 52; ML 51.277–426); a summary of Augustine's *Enarrationes in psalmos* entitled *Liber sententiarum ex operibus sancti Augustini delibatarum* (392 propositions, taken partly from his own *Expositio,* partly from the many works of Augustine; ML 51.417–96); and a versified edition of these *Sententiae,* under the title *Epigrammata ex sententiis sancti Augustini* (ML 51.497–532).—As to the place the *De vocatione omnium gentium* holds in Prosper's defense of Augustine against the Semi-Pelagians, we may refer to ACW 14.11, 165.

[51] Cf. J. Chéné, "Que signifiait 'initium fidei' et 'affectus credulitatis' pour les semipélagiens?" RSR 35 (1948) 566–88.

[52] Cf. J. Chéné, "Le semipélagianisme du midi de la Gaule," RSR 43 (1955) 321–41; also *id.*, "Les origines de la controverse semipélagienne," ATA (1953) 56–109.

[53] It strikes one how Cassian reduces to as little as possible the part of free will and of faith before the advent of grace: "No sooner does God perceive in man the least good move than He comes with His grace . . ." (*Conlatio* 13.11.4 [CSEL 13.371]), while Prosper magnifies it (*Contra collat.* 2.3f.). Setting aside rhetoric, the fact remains that in Cassian's position human initiative provokes and determines God's giving of grace. Grace, then, is rendered, not given.

[54] It may be well to note that the more basic reason for the necessity of grace for every salutary act, also for the beginning of faith, is not the Fall with its consequences for human nature, but the supernatural character of salutary activity, to which man needs to be raised by grace (and would have to be even apart from the Fall). Augustine and Prosper after him mainly stress, in the dispute against the Semi-Pelagians, the *healing* character of grace.

[55] It is this setting against the background of original sin that gives the doctrine of predestination its Augustinian and rigid character, as though it were a purely arbitrary picking-out of the predestined from among the condemned lot of men. Loosened from this, and taken as meaning the divine initiative and all-embracing priority and causality in the salvation of those who are saved, predestination expresses a doctrine of the faith (but then it is no longer "Augustinian").

[56] This was the Jansenist interpretation of Augustinian pessimism, which was repeatedly condemned by the Church's magisterium; cf. ES 1092, 1297f., 1394–96, 1523.

[57] Cf. J. Wang-Tchang-Tche, *Saint Augustin et les vertus des païens* (Paris 1938).

[58] Cf. Cassian, *Conlatio* 13.12.2 and 7 (CSEL 13.378, 380).

[59] When the Church condemned the proposition of Baius, supposedly Augustinian, "Omnia opera infidelium sunt peccata, et philosophorum virtutes sunt vitia" (ES 1025), she implicitly sanctioned the idea of naturally good acts.

[60] This insistence on the fixed number of the predestined, typical of Augustine, is another aspect of the unnecessary rigidity of his teaching on predestination. The Catholic doctrine, though granting evidently that God knows infallibly the number of the elect, does not say that this number is settled *now* once for all; this is too human a way of conceiving things, one which brings the divine action down to the temporal level of human events. One should rather say that predestination is not

"finished," it is *in fieri*. Cf. H. Rondet, "Prédestination, grâce et liberté," NRT 69 (1947) 449–74.

[61] We may concede to the Semi-Pelagians that Augustinian predestination and universal salvific will do not go together. History is there to show that the more Augustine insisted on predestination, the more definite he was in interpreting the salvific will in the sense of a restricted universality. On this Augustinism, cf. O. Rottmanner, *Der Augustinismus. Eine dogmengeschichtliche Studie* (Munich 1892), translated and prefaced by Liebaert in MSR 6 (1949) 29–48.

[62] Prosper does not seem to have modified Augustine's idea of the damnation of unbaptized infants. To the problem of the universal salvific will in their behalf, he answers in the negative. Even today, after Augustine's views have been softened down and the doctrine on Limbo commonly accepted, a difficulty remains.

[63] K. Rahner, "Augustin und Semipelagianismus," ZKT 62 (1938) 171–96.

[64] As shown by K. Rahner, *art. cit.*, Augustine is not (or was not) unaware of these graces. Texts of his can be quoted (cf. Rahner 181, 185), at least from his early writings, to show that he knew sufficient graces. But in his exposition and defense of predestination, he never appeals to these in order to make his teaching more acceptable, and this one-sidedness adds to the harshness of his teaching.

[65] He did speak—and would speak more so in *De vocatione* (cf. ACW 14, Index *s.v.* salvific will)—of the help of nature and the law, by which God calls all men, but here only in passing, and without developing the implications. In the setting of his idea on grace, he could not have developed them.

[66] Cf. Jacquin, *art. cit.* 298.

[67] As we shall say presently, owing to this idea of ever-efficacious grace, they could not conceive otherwise the universality of the salvific will. If grace is always efficacious, a universal distribution of this grace would have meant a universal answer to God's call. But too many, it appeared evident to them, do not in fact come to the faith but live and die outside the fold of the believers. These, therefore, cannot have received grace. They must have been called, if God wants all men to be saved, but without grace.

[68] As explained elsewhere (ACW 14.158 n. 7), the Semi-Pelagians were not half-faithful followers of Pelagius; they repudiated his errors frankly, and as appears from Prosper's letter to Augustine (8.9), wished to remain faithful to the Catholic faith.—On Pelagius and his errors, cf. G. de Plinval, *Pélage. Ses écrits, sa vie et sa réforme* (Lausanne

1943); J. Ferguson, *Pelagius. A Historical and Theological Study* (Cambridge 1956).

[69] So it appears how the Semi-Pelagian concept of the universal salvific will logically required the nonnecessity of grace (as they conceived grace) for the *initium fidei*. The false presupposition of this connection is the narrow concept of grace as being always efficacious. To break that connection, it is enough to broaden that concept so as to include sufficient grace as well.

[70] It would seem as unnecessary as it is unhistorical to interpret Augustine's teaching on the salvific will, particularly at the time of the Semi-Pelagian controversy, in another meaning than that of a restricted universality. The principles that entail a real universalism of the salvific will may be latent in Augustine's writings, especially in the earlier ones, but at the time of these controversies he left them unexploited.

[71] Cf. his references to nature and to the law as means of God's call to salvation addressed to all men: *Resp. cap. Gall.* 8 (perhaps borrowed from the Semi-Pelagians; cf. *Epist. ad August.* 4).

[72] Cf. *Epist. ad Rufin.* 11. At the time he wrote the *Auctoritates*, he apparently no longer considered it so, but rather as one of the difficult questions which could be left aside without any harm to the profession of the faith (*ibid.* 10).

[73] The *Auctoritates* state the necessity of grace for every salutary good action and its absolute gratuity without mentioning predestination. These, therefore, can be held without explicit acceptance of the latter.

[74] For the history of this edition—and of other editions—of Prosper's works, cf. Valentin, *op. cit.* 205–21, or L. Couture, "Saint Prosper d'Aquitaine," BLE 1900, 269–82. Prepared by Le Brun des Marettes, the edition was actually done by L. U. Mangeant (Paris 1711). Another edition of the works, by P. F. Foggini, followed (Rome 1758). For C. Lequeux cf. n. 77 below.

[75] CSEL 57 (1911) 454–68.

[76] M. Cappuyns, "Premier représentant" 311 n. 5 (*Epist. ad Rufin.*), 317f. n. 22 (*Resp. exc. Gen.*), 321 n. 34 (*Contra collat., Resp. cap. Gall., Resp. cap. Vinc.*); for the *Auctoritates* cf. *id.*, "L'Origine des capitula . . . ," RB 41 (1929) 156 n. 2 (about editions).

[77] The complete title is: *Oeuvres de saint Prosper d'Aquitaine, secrétaire de saint Léon le Grand, sur la grâce de Dieu, le libre arbitre de l'homme et la prédestination des saints, fidèlement traduites sur la nouvelle édition publiée à Rome en 1758 avec les permissions ordinaires et dédiée au pape Clément XIII.*

TEXT

LETTER TO RUFINUS

[1] This common friend of Prosper and Rufinus seems to be unknown to history.

[2] They are the monks of Marseilles, Semi-Pelagians.

[3] The denial of the gratuity of grace, which Prosper says is the root of the whole Pelagian heresy, is precisely the point in which the Semi-Pelagians offend when they ascribe the *initium fidei* to unaided free will.

[4] The Pelagian heresy rejected original sin; cf. Augustine, *De gratia Christi et de peccato originali* (ML 44.359–410; CSEL 42.133–206); G. de Plinval, *Pélage* 236ff.

[5] On the Catholic opposition to Pelagius, especially in Africa, cf. de Plinval, *Pélage* 252–384; ES 101–8.

[6] For the variations of the Pelagian opinions, cf. Augustine, *op. cit.* (n. 4). In his *De gestis Pelagii* (ML 44.319–60; CSEL 42.49–122) Augustine exposed Pelagius' changes of opinion or of expression at the Council of Diospolis (415). Cf. also de Plinval, *Pélage* 286–92.

[7] Cf. Rom. 9.22f.

[8] Cf. Council of Carthage, can. 4 (ES 104); Augustine, *De grat. Christi* 1.7–14.

[9] Cf. Augustine, *ibid.* 1.22f.

[10] *Frustra gratia nominatur;* cf. *De voc.* 1.1; Rom. 11.6; Augustine, *Epist. 194 ad Sixt.* 3.7.

[11] At the Council of Diospolis; cf. n. 6 above.

[12] *Epist. tractoria* of Pope Zosimus (an. 418); cf. Amann, "Zosime," DTC 15 (1950) 3708–16; and Floëri, *art. cit.* (Intro. n. 48).

[13] For the list of these African Councils, cf. H. Froidevaux, "Afrique," DHG 1 (1912) 815ff. The first of the anti-Pelagian councils was held in 411; the most important of them was the Sixteenth of Carthage, held in 418; cf. ES 101ff.; de Plinval, *Pélage* 252–332.

[14] The chronological list of Augustine's anti-Pelagian writings is as follows: *De peccatorum meritis* (412), *De spiritu et littera* (412), *De natura et gratia* (415), *De perfectione iustitiae hominis* (415), *De gestis Pelagii* (417), *De gratia Christi et de peccato originali* (418), *De anima et eius origine* (419/20). Later, against Julian of Eclanum, *De nuptiis et concupiscentia* (419/20), *Contra duas epistulas Pelagianorum* (420), *Contra Iulianum* (421), and *Contra Iulianum opus imperfectum* (429/30). Cf. F. Cayré, *Précis de patrologie* 1 (Paris 1927) 614ff.

[15] *In suis detruncationis partibus palpitantem:* still alive in those parts

cut off from it by the Semi-Pelagians, who did not wish to have anything to do with Pelagius' ideas, they are offshoots of Pelagianism.

[16] Cf. the same accusation of fatalism in *Epist. ad August.* 3 and *Resp. cap. Gall.* 1.

[17] Cf. the same accusation of Manichean dualism in *Epist. ad August.* 3.

[18] This shows that Prosper was not alone in defending Augustine against the monks of Marseilles, though he was soon to be the leader of the Augustinians.

[19] Cf. Rom. 3.21-31.

[20] Prosper knew of Cassian's conferences even before their publication. It is the thirteenth conference which, when published, was the theme of his *Contra collatorem*.

[21] *Centenis voluminibus*: this general reference to Augustine's writings against the Pelagians (cf. n. 14 above) suggests that Prosper did not yet know of the *De correptione et gratia* (written 426/27), of which he did know when he wrote his *Epist. ad August.* (*q.v.* 2).

[22] Prosper, though sensing a lack of humility in the anti-Augustinians (contamination of "Pelagian pride"), yet acknowledges their moral integrity and virtue. Cf. also *Epist. ad August.* 3.

[23] Of these two Pelagian errors, namely, that virtue is a gift of nature, and due to grace which is given for merit, a trace is found in Cassian's ideas: the seeds of the virtues remain after the Fall, and the beginning of faith sometimes originates from the unaided free will; cf. *Contra collat.*, propositions 8 and 9, and 5.

[24] Matt. 11.28-30.

[25] John 15.5.

[26] John 6.44.

[27] John 6.66.

[28] John 5.21.

[29] Luke 10.22.

[30] Prov. 8.35 (LXX).

[31] Phil. 2.13.

[32] Acts 10.1-48; cf. *Contra collat.* 15.1 and 19.12; Augustine, *De praed. sanct.* 12: Cornelius' acts were not "sine aliqua fide."

[33] Acts 10.2 (ancient version).

[34] Acts 10.10-12, 28, 43, 47.

[35] Acts 10.14.

[36] Acts 10.15.

[37] 2 Thess. 3.2.

[38] Rom. 10.16.

[39] Eph. 2.8f.

[40] 1 Cor. 1.31.

[41] The point Prosper makes is that the beginning of faith is not man's initiative but a gift of grace.

[42] Rom. 1.17.

[43] Heb. 11.6 (ancient version).

[44] Rom. 4.23.

[45] Augustinian idea: no true virtue without faith; cf. *Epist.* 217 *ad Vital.* 9.11: "habere nonnulla *velut* opera bona"; cf. *De voc.* 1.6; cf. Intro. n. 57.

[46] 1 John 4.10.

[47] 1 John 4.9.

[48] 1 John 4.7f.

[49] Gal. 5.6.

[50] Phil. 1.29.

[51] Rom. 5.5.

[52] Cf. 1 Cor. 13.3.

[53] Cf. n. 45 above.

[54] Col. 1.12f.

[55] 2 Tim. 1.8f.

[56] Tit. 3.3–5.

[57] Cf. the same idea in *De voc.* 1.8.

[58] The correction suggested by Mangeant, *iustitiam* instead of *industriam*, is unnecessary. Lequeux, *op. cit.* 45, seems to combine both: "l'amour et la pratique de la justice."

[59] The same reflections on St. Peter's temptation and fall are found in *De voc.* 2.28 (ACW 14.138ff.), with the same Scripture texts commented on, to prove that steadfastness in virtue is a gift of grace.

[60] Luke 22.31f.

[61] Luke 22.40.

[62] Luke 22.33.

[63] Luke 22.34.

[64] For Augustine's teaching on the fixed number of the predestined, cf. *De corr. et grat.* 23.39: "numerus clausus neque augendus neque minuendus"; and Prosper, *Resp. cap. Gall.* 8.

[65] In Prosper's mind, at this stage of his doctrinal development, the gratuity of grace and the Augustinian teaching on the fixed number of the predestined are inseparably linked with one another as two points of faith. (Augustine connected them, e.g., in *De dono persev.* 13.33.) Cf. Cappuyns, "Premier représentant" 312f. Later on, in the *Auctoritates* and in *De voc.* (cf. ACW 14.12), he dissociates them. Prosper's proof for this connection is drawn from the Scripture texts which seem to say that, according to God's decree, many die without having known the true faith.

⁶⁶ Acts 14.14–16.

⁶⁷ We may contrast with this the different tone and setting of the same consideration about God's gifts seen as a "universal grace" in *De voc.* 1.5 and 2.4: there, to allow a universal salvific will; here, to show rather a restricted universalism of that salvific will.

⁶⁸ Cf. 1 Tim. 2.5.

⁶⁹ Cf. Acts 4.12.

⁷⁰ Cf. Ps. 99.3.

⁷¹ The case of infants, of whom some die baptized, others without baptism, is given here as a proof of the gratuity of grace and of predestination. The same idea appears in *De voc.*, but as a difficulty against the universal salvific will; cf. *De voc.* 2.20, answered *ibid.* 23 by the idea of a general grace (ACW 14.205 n. 180, 207 n. 215). We should remember that for Prosper as for Augustine (cf. *Enchir.* 23.93; ACW 3.88), infants dying without baptism are lost though "damnatione mitissima."

⁷² 1 Tim. 2.4. At this stage, Prosper apparently sees no difficulty in holding both the universal salvific will and the Augustinian fixed number of the predestined (he interprets the salvific will, after Augustine, in a restricted sense). Later, in *De voc.*, he labors to reconcile the two points and interprets the salvific will in a universal sense, thus sacrificing "Augustinian" predestination. Cf. ACW 14, Index *s.v.* salvific will.

⁷³ Compare *De voc.* 1.16 and 2.20.

⁷⁴ Cf. 1 Tim. 2.4. Restricted universalism in the sense that all those who are saved, are saved through grace or through God's will; or that none are saved unless God wills. Cf. Augustine, *De pecc. mer.* 1.28.55.

⁷⁵ 1 Cor. 3.7.

⁷⁶ Acts 13.48. Compare this chapter with Augustine, *Contra Iul.* 4.42.

⁷⁷ Acts 16.14.

⁷⁸ 1 Tim. 2.4.

⁷⁹ Acts 16.6f. All these Scripture texts are quoted to prove a restricted salvific will.

⁸⁰ Ps. 32.15.

⁸¹ Matt. 3.9.

⁸² Acts 13.48.

⁸³ Ps. 2.8.

⁸⁴ Ps. 21.28.

⁸⁵ Matt. 24.14.

⁸⁶ Acts 13.48.

⁸⁷ Eph. 1.11. Prosper thus reconciles predestination and salvific will by interpreting the latter in the sense of a restricted universality: God wills the salvation of all the elect.

⁸⁸ Ps. 75.2.

[89] Eph. 3.5f.

[90] Acts 10.45.

[91] Compare *Resp. cap. Gall.* 6.

[92] Cf. *De voc.* 1.17: deathbed conversions as a proof of the gratuity of grace.

[93] *Conversam non eversam:* turned back (to God), not destroyed.

[94] Cf. *De voc.* 1.8.

[95] James 1.17.

[96] James 3.14–17.

[97] Prov. 1.6 (ancient version).

[98] Cf. 2 Cor. 10.17f.

[99] Cf. 3 and nn. 16f. above.

[100] Against fatalism cf., among others, *De civ. Dei;* against the Manichees, *De Gen. contra Manich., De mor. eccl. cath. et de mor. Man., Contra Fortun. Man., Contra epist. Man., Contra Faust. Man.,* and *De natura boni.*

[101] Rom. 5.12. The answer to Manicheism is the Catholic doctrine on original sin, which sees there the source of what is evil in men.

[102] We may note here that Prosper stresses the grace needed for perseverance. In his *Epist. ad August.* he develops only the Semi-Pelagian error about the beginning of faith.

[103] *In confitenda gratia Dei:* for professing faith in the grace of God—concerning the Catholic doctrine of grace.

LETTER TO AUGUSTINE

[1] This letter and Augustine's answer have not been preserved. "The history of theology has no doubt lost little with them" (Cappuyns, "Premier représentant" 314 n. 13). On the present letter cf. Chéné, "Le semipélagianisme du midi de la Gaule," RSR 43 (1955) 321–41.

[2] *Servi Christi* = monks.

[3] The complaint, though greatly exaggerated, was not altogether unfounded: Augustine did "innovate" by his teaching on predestination; cf. F. Prat, *The Theology of Saint Paul* 1 (Westminster, Md. 1952) 443–55: Note H, "Predestination and Reprobation."

[4] The monks of Hadrumetum are meant here, for whom Augustine wrote two tracts, *De gratia et libero arbitrio* and *De correptione et gratia;* cf. Amann, "Semi-pélagianisme," DTC 14.1800–1802; Intro. n. 12; ACW 14.3f.

[5] From this indication it would appear that Prosper did not know of the *De corr. et grat.* when he wrote his letter to Rufinus.

[6] This shows that the Semi-Pelagians held the dogmas of original sin and the universal necessity of grace (unlike the Pelagians), together with the universal salvific will (unlike Augustine).

[7] A predestination which later theology would call *ex praevisis meritis*, as stated here, goes together with the universal salvific will.

[8] This is predestination *ante praevisa merita*, as taught by Augustine.

[9] Cf. Rom. 9.21.

[10] This is the same objection of fatalism as in *Epist. ad Rufin.* 3 and in *Resp. cap. Gall.* 1.

[11] On this objection of Manichean dualism, cf. *Epist. ad Rufin.* 3 and 18.

[12] As noted n. 3 above, there is some truth in saying that Augustine's teaching on predestination is not found in the tradition before him: it is not there in the form he gave it. Cf. also H. de Lubac, *Méditation sur l'église* (2nd ed. Paris 1953) 211 n. 20.

[13] Rom. 9.14–21. Here also the objection is partly founded; cf. n. 3 above.

[14] For the answer to this difficulty, not altogether unfounded (Augustine's teaching on predestination is not, as such, of faith, and if misrepresented can lead to wrong practical conclusions), cf. the sample of "sermon" on predestination in *Resp. exc. Gen.*, extract 9.

[15] If the monks of Marseilles really taught what Prosper here ascribes to them, then they actually followed Pelagius, who called nature or free will itself by the name of grace and in that sense attributed to grace the beginning of salvation. Cf. above, *Epist. ad. Rufin.* 6.

[16] This explanation of the universal salvific will is echoed by Prosper himself in *Resp. cap. Gall.* 8 and *De voc.;* cf. Intro. n. 63.

[17] The Semi-Pelagian explanation of the salvific will is erroneous when they say that man can answer God's call to salvation without the help of grace. Cf. Intro. n. 65.

[18] This is exactly the Pelagian concept of freedom; cf. de Plinval, *Pélage* 234–36. But, as stated immediately in the text, the Semi-Pelagians held the need of the help of grace in the actual practice of virtue.

[19] The case of dying unbaptized infants is a difficulty against the salvific will even today. The Semi-Pelagian answer, however, taken from *praevisis meritis futuribilibus* (which never exist) is purely verbal; cf. Augustine's criticism in *Contra duas epist. Pelag.* 2.7.14 or in *Epist. 194 ad Sixt.* 8.35 and 9.41f., and later in *De praed. sanct.* 12–16, 23–29. Cf. ACW 14.187 n. 213.

[20] Prosper's criticism of the Semi-Pelagian argument is justified: God does not foreknow what will never be. But though the argument is

wrong, if it is not replaced by another valid one, the universal salvific will on behalf of unbaptized infants remains unexplained.

21 Acts 14.15.

22 Cf. Matt. 4.16; Isa. 9.2.

23 Cf. Rom. 9.25; Osee 2.24.

24 *Ibid.*

25 This states predestination *ex praevisis meritis*, against Augustine, who held predestination *ante praevisa merita.*

26 1 Tim. 2.4.

27 Here appears the Semi-Pelagian idea of the universal salvific will, explained without grace. Cf. Intro. n. 67.

28 This explanation of the delay in preaching the gospel is also purely verbal; cf. n. 19 above.

29 Contrast with this explanation of the universality of the redemption Prosper's answer to the objection that predestination entails the nonuniversality of the redemption, in *Resp. cap. Gall.* 9. and in *Resp. cap. Vinc.* 1.

30 The Semi-Pelagian error about the *initium fidei:* man believes of himself, grace is a reward for his faith.

31 Rom. 9.21.

32 Cf. Augustine, *De corr. et grat.* 9.20–25: "numerus clausus. . . ." The Semi-Pelagians felt reluctant to admit this predestination because it goes against the universal salvific will.

33 This Semi-Pelagian position, *initium salutis ab homine*, logically flows from their concept of ever-efficacious grace and of the universal salvific will; cf. Intro. n. 67.

34 Hilary of Arles was made a bishop of that town at the end of 428; cf. Cappuyns, "Premier représentant" 313f. n. 13., and below, *Letter to Augustine* 9.

35 *Pelagianae pravitatis reliquiae:* Prosper's label for Semi-Pelagianism and historical origin of this name; cf. ACW 14.178 n. 7.

36 Mangeant reads *collatus* for *collocatus*, a negligible nuance of meaning.

37 Prosper's first request: show that a point of faith is at stake. In fact, there was: the *initium fidei* is from grace, not from nature.

38 His second request: how efficacious grace does not suppress free will. Augustine had already shown this in *De grat. et lib. arb.* and *De corr. et grat.*

39 Prosper's third request: about predestination, particularly about the relation that exists between God's foreknowledge and His decree. He asks three questions: (1) Is God's prescience determined by His decree (foreknown is what was decreed)? (2) Or is the decree different for dif-

ferent cases: of those who are saved without works of their own (*sine praevisis meritis*) and those who have to co-operate freely (*ex praevisis meritis*)? (3) Or is it the same in all cases: God's decree "depending" on His foreknowledge? Prosper has visibly been impressed by the Semi-Pelagian reasonings. Augustine's answer is in *De dono persev.* 14.35; cf. *Resp. exc. Gen.* 8.

⁴⁰ How preach about predestination without causing harm? Cf. n. 14 above. Augustine's answer is given in *De praed. sanct.* 17.34f.; cf. *Resp. exc. Gen.* 9.

⁴¹ Prosper's last question: Does traditional teaching have predestination *post praevisa merita?*

⁴² They are found in Augustine's double tract, *De praed. sanct.* and *De dono persev.*, which however was a source of new difficulties; cf. *Resp. exc. Gen.* praef.

⁴³ Cf. n. 34 above.

ANSWERS TO THE EXTRACTS OF THE GENOESE

¹ From this text it appears that the two tracts, *De praed. sanct.* and *De dono persev.*, Augustine's answer to the letters of Prosper and Hilary, were originally one work. Cf. Intro. n. 20.

² Prosper's modesty appears in most of his writings; cf., e.g., *Epist. ad August.* 7. Here it naturally suits the lay theologian writing to priests.

³ James 1.17.

⁴ Ps. 18.8.

⁵ Rom. 9.3; Mal. 1.3.

⁶ *De praed. sanct.* 1.3.

⁷ Cf. 1 Cor. 12.4.

⁸ *De praed. sanct.* 1.3.

⁹ Rom. 9.12.

¹⁰ *De praed. sanct.* 1.3. Augustine had corrected these three passages, taken from *Expos. quor. prop. epist. apost. ad Rom.*, written *ca.* 394, in *Retract.* 1.23.2 and 3.

¹¹ *Et praecedentibus, et mediis, et subsequentibus:* the mediate and immediate context.

¹² This is the Semi-Pelagian idea of the *initium fidei.*

¹³ 1 Cor. 4.7.

¹⁴ Cf. Rom. 9.13. Formerly Augustine considered God's foreknowledge of future merits as determining His decree electing one for grace and not electing another; this opinion he abandoned in his later works.

¹⁵ Cf. *De div. quaest. ad Simplic.* (year 397; ML 40.111–28).

[16] Cf. Rom. 11.6.

[17] Rom. 9.13.

[18] *Retract.* 2.1.

[19] This is one position of the Pelagians: retaining the name grace, they say it is given in answer to merit; cf., e.g., Augustine, *De grat. Christi* 1.22.

[20] By attributing the *initium fidei* to man's unaided will and saying God awaits it before giving grace, the Semi-Pelagians logically implied that grace is given in answer to human merit. Cf. Intro. n. 51.

[21] If the *initium fidei* is from man and not from grace, then it is a gift of God in a broad sense only, and this leads to another Pelagian position, which said that free will itself is grace; cf. *De gest. Pel.* 30: "Gratiam Dei . . . esse in libero arbitrio"; de Plinval, *Pélage* 288f.

[22] Prosper reasons on the supposition that his Semi-Pelagian opponents do not deny original sin. Faith is among the gifts which Adam lost by sin —he did so by believing the devil—and his posterity lost it in him.

[23] Wisd. 8.21.

[24] Rom. 5.5.

[25] Isa. 11.2.

[26] 1 Cor. 12.6.

[27] Rom. 5.12.

[28] Prosper's proof that faith is a gift of grace is based on the fallen state of men and the healing character of grace. As noted, Intro. n. 52, there is a more basic reason for it, namely, the elevating character of grace. The denial that faith is a gift of God and the affirmation that it is initiated by man logically lead to the Pelagian error that grace is given in answer to merit, namely, to the merit of faith.

[29] To sum up Prosper's answer to the first three excerpts: it is not right to follow an opinion of Augustine which he held when he was young and disowned later.

[30] Prov. 8.35 (LXX); *De praed. sanct.* 5.10.

[31] 1 Cor. 4.7.

[32] Rom. 11.7.

[33] Rom. 11.8; cf. Isa. 6.9f.

[34] Ps. 48.23f.

[35] Rom. 11.5f.

[36] Ps. 55.8.

[37] Ps. 55.10.

[38] Rom. 11.33.

[39] *De praed. sanct.* 5.10—6.11.

[40] Prov. 8.35 (LXX).

[41] Rom. 8.14.

[42] This answers the accusation of Manichean dualism leveled against Augustine; cf. *Epist. ad August.* 3; *Epist. ad Rufin.* 3.

[43] Cf. Rom. 11.7.

[44] Ps. 55.8.

[45] Ps. 24.10.

[46] Rom. 11.13.

[47] This answer hardly diminishes the harshness of Augustine's view on predestination and reprobation. Augustine says that the effective call of the elect is due to grace, its absence in the case of the reprobate is due to God's justice, no one deserving to be called because of original sin. As pointed out, Intro. n. 63, it is only by considering what we now call sufficient grace offered to all that this harshness can be remedied.

[48] *De praed. sanct.* 8.16.

[49] Cf. Hab. 2.4.

[50] Gal. 2.21.

[51] Cf. 2 Thess. 2.12.

[52] Cf. Eph. 6.23.

[53] Eph. 2.8.

[54] Phil. 1.29.

[55] Heb. 12.1f.

[56] 2 Thess. 3.2.

[57] Prosper did not answer the difficulty implied in this excerpt: Why is the gift of faith not given to all? This is tackled in the answer to the following extract.

[58] Cf. Rom. 5.18.

[59] 1 Cor. 1.31; cf. 2 Cor. 10.17.

[60] Rom. 11.33.

[61] Rom. 9.20.

[62] *De praed. sanct.* 8.16. The doctrine of the Fall is the background of Augustinian predestination and reprobation; the reason of the discrimination is a mystery. Prosper's consultants looked, no doubt, for a way of making this teaching less rigid and harsh. Prosper, however, fails to show this; he only reaffirms Augustine's position.

[63] Prosper's reasoning holds good only when no account is taken of sufficient grace. If sufficient grace were offered to all, those who come to the faith do so thanks to grace; those who do not, fail to come through their own fault. But this solution, as noted, Intro. n. 62, lies outside both Augustine's and Prosper's perspective.

[64] Col. 1.13.

[65] Cf. Acts 14.15.

[66] 2 Tim. 1.9.

[67] *De praed. sanct.* 16.33.

[68] Ps. 2.1f.

[69] Acts 4.23–28; *De praed. sanct.* 16.33.

[70] This is a typically Augustinian idea about God's providence: in their very sins the wicked carry out God's designs; cf., e.g., *De grat. et lib. arb.* 20.40 and 21.42.

[71] Rom. 8.32.

[72] John 19.10.

[73] John 19.11.

[74] Book 2 = *De dono persev.*; cf. n. 1 above.

[75] Cf. John 18.9.

[76] Cf. Matt. 11.21.

[77] *De dono persev.* 14.35. This definite statement about predestination and reprobation is Augustine's answer to Prosper's question in *Epist. ad August.* 8 (cf. *ibid.* n. 39 above).

[78] Prosper's answer shows the connection between gratuitous predestination and the gratuity of the first grace, which is faith. Rejection of the latter leads to rejection of the former. Both of them are, in Prosper's mind, points of faith. Cf., however, Intro. n. 53.

[79] 1 Cor. 12.6.

[80] Heb. 11.6.

[81] Ps. 126.1.

[82] 2 Tim. 2.19.

[83] Cf. John 18.9.

[84] This explanation of the reprobation, acceptable to Prosper as it was to Augustine, seems to us today rather rigid and incompatible with a universal salvific will. Cf. Intro. n. 59.

[85] 2 Par. 19.7.

[86] *De grat. et lib. arb.* 23.45.

[87] Compare a similar avowal of ignorance of the reason of God's discrimination between the elect and the reprobate in *De voc.* 1.21 and 23 (ACW 14.69, 87f.).

[88] Cf. Matt. 11.21; Luke 10.23.

[89] Cf. Matt. and Luke, *loc. cit.*

[90] John 6.66.

[91] Matt. 13.11.

[92] Matt. 11.27.

[93] John 5.21.

[94] 1 Cor. 12.3.

[95] 1 Cor. 12.6.

[96] Rom. 1.21.

[97] *De dono persev.* 15.38. This parody of a sermon on predestination is not found in the letters of Prosper or Hilary, both of whom merely say

that the teaching of Augustine on predestination renders exhortation to virtue useless. Cf. *Epist. ad August.* 8, and Hilary, *Epist. ad August.* 5.
[98] Cf. *Epist. ad August.* 8 n. 40.
[99] Rom. 3.8.
[100] *De dono persev.* 22.61.
[101] James 1.17.
[102] Jer. 17.5.
[103] Ps. 117.8.
[104] Ps. 2.11.
[105] Matt. 6.13.
[106] *De dono persev.* 22.62. There is, no doubt, a world of difference between Augustine's sample of a sermon on predestination and the parody quoted above. Yet, even this leaves one with the impression that a misunderstanding is not altogether warded off, however much he may have attenuated the idea of reprobation.
[107] *De dono persev.* 22.57.
[108] *Ibid.* 22.61.
[109] Prosper considers as of faith Augustine's teaching on predestination. Hence his practical conclusion about preaching it, to which not everyone would subscribe; cf., e.g., despite the distance in time, St. Ignatius of Loyola, *Spiritual Exercises*, "Rules for Thinking with the Church" 14–15. As explained in the Intro. n. 53, not everything in Augustine's teaching is of faith.
[110] This extract, Prosper says, follows immediately on excerpt 8 in *De dono persev.* 14.35; it reads: "Ex quo apparet habere quosdam in ipso ingenio divinum naturaliter munus intelligentiae, quo moveantur ad fidem, si congrua suis mentibus, vel audiant verba vel signa conspiciant; et tamen si Dei altiori iudicio a perditionis massa non sunt gratia praedestinationis discreti, nec ipsa eis adhibentur vel dicta divina vel facta, per quae possent credere, si audirent utique talia vel viderent." The excerpt would have deserved a word of comment beyond Prosper's answer to excerpt 8.

ON GRACE AND FREE WILL, AGAINST CASSIAN THE LECTURER

[1] The full Latin title reads *De gratia et libero arbitrio liber contra collatorem, id est, pro defensione s. Aurelii Augustini, Hipponensis episcopi, contra Cassiani presbyteri librum qui titulo de protectione Dei praenotatur.* Cassian's thirteenth Conference, *On the Protection of God,* is in CSEL 13.361–96; ML 48.897–954. For the *Contra collat.* cf. Lequeux, *op. cit.* 183–328.

[2] Semi-Pelagianism was a reaction against Augustine's teaching on the divine election and predestination, particularly in his last writings against the Pelagians; cf. *Epist. ad August.* 2.

[3] The Massilians, later to be known as Semi-Pelagians, meant to remain within the Church; the Pelagians had been severed from the Church by their condemnation at the Council of Carthage, 418.

[4] By attacking Augustine, Prosper says, the Semi-Pelagians attack the bishops of Africa, who approved of his teaching, and the Roman pontiffs, who gave their sanction to the Council of Carthage. It should be noted, however, that he exaggerates: Augustine's later teachings, against which the Massilians protested, had never been officially approved—nor would they ever be without considerable toning down of some of their expressions.

[5] This shows the time when the *Contra collat.* was written: about 432. Augustine's first formal writing against the Pelagians was the *De peccat. mer.* of 412.

[6] At the Council of Carthage, 418; cf. ES 101ff.

[7] Celestius was excommunicated at the Council of Carthage, 411/12 (cf. de Plinval, *Pélage* 258f.); Pelagius and Celestius were again excommunicated by Pope Innocent I in 417 (*ibid.* 303); and the Pelagians, Celestius, Pelagius, Julian, etc., were condemned by the *epistola synodalis* of the Council of Ephesus, 431 (*ibid.* 353).

[8] "Our writers," especially Augustine; "our judges" (in the faith): the Fathers of the councils and the Roman pontiffs.

[9] Prosper means Cassian, abbot of a Marseilles monastery. On Cassian cf. the works of Cristiani and Chadwick, cited Intro. n. 3.

[10] *Conlatio* 13 (CSEL 13.361–97).

[11] James 1.17.

[12] 2 Cor. 9.10; Cassian, *Conlatio* 13.3.5 (CSEL 13.364).

[13] Cf. Acts 7.51.

[14] Jer. 8.4.; Cassian, *Conlatio* 13.3.6 (CSEL 13.364).

[15] Cassian, *ibid.* 13.6.3 (CSEL 13.367).

[16] *Ibid.* 13.8.3 (CSEL 13.371).

[17] *Ibid.* 13.8.4.

[18] Already here Cassian's idea is rather that the good efforts spring from man's own unaided will; Prosper's interpretation is "charitable."

[19] Cf. Rom. 10.20f.; Isa. 66.1f.

[20] Cassian, *Conlatio* 13.9.1 (CSEL 13.372).

[21] The discrimination lies in the ways of divine grace; some men are called willing, others unwilling. Cassian interprets: some come to grace of their own accord, others God prevents with His grace. Prosper rejects this interpretation: grace it is that produces the willingness.

[22] Cf. 2.2 above and n. 12 above.

[23] So the Pelagians understood grace; cf. Augustine, *De grat. Christi* 1.7–14.

[24] James 1.17.

[25] Cf. 2.2 above and n. 12 above. Prosper's reasoning in what follows supposes that no good comes from fallen nature. He is unaware of what later would be called naturally honest or good acts.

[26] This is the Pelagian position; cf. Augustine, *De praed. sanct.* 2.3; and cf. 5.1 below.

[27] John 6.44.

[28] Ps. 84.13.

[29] Isa. 1.19.

[30] Rom. 9.16.

[31] Matt. 16.17.

[32] Phil. 2.13.

[33] Eph. 2.13; cf. Cassian, *Conlatio* 13.9.2 (CSEL 13.372).

[34] Compare Augustine, *De spir. et lit.* 14.23: "Decalogus occidit, nisi adsit gratia."

[35] Cassian, *Conlatio* 13.9.4 (CSEL 13.373).

[36] Cf. 2.2 above and n. 12 above.

[37] Cassian, *Conlatio* 13.9.5 (CSEL 13.373f.).

[38] We may note here the presuppositions of the reasoning: fallen nature is considered as capable of no good, and grace as ever-efficacious; cf. Intro. nn. 52, 61ff.

[39] Rom. 7.18; Cassian, *loc. cit.*

[40] Cf. 2.2 above and n. 12 above.

[41] Rom. 7.18.

[42] 2 Cor. 3.5.

[43] Phil. 2.13.

[44] Rom. 7.18.

[45] Cf. Rom. 7.22f.

[46] Cassian, *Conlatio* 13.11.1 (CSEL 13.375f.).

[47] Cf. n. 26 above.

[48] This is not a literal quotation from Cassian, but a summary of *op. cit.* 13.11.4.

[49] This alludes to Cassian's teaching on lying in *Conlatio* 17.20 (CSEL 480ff.), where he says that it is sometimes allowed to speak or act untruthfully—"utilis ac salubris hypocrisis."

[50] Cassian, *Conlatio* 13.11.1 (CSEL 13.376).

[51] *Epist.* 29.3 (ML 20.584), addressed to the Council of Carthage of 416; cf. *Auctoritates* 2 (ES 131).

[52] *Epist.* 29.6 (ML 20.586); cf. *Auctoritates* 1 (ES 130).

53 Cf. Augustine, *De gest. Pel.* 14.33–35; cf. de Plinval, *Pélage* 290.

54 These are the Councils of Mileve and Carthage; cf. Mansi 3.1071, 811; ES 104.

55 Cf. 1 Cor. 8.1.

56 Ps. 93.10.

57 1 John 4.7.

58 Of the great Council of Carthage, 418.

59 Cf. Mansi 4.376.   Only the passage quoted by Prosper has been preserved.

60 The famous *Epistula tractoria,* of which only some excerpts are extant; the present quotation is found also in *Auctoritates* 5 (ES 134).

61 Prov. 8.35 (LXX).

62 Rom. 8.14.

63 Cf. Prosper, *Auctoritates* 5 (ES 134).

64 Allusion to Jos. 6.20.

65 Luke 1.51–53.

66 Luke 1.72–75.

67 I Cor. 2.12.

68 Cf. Prosper, *Auctoritates* 5 (ES 134).

69 Rom. 8.14.

70 Cf. Isa. 11.2.

71 Cf. Rom. 9.8; Gal. 4.28.

72 Cassian, *Conlatio* 13.11.1f. (CSEL 13.376).

73 Cf. Ps. 76.11.

74 John 6.44.

75 Rom. 1.20.

76 Ps. 77.4.

77 Prov. 1.7; Ps. 110.10.

78 Ps. 121.1.

79 Ps. 83.3.

80 Ps. 118.103; another reading has *divinae lectiones* for *delectationes.*

81 1 Cor. 12.11.

82 2 Cor. 4.6.

83 Luke 19.5.

84 Luke 19.9.

85 Luke 19.10.

86 Luke 10.22.

87 John 12.32.

88 Luke 23.42.

89 1 Cor. 12.3.

90 1 Cor. 12.6.

91 Cassian, *Conlatio* 13.11.2 (CSEL 13.376).

92 Cf. Num. 22.5ff.
93 Cf. Gen. 20.6.
94 Cf. Gen. 37.28.
95 Cassian, *Conlatio* 13.11.4 (CSEL 13.377).
96 1 Cor. 12.3.
97 1 Cor. 4.7.
98 1 Cor. 15.10.
99 1 Cor. 7.25.
100 2 Cor. 4.7.
101 Eph. 2.8.
102 Phil. 1:28f.
103 Phil. 2.12f.
104 2 Cor. 3.5.
105 John 6.66.
106 John 6.37.
107 John 15.5.
108 John 15.16.
109 Matt. 11.27.
110 John 5.21.
111 Matt. 16.17.
112 Cf. Eph. 3.8.
113 Cf. Col. 1.13.
114 James 1.17.
115 Cf. 2.2. above and n. 12 above.
116 Isa. 30.19.
117 Ps. 49.15; Cassian, *Conlatio* 13.11.5 (CSEL 13.377).
118 Cf. Augustine, *De gest. Pel.* 14.30f.; *De praed. sanct.* 2.3; cf. n. 53 above.
119 Ps. 36.23.
120 Prov. 21.2.
121 Prov. 20.24.
122 Rom. 8.15.
123 Gen. 3.22.
124 Eccli. 7.29 (LXX).
125 Cf. *ibid.*
126 Cf. Gen. 3.22.
127 Cassian, *Conlatio* 13.12.1f. (CSEL 13.378).
128 The possibility of perseverance for Adam, without any need of the great "gift of perseverance" which men after the Fall are in need of, is the teaching of Augustine, e.g., in *De corr. et grat.* 11.31f., with his well-known distinction between *auxilium sine quo non*, given to Adam, and *auxilium quo*, given to the fallen and redeemed elect.

[129] Ambrose, *In Lucam* 7.15 (ML 15.1852).

[130] Luke 19.10.

[131] Eph. 2.3.

[132] Eph. 5.8.

[133] Col. 1.13. Prosper considers no other goodness than that of salutary acts; he knows of no natural goodness.

[134] Cf. Rom. 5.12.

[135] Cf. John 6.54.

[136] Cassian, *Conlatio* 13.12.1. Prosper's criticism of this statement is that to admit man's fallen state is not the same as saying that God created man in this fallen state. To say the opposite leads to denying the Fall, since God cannot be the author of this fallen state.

[137] Man's fallen state supposes that all share in Adam's sin and not only in his punishment. This is precisely the dogma of original sin. Accordingly, the Creator is not the cause of man's misery: man incurred it by sin.

[138] Gen. 3.22; cf. Cassian, *Conlatio* 13.12.1.

[139] Cassian, *ibid.* 13.12.2 (CSEL 13.378).

[140] Luke 16.13.

[141] John 8.34.

[142] 2 Peter 2.19.

[143] Rom. 6.20–22.

[144] Prosper rather magnifies Cassian's statement about the soundness of free will in fallen man; this statement need not be equivalent to a denial of original sin—original sin has not taken away free will but only weakened it. Cf. ES 793 and 181.

[145] Rom. 2.14–16; Cassian, *Conlatio* 13.12.3 (CSEL 13.378).

[146] Eph. 2.13.

[147] Cf. 1 Peter 2.10.

[148] Rom. 3.30.

[149] Cf. Eph. 2.14.

[150] Gal. 3.22.

[151] Prosper here understands St. Paul's text as referring to the Gentiles converted to Christ—wrongfully, however. There is a natural goodness which he does not, and could not, consider. Cf. Intro. n. 57.

[152] Rom. 3.23.

[153] Rom. 11.35.

[154] This is the real meaning of St. Paul's text; cf. Prat, *Theology of Saint Paul* 1.198ff.

[155] Eccli. 24.5.

[156] This is the Augustinian idea of the virtues of pagans; cf. Intro. n. 57.

[157] Rom. 3.20.
[158] Gal. 6.15; cf. 5.6.
[159] Cf. Rom. 5.5. Note again that Prosper only considers salutary acts.
[160] Heb. 11.6.
[161] Rom. 14.23.
[162] Gal. 5.6.
[163] Cf. Isa. 42.18.
[164] Ezech. 11.19f.; cf. 36.26f.
[165] Luke 12.37.
[166] Cassian, *Conlatio* 13.12.5 (CSEL 13.379). Cassian's reasoning holds good only in the supposition of ever-efficacious grace. If sufficient grace is considered also, then men are blameworthy for not using it, and not only because they omitted the good works they could do of themselves.
[167] Cf. 2 Cor. 3.6.
[168] Cassian, *Conlatio* 13.12.5 (CSEL 13.379). Prosper interprets this in an altogether Pelagian sense, when it could also be understood as meaning that free will positively co-operates with grace.
[169] Cf. Augustine, *De praed. sanct.* 2.3.
[170] Cf. Augustine, *De gest. Pel.* 14:30: "gratiam Dei et adiutorium non ad singulos actus dari."
[171] Prosper interprets Cassian's statement: grace is not the principle of merit, since, in Cassian's mind, free will is; and when grace does everything, then free will does not do anything, and so there is no merit then. But this does not follow necessarily from Cassian's text; all he may mean to say is that free will co-operates with grace.
[172] Cf. Pelagius, *De lib. arb.* quoted by Augustine, *De grat. Christi* 29.30. Cf. Council of Carthage, can. 9 (ES 105). Again, this does not necessarily follow from Cassian's text.
[173] As just noted, Prosper imputes to Cassian a good deal more than follows from his text with strict logical necessity. He himself seems to be aware of it; cf. 12.1 below.
[174] Cf. 2.2 above and n. 12 above; Cassian, *Conlatio* 13.3.5 (CSEL 13.364).
[175] 3 Kings 8.17–19; cf. Cassian, *Conlatio* 13.12.5 (CSEL 13.380).
[176] Cassian, *Conlatio* 13.12.6 (CSEL 13.380).
[177] Prosper's remark is to the point: grace at times inspires "impossible desires."
[178] Ps. 131.3–5.
[179] John 2.19, 21.
[180] This spiritual exegesis is borrowed from Augustine, *Enarr. in ps.* 126.2 (ML 37.1668), *De civ. Dei* 17.8. It is not needed to show that God can inspire in man a good desire which nevertheless He gives him no

chance to carry out; the good desire itself has a spiritual effect of its own.

[181] Matt. 28.19–20.

[182] Cf. Acts 16.6f.; cf. *De voc.* 2.3 (ACW 14.93).

[183] Luke 18.19.

[184] Compare *De voc.* 1.4 (ACW 14.29). This idea, Augustinian in origin (cf. *De civ. Dei* 5.15), expresses the equivalent of what later theology called "natural goodness" and "naturally honest acts"; these acts are not evil, yet ineffective for salvation and life eternal.

[185] Rom. 1.21. Cf. *De voc., loc. cit.,* and Intro. n. 55.

[186] Compare *De voc.* 1.8 (ACW 14.35). The need of grace for free will to turn to God is here again derived mainly from man's fallen state and the healing character of grace. The Fall made free will incapable of any (salutary) good acts; only grace enables him to do these.

[187] Eph. 2.10.

[188] 1 Cor. 3.7.

[189] *Pastor Hermae,* Mandat. 6.2.

[190] Cassian, *Conlatio* 13.12.7f. (CSEL 13.380f.).

[191] Cf. Ps. 50.7.

[192] Cf. Eph. 2.3.

[193] Cf. Col. 1.13. Prosper sees in Cassian's text the equivalent of a denial of original sin. In this he rather magnifies its implications. Cassian's text is ambiguous: the "seeds of the virtues" may mean just nature basically unspoiled, and then it is right; or a grace not lost by sin, and then it is wrong. Prosper understands the text in the second meaning.

[194] 2 Cor. 6.14.

[195] 1 Cor. 1.24.

[196] Cf. 1 Tim. 2.5.

[197] John 12.13.

[198] Mark 3.27.

[199] 1 Cor. 2.12.

[200] Rom. 8.9.

[201] Cf. *De voc.* 1.4 (ACW 14.29).

[202] For this Augustinian view of pagan virtues as always vitiated somehow, cf., e.g., *De civ. Dei* 19.25; or *In Ioan. ev. tract.* 45.2. As explained in Intro. nn. 54f., this judgment should be toned down. Cf. also ACW 14.175 n. 34.

[203] Cassian, *Conlatio* 13.12.7 (CSEL 13.380).

[204] This is the Pelagian idea of external grace. It may be doubted whether Prosper is fair to Cassian in thus interpreting his text. He certainly magnifies his idea of the seeds of the virtues which remain in fallen man; cf. n. 193 above.

[205] 1 Cor. 3.11.

206 Prov. 1.7.
207 Cf. *ibid.* 9.10.
208 Eccli. 25.14f.
209 This implies: and so every virtue is or originates in a gift of God.
210 2 Peter 1.2 (other version).
211 1 Cor. 4.7.
212 Note again the stress on *gratia sanans*.
213 Augustinian idea: the virtues of pagans are not true virtues; cf. n. 202 above.
214 1 Cor. 3.19.
215 1 Cor. 3.18.
216 1 Cor. 1.21.
217 Cassian, *Conlatio* 13.12.7 (CSEL 13.380).
218 *Ibid.* 13.12.8 (CSEL 13.381).
219 The case of infants and that of the insane, who are saved through baptism without any co-operation of their free wills, is a classical argument of Augustine and Prosper for predestination. But, as Prosper seems to sense, it is rather beside the point in his dispute with Cassian.
220 Prosper hints at the Pelagian concept of freedom: equal power for good and evil.
221 Luke 12.49.
222 Lovers of grace—ironically; another reading has *in istis gratiae damnatoribus*.
223 Luke 24.32.
224 Acts 16.14.
225 Prosper manifestly exaggerates Cassian's "seeds of the virtues."
226 Cf. 1 Cor. 13.2f.
227 Rom. 5.5.
228 Eph. 6.23.
229 1 John 4.7.
230 1 John 4.10.
231 1 John 4.19.
232 1 Cor. 4.7.
233 Prosper aims at what Cassian says, *Conlatio* 13.13.2 (CSEL 13.383), of the good thief on the cross or of the repentance of David.
234 John 15.5.
235 Job 1.9–11 (LXX).
236 Cassian, *Conlatio* 13.14.1f. (CSEL 13.384f.).
237 James 1.17.
238 Cf. 2.2 above; Cassian, *Conlatio* 13.3.5 (CSEL 13.364).
239 *Hostilium reliquiarum;* cf. *reliquiae Pelagianorum* or *Pelagianae pravitatis reliquiae* in *Epist. ad August.* 7.

²⁴⁰ Cf. 2.2 above; Cassian, *Conlatio* 13.3.5 (CSEL 13.364).

²⁴¹ Cf. 3.2 above; Cassian, *ibid.* 13.9.4 (CSEL 13.373).

²⁴² Cf. 4.2 above; Cassian, *ibid.* 13.9.5 (CSEL 13.373f.).

²⁴³ Cf. 5.1 above; Cassian, *ibid.* 13.11.1 (CSEL 13.375f.).

²⁴⁴ For St. Paul cf. Acts 9.1-8; for St. Matthew cf. Matt. 9.9, Mark 2.14, Luke 5.27; for Zacchaeus cf. Luke 19.2-10; for the good thief, Luke 23.40-43.

²⁴⁵ Cf. 7.1 above; Cassian, *Conlatio* 13.11.1f. (CSEL 13.375f.).

²⁴⁶ Cf. 9.2 above; Cassian, *ibid.* 13.12.2 (CSEL 13.378).

²⁴⁷ Cf. 11.2 above; Cassian, *ibid.* 13.12.5 (CSEL 13.379f.).

²⁴⁸ Cf. 13.1 above; Cassian, *ibid.* 13.12.7 (CSEL 13.380).

²⁴⁹ *Fallaciter:* Prosper's accusation against Cassian implies duplicity on the Lecturer's part; this is oversevere and may well be unjust.

²⁵⁰ Cf. 4.2 above; Cassian, *Conlatio* 13.9.5 (CSEL 13.373f.).

²⁵¹ Cf. Cassian, *ibid.* 13.14.1f. (CSEL 13.384f.).

²⁵² Cf. Cassian, *ibid.* 13.14.2 (CSEL 13.385).

²⁵³ Cf. Augustine, *De nat. et grat.* 26.29: "Deus non deserit, nisi prius deseratur" (ML 44.261).

²⁵⁴ Job 19.25-27.

²⁵⁵ 1 Cor. 15.20.

²⁵⁶ Matt. 10.19f.

²⁵⁷ Job 12.4.

²⁵⁸ Job 12.13.

²⁵⁹ Job 12.10.

²⁶⁰ Job 14.14-17.

²⁶¹ Ps. 22.4.

²⁶² Ps. 36.39.

²⁶³ Rom. 5.1-5.

²⁶⁴ Rom. 8.35-37; cf. Ps. 43.22.

²⁶⁵ Luke 22.31.

²⁶⁶ Matt. 6.13. The Lord's Prayer was in daily use with the Christians.

²⁶⁷ Ps. 96.10.

²⁶⁸ Cassian, *Conlatio* 13.14.2 (CSEL 13.385).

²⁶⁹ Cf. n. 172 above.

²⁷⁰ John 15.5; Council of Carthage, can. 5 (ES 105).

²⁷¹ Cf. Cassian, *Conlatio* 13.14.3 (CSEL 13.385).

²⁷² Matt. 8.8; Cassian, *ibid.*

²⁷³ Matt. 8.10.

²⁷⁴ Cassian, *Conlatio* 13.14.4 (CSEL 13.385f.).

²⁷⁵ Wisd. 8.21.

²⁷⁶ 1 Cor. 7.7.

[277] James 1.5.
[278] James 1.17.
[279] John 3.27.
[280] Cf. Phil. 1.29.
[281] Cf. 1 Cor. 1.31; 2 Cor. 10.17.
[282] Jer. 17.5.
[283] Ps. 17.1.
[284] Ps. 33.3.
[285] Ps. 117.14.
[286] But these virtues gain no merit or praise without man's free co-operation. Prosper rather tendentiously leaves aside the consideration of the role of free will.
[287] Rom. 1.8.
[288] 1 Cor. 1.4.
[289] Eph. 1.15–18.
[290] Phil. 1.3–6.
[291] Ps. 88.16f.
[292] Cf. n. 169 above; also *Epist. Pelagii ad Demetr.* 3 (ML 30.18).
[293] Cassian, *Conlatio* 13.16.1 (CSEL 13.391).
[294] Cassian, *ibid.* 13.16.3 (CSEL 13.391f.).
[295] Rom. 1.17.
[296] John 5.24.
[297] John 6.40.
[298] John 17.3.
[299] Prosper's argumentation is to the point: Cassian is inconsistent when he both condemns the Pelagians who say that grace is given for merit, and attributes faith to unaided free will and not to grace; faith (living faith) is meritorious and so cannot but come from grace.
[300] Cf. 2.2 above; Cassian, *Conlatio* 13.3.5 (CSEL 13.364).
[301] Cf. 15.1 above; Cassian, *ibid.* 13.14.4 (CSEL 13.385).
[302] Cassian, *ibid.* 13.17.1f. (CSEL 13.392f.).
[303] Matt. 1.21.
[304] Acts 4.12.
[305] John 15.16.
[306] John 6.66.
[307] John 1.9.
[308] Col. 1.13.
[309] Prosper is right in pointing out Cassian's inconsistency: one cannot hold both the necessity and the nonnecessity of grace for answering the call to the faith—or be both Pelagian and Catholic according to different cases.
[310] Cf. 1 Cor. 15.10.

311 Cf. Matt. 18.11.

312 Rom. 12.16.

313 Cassian's distinction between Christ Saviour of some and refuge or helper of others means to say that the second begin the work of their salvation of themselves and are then helped by the grace of Christ, while in the first grace starts the process of their salvation. It is another way of attributing the *initium fidei* to free will in the case of the latter, and to grace in the case of the former.

314 As noted repeatedly, it is the healing character of grace which Prosper after Augustine stresses, particularly in this adage, which sums up his position concerning grace and free will. That grace does not set aside free will is also shown in *De voc.* 1.8 (ACW 14.35f.).

315 Gal. 4.6.

316 Cf. Matt. 10.20.

317 Phil. 2.13.

318 1 John 4.7.

319 Rom. 5.5.

320 Compare *De voc.* 1.7 (ACW 14.33f.).

321 James 1.17.

322 Cf. 2.2 above; Cassian, *Conlatio* 13.3.5 (CSEL 13.364).

323 Ps. 58.11.

324 Cf. 2.3 above; Cassian, *Conlatio* 13.8.3f. (CSEL 13.371f.).

325 Cf. 3.2; 4.1 above; Cassian, *ibid.* 13.9.4f. (CSEL 13.373f.).

326 Rom. 7.18; cf. 4.2 above; Cassian, *ibid.* 13.9.5 (CSEL 13.373f.).

327 Cf. 5.1; 7.1 above; Cassian, *ibid.* 13.11.1f. (CSEL 13.375f.).

328 Cf. 8.1 above; Cassian, *ibid.* 13.11.4 (CSEL 13.377).

329 Cf. 9.2 above; Cassian, *ibid.* 13.12.2 (CSEL 13.378).

330 Cf. 11.2 above; Cassian, *ibid.* 13.12.5 (CSEL 13.379f.).

331 Cf. 13.1 above; Cassian, *ibid.* 13.12.7 (CSEL 13.380f.).

332 Job 1.9–11.

333 Cf. 14.1 above; Cassian, *Conlatio* 13.14.1f. (CSEL 13.384f.).

334 Matt. 8.10.

335 Cf. 16.1 above; Cassian, *Conlatio* 13.14.4 (CSEL 13.385).

336 Cf. 18.1 above; Cassian, *ibid.* 13.17.2 (CSEL 13.393).

337 This synthesis of Cassian's errors clearly indicates Prosper's inclination to magnify them. His basic argument against attributing the beginning of faith to free will and not to grace is correct: this position logically leads to the Pelagian heresy, merit preceding and deserving grace. But there does not seem to be any need to read in Cassian's text that Adam suffered no spiritual harm from his sin—he did, Cassian says, but not to the extent of being unable to do any good whatever; nor that every man is able to anticipate grace if he wishes—Cassian said some do, but nothing

more; nor that all men are by nature able to practice all the virtues without the help of grace—Cassian only said: some did practice virtues not only with the help of grace, but also by their unaided will; nor that free will is as hale in us as it was in Adam before his sin—Cassian said it is not altogether destroyed and can still do some good even without the help of grace. But Prosper is right in refusing Cassian's position that in some people free will begins to believe of itself without the help of grace. This admission introduces a discrimination among the faithful which is inconsistent with the Catholic faith on the gratuity of our salvation. And so it logically leads to a partial (and why, then, not complete?) acceptance of the Pelagian principle: human merit determines divine grace.

[338] Augustine is meant.

[339] 2 Tim. 2.19.

[340] Julian of Eclanum. In his two works against him, *Contra Iul.* (year 421) and *Op. imp. contra Iul.* (year 429/30), Augustine often refers to his insolence and loquacity.

[341] Compare Matt. 7.16.

[342] *Epist.* 29.6 (year 416; ML 20.586; ES 130); *Epist.* 30.3 (ML 20.591; ES 133).

[343] Synod of Diospolis, of the year 415; cf. 5.3 n. 53 above.

[344] *Epist. tractoria* (418), fragments of which were preserved in Prosper's *Auctoritates* 5f. (cf. ES 134f.).

[345] Cf. de Plinval, *Pélage* 343.

[346] Cf. *Epist. Augustini ad Bonifacium* (ML 20.763f.), from which it appears that Augustine wrote his *Contra duas ep. Pelag.*, of which this letter constitutes the preface, at the invitation of Pope Boniface, who had forwarded the letters to Augustine.

[347] Prosper is the main authority for this history of Pelagianism; cf. de Plinval, *Pélage* 347f.

[348] Cf. Prosper, *Chronicon* (ML 51.594C–95A).

[349] Allusion to Pelagius, who was a native of Britain; cf. de Plinval, *Pélage* 57–63.

[350] Cf. *Chronicon* (ML 51.595B).

[351] Cf. letter of Celestine, *Aliquantis diebus* (Mansi 4.1026; de Plinval, *Pélage* 352).

[352] Prosper and Hilary; cf. Intro. n. 24.

[353] Cf. Pope Celestine's letter, *Ad episcopos Gallorum,* Intro. n. 25.

[354] *Epist.* 21 (ML 50.530A; cf. ES 128).

[355] There is some foundation to this complaint: Pope Celestine gave no more than a general approval of Augustine's work (cf. text quoted above to n. 354). Cf. also Intro. n. 26; Cappuyns, "Premier représentant" 318f.

356 Cf. n. 353 above.

357 *De pecc. mer.* (ML 44.109–200).

358 *Epist.* 186 (ML 33.815–32).

359 *Epist.* 194 (ML 33.874–91).

360 *De grat. Christi* (ML 44.359–410).

361 *De nupt. et concup.* (ML 44.413–74).

362 *De nat. et grat.* (ML 44.247–90).

363 *Contra Iul.* (ML 44.641–874).

364 *De gest. Pel.* (ML 44.319–60).

365 *De perf. iust. hom.* (ML 44.291–318).

366 *Contra duas epist. Pelag.* (ML 44.549–638).

367 Prosper's argument is not altogether stringent. Augustine himself corrected his earlier ideas about the *initium fidei* (cf. *Resp. exc. Gen.* 1–3). It is a fact that in the latest works of Augustine, which Prosper is defending, some ideas are proposed, particularly about predestination, which appeared new and which did not obtain an explicit approval of the Holy See; rather, as Prosper himself will say in the *Auctoritates* 10, the "profundiores et difficiliores quaestiones" could be left aside (and they refer precisely to the mystery of predestination), because the Catholic doctrine can be held without entering into these.

368 This is confirmed by the variations of Pelagius' opinions, as related by Augustine in the *De gest. Pel.*

369 What Pope Sixtus did against Pelagius (he was Pope from 432, two years after Augustine's death, till 440) is related by Prosper in the *Chronicon* (ML 51.598B).

370 Augustine, *Epist.* 94.1.2 (ML 33.874), written fifteen years before Sixtus became Pope.

371 The Semi-Pelagian controversy was not settled definitively till much later, at the second Council of Orange (529), which defined the point made here by Prosper, against Cassian, concerning the beginning of faith. Cf. ES 178. The first phase of the controversy, in which Prosper took a leading part, did not end with any such official sanction.

372 Rom. 11.36.

ANSWERS TO THE OBJECTIONS OF THE GAULS

1 The full title is *Pro Augustino responsiones ad capitula obiectionum Gallorum calumniantium.* For an incomplete catalogue of Augustine's anti-Pelagian writings, cf. *Contra collat.* 21.3.

2 The text of the pamphlet is known only from Prosper's answer. Cf. Cappuyns, "Premier représentant" 322. Its author is unknown but does

not seem to be the same as the author of the Vincentian objections; cf. Amann, "Semi-pélagiens" 1825 (against Koch).

[3] Prosper's intention is to keep faithfully to Augustine's teaching. According to Cappuyns, "Premier représentant" 323, he partly betrays that intention; cf. nn. 11, 15, 19 below.

[4] Predestination, to Prosper's mind, is a doctrine of faith. Cf. Intro. n. 53; *Resp. exc. Gen.* n. 109.

[5] Eccli. 15.20.

[6] Ps. 5.7.

[7] *Tam non est probandus:* not "less blameworthy" (cf. Cappuyns, "Premier représentant" 323) but "as blameworthy" (*tam non probandus,* and not *non tam probandus*). Augustine himself had already answered the accusation of fatalism leveled against him by the Pelagians in *Contra duas epist. Pelag.* 2.5.9. Cf. also Prosper's *Epist. ad Rufin.* 3 and *Epist. ad August.* 3.

[8] Cf., e.g., *Epist. ad August.* 3 (Rom. 9.14–21); *Resp. exc. Gen.* 6 (Rom. 9.20; 11.33).

[9] Predestination is not fatalism, especially because there is no predestination of evil. God only foresees, He does not predestine, evil (cf. art. 15 below). Man's natural inclination to evil originates in the Fall.

[10] This conclusion from the theory of nonpredestination is a *latius hos,* which Augustine never taught or insinuated. Cf. a similar idea condemned in Trent (ES 827).

[11] This answer implies reprobation *post praevisa demerita* and goes beyond Augustine's explicit teaching.

[12] This objection is inconsistent with the previous one; it supposes the effect of baptism in the nonelect, but points out its precariousness.

[13] The objection suggests positive reprobation, which is not found in Augustine.

[14] Prosper's answer: "concedo antecedens, nego consequens et consequentiam."

[15] Note again reprobation *post praevisa demerita.*

[16] The reason for God's disposition allowing nonpredestined men to live till they fall into sin is hidden from us, as are many of His dispositions.

[17] Cf. *De voc.* 2.21 (ACW 14.121f.).

[18] Part of Prosper's answer: a long life is good and a gift of God, a bad life is evil and comes from man's fault.

[19] Again, nonpredestination is said to be dependent on God's foreknowledge of demerits. Cf. nn. 11 and 15 above.

[20] The denial of the universality of grace flows, the anti-Augustinians say, from Augustine's doctrine on predestination.

[21] The answer grants the objection in part (for those, namely, who

never heard of the gospel) and explains God's salvific will in a restricted sense, after the manner of Augustine. Cf. Intro. n. 68.

[22] Cf. Matt. 24.14.

[23] Today theology would rather look for substitutes to the gospel preaching by which God reaches all men to call them to salvation.

[24] Prosper grants that the gospel was or is not preached at all.

[25] Cf. Acts 16.7.

[26] Cf. *ibid.*

[27] Matt. 24.14.

[28] Prosper understands the text as a positive sign of Christ's second coming, and not only as a negative one, as it is generally understood—the Parousia will not take place before (negative), or it will happen at once after, the gospel has been preached everywhere.

[29] The death of unbaptized infants is given here as a proof for God's restricted salvific will; in the *De voc.* 2.23, Prosper labors to show that even for them God's salvific will holds good; cf. ACW 14.130f., 207f.

[30] Cf. 1 Cor. 3.7.

[31] The objection implies that Augustine taught positive reprobation.

[32] Cf. 1 Cor. 3.7.

[33] Cf. Augustine on the interior Master in *De praed. sanct.* 8.13.

[34] 2 Cor. 2.16.

[35] 2 Cor. 2.15.

[36] 1 Cor. 2.23f.

[37] The answer comes to this: unbelief following on the preaching of the gospel is not due to the preaching but to man's free refusal to accept the message, while faith that follows on it is due to grace.

[38] Objection: predestination destroys free will, the reprobate are not free (= able) to do good, while the elect are, apparently, compelled to do good. The objection presupposes the Pelagian idea of freedom as ability to do equally good or evil, and the Augustian idea of ever-efficacious grace.

[39] Ps. 106.10.

[40] Against the Pelagian idea: man is naturally good (even after Adam's sin).

[41] Grace originates merit and is, together with man's free co-operation, the principle of its growth and of perseverance.

[42] The answer to the difficulty: neither the presence nor the absence of grace destroys free will; man merits freely (with the help of grace) and sins freely (unaided by grace).

[43] The objection implies positive reprobation, which entails the denial by God of final perseverance.

[44] The answer: God's foreknowledge of the sins of Christians is the reason of their nonpredestination, and not inversely: their nonpredestina-

tion is not the cause of their sins. Note, again, nonpredestination *post praevisa demerita.*

45 God is not unjust in withholding from sinners the grace of final perseverance, which they did not deserve; they rather deserve not to have it.

46 The difficult doctrine on final perseverance, denied by Pelagians and Semi-Pelagians, is developed by Augustine in *De praed. sanct.* et *De dono persev.* Cf. Chéné, *art. cit.* (RSR 43; cf. Intro. n. 52) on the Semi-Pelagian ideas.

47 The objection that Augustine's predestination theory is incompatible with a universal salvific will is not unfounded; cf. Intro. nn. 61f.

48 Prosper's answer developed in this chapter comes to this: thesis = universal salvific will; antithesis = apparent restriction in the gospel; synthesis = the universal salvific will is fulfilled in the salvation of the elect the world over, that is, he proposes here a restricted universalism.

49 Acts. 14.15.

50 Ps. 134.4.

51 Ps. 147.20.

52 Cf. Osee 2.23; 1 Peter 2.10.

53 Rom. 11.7.

54 2 Par. 19.7.

55 Luke 19.10.

56 The absence of every free act in the case of the salvation or nonsalvation of dying infants is a proof, Prosper implies, that man's free actions do not determine their election or nonelection.

57 Cf. Rom. 11.33.

58 Compare *De voc.* 1.13; 1.21; 2.9 (ACW 14.53f., 68f., 103).

59 This Pelagian error is not necessarily involved in the concept of predestination *ex praevisis meritis;* it is so only in the supposition (which is also Prosper's) of an ever-efficacious grace.

60 1 Tim. 2.4.

61 Matt. 28.19f.

62 Gen. 12.3.

63 Rom. 4.20.

64 Rom. 4.20f.

65 Ps. 21.28.

66 Ps. 71.17.

67 Ps. 85.9.

68 Rom. 4.21.

69 Note the restricted universalism of the salvific will. Cf. n. 48 above.

70 Cf. 1 Peter 2.5.

71 Eph. 2.20f.

[72] John 6.37.

[73] John 10.26–28.

[74] Is this a foreshadowing of a more universalistic interpretation of the salvific will and of the general grace of which *De voc.* 2.25 (cf. ACW 14.133, 209)? It is, moreover, rather inconsistent with the restricted universalism which Prosper states here so definitely.

[75] Council of Carthage (418); cf. *Contra collat.* n. 58.

[76] The text quoted here (freely?) has not been preserved; for its equivalent cf. ES 104f.

[77] Pelagius understood grace as meaning nature or free will itself (= God's gift).

[78] Prosper, after Augustine, conceives grace mainly as "healing."

[79] Cf. 2 Cor. 5.17.

[80] Cf. Rom. 9.22f.

[81] Cf. the same objection in *Resp. cap. Vinc.* 1: denying the universality of the redemption. Compare the Jansenist proposition (ES 1096). Cf. also *De voc.* 2.16 (ACW 14.118ff.).

[82] Rom. 8.3.

[83] Cf. Heb. 4.15.

[84] Pauline symbolism of baptism; cf. Rom. 6.4; Gal. 3.27; Col. 2.12.

[85] Rom. 6.5.

[86] Cf. Gal. 5.24; Eph. 5.30.

[87] Cf. Gal. 3.27; John 3.5.

[88] Prosper's answer: Christ died for all men, but not all profit by His death; in the first sense the redemption is universal, in the second it is not.

[89] John 11.51f.

[90] John 1.11–13.

[91] John 1.10.

[92] John 1.5.

[93] Eph. 5.8.

[94] Luke 19.10.

[95] Matt. 15.24.

[96] Gen. 21.12.

[97] Rom. 9.6–8.

[98] John 11.51f.

[99] Rom. 4.17.

[100] Ps. 146.2.

[101] Gen. 12.3. Note Prosper's restricted universalism of the redemption.

[102] Cf. art. 4 above.

[103] Prosper does not believe that the gospel has been preached to all men already; cf. above, his answer to art. 4.

[104] The reason for the delays in announcing the gospel to some peoples (or individuals) is hidden from us.

[105] Compare *Resp. cap. Vinc.* 5.

[106] Ps. 144.14.

[107] 2 Tim. 2.25f.

[108] Rom. 1.24.

[109] God forsakes only those who forsake Him first; cf. Augustine, *De nat. et grat.* 26.29.

[110] Only in that sense does God permit sins: He forsakes those who have forsaken Him.

[111] The objection supposes "positive" reprobation, by which God deprives of grace the justified who are not predestined.

[112] A first answer: the objection contradicts God's justice.

[113] Second answer: the root of the objection is the failure to distinguish foreknowledge and predestination: God's foreknowledge of sin does not mean predestination to sin.

[114] Prosper explains nonpredestination *ex praevisis demeritis,* adding to Augustine; cf. Intro. 9.

[115] Cf. *De voc.* 1.4 and 2.15 (ACW 14.29, 116). Here this idea that the nonpredestined serve a temporal purpose is twisted to mean that they are not meant for eternal life.

[116] Prosper's answer grants that the reprobate serve a temporal purpose, but says that their reprobation is not due to the Creator but to their own fault.

[117] Augustinian idea, and cf. *De voc.* (ACW 14.202 n. 131).

[118] Cf. *De voc.* 2.15 (ACW 14.115f.).

[119] Acts 4.27f.; cf. *De voc., ibid.*

[120] Cf. *De voc.* 2.15 (ACW 14.117f.).

[121] Phil. 1.28f.

[122] 1 Cor. 11.19.

[123] The objection supposes a positive predestination to unbelief, or positive reprobation.

[124] The answer is perfect: God never predestines (wills), He only foreknows, evil.

[125] Ps. 24.10.

[126] Further answer: distinguish foreknowledge and decree. God's infallible foreknowledge does not entail that evil is necessary.

[127] Eph. 2.8–10.

[128] Two errors set aside: that there is a predestination of evil, and that there is no predestination of what is good.

[129] Sin deprived man of grace; God is the giver who restores grace. The antithesis is rather artificial.

[130] The last objection formulates what underlies most of the previous ones: confusion or identification of prescience and predestination—when actually predestination adds to prescience an act of the will.

[131] The reason for the distinction is that foreknowledge does not imply that God is the author of what He foreknows, while predestination does. What is good is object of both prescience and predestination, but what is evil is object of prescience only.

[132] First article: an error against the faith.

[133] Second article: same qualification.

[134] Third article: same qualification—positive reprobation is against the faith.

[135] Fourth article: granted in one sense—the gospel message has not reached all nations. Prosper is not aware, any more than are his contemporaries, of the possibility of (implicit) baptism of desire and graces given outside, though not independently of, the visible Church.

[136] Fifth article: to say that there is a positive call to unbelief is an error (whether or not against the faith is not explicitly said).

[137] Sixth article: error against the faith.

[138] Seventh article: error against God's justice.

[139] Eighth article: God's salvific will is restricted to the fixed number of the elect: rigorist expression; rather insist on the universalism (restricted, though) of the election.

[140] 1 Tim. 2.4.

[141] Cf. Rom. 8.30.

[142] Expression of restricted universalism of the salvific will; cf. De voc. 1.9 (ACW 14.46, 182 n. 138).

[143] Gen. 22.18.

[144] Rom. 4.21.

[145] Ninth article: incomplete statement. Christ died for all, but not all profit by His redemption, through their own fault.

[146] Cf. Rom. 9.22f.

[147] Col. 1.13.

[148] Tenth article: answered by admitting a restricted universalism of the salvific will.

[149] Cf. Matt. 11.21.

[150] Cf. Matt. 10.5.

[151] Cf. Matt. 24.10.

[152] Phil. 2.11.

[153] Eleventh article: rejected, but no qualification given.

[154] Twelfth article: the qualification could be severer: error against God's goodness and justice—or even against the faith.

[155] Cf. 1 Cor. 6.17; Rom. 8.14.

[156] Thirteenth article: partly corrected—God has a purpose in creating those who will not attain to eternal life, He foresees their reprobation but does not intend it; partly granted—the reprobate are of use to the world.

[157] Cf. *De voc.* 2.10, 33 (ACW 14.104, 146): the unbelievers serve the purpose of God's providence.

[158] Cf. Matt. 5.45.

[159] Fourteenth article: positive reprobation is an error against the faith.

[160] Gal. 5.6.

[161] Fifteenth article: partly granted—prescience and predestination go together with regard to what is good; partly rejected—there is no predestination, but only prescience, of evil.

ANSWERS TO THE VINCENTIAN ARTICLES

[1] This pamphlet, too, has not been preserved except in Prosper's answer. Cf. Cappuyns, "Premier représentant" 320. Its author is the same as that of the *Commonitorium*, Vincent of Lerins; cf. H. Koch, *op. cit.* (Intro. n. 28), and Amann, "Semi-pélagiens," DTC 14.1821. The full title of Prosper's answer is *Pro Augustino responsiones ad capitula obiectionum Vincentianarum.*

[2] It is no exaggeration to call the pamphlet a "devilish catalogue" of "shocking propositions," so plain is it that they are against the faith.

[3] Did Prosper get a commission from the Holy See to answer these blasphemies? Perhaps implicitly, at his visit to Rome. Yet, his answers do not draw on the authoritative teachings of the Holy See.

[4] Cf. *Resp. cap. Gall.* 9. As noted (Intro. 12), the objections of Vincent "improve" on those of the Gauls in violence and in blasphemous character.

[5] The answer is: the objective redemption is universal, as theologians would say today, *in actu primo,* but not *in actu secundo;* only those to whom the merits of Christ are actually applied in baptism are actually saved. Compare *Resp. cap. Gall., loc. cit.*

[6] Cf. John 12.31.

[7] Denial of the universal salvific will.

[8] Matt. 7.11.

[9] Prosper grants that not all are saved, not because God does not want them to be saved but for some mysterious though just reason. Examples of this bowing down before the mystery, in which Prosper follows Augustine, are found also in the *De voc.* (cf. ACW 14.15, 68, 87f.).

[10] 1 Tim. 2.4.

[11] 1 Tim. 2.1f.

[12] An improvement on *Resp. cap. Gall.* 13: there it was "quidam," here "maior pars."

[13] Rom. 5.12 (according to the Latin: *in quo*).

[14] Cf. John 3.5; Col. 2.12.

[15] Rom. 5.19. Answer to the objection: distinguish nature and guilt; the first is the work of the Creator and is not the cause of men's reprobation; the second is from man only and is the reason for the reprobation of those who are not freed from it by baptism.

[16] Objection; many (not only some) are created for the slavery of the devil (not only to cease obeying God); compare *Resp. cap. Gall.* 12.

[17] For Pelagius' denial of original sin, cf. his commentary on *Ep. ad Rom.* 5.12ff.; A. Souter, *Pelagius' Exposition of Thirteen Epistles of St. Paul* (Cambridge 1926) 389.

[18] In the Pelagian hypothesis that there is no original sin, the reprobation of infants is inconceivable and leads to the objection that God creates them for the slavery of the devil. In the Catholic position that all men are born in original sin, the negative reprobation of infants has its reason, Prosper says, in original sin.

[19] Luke 19.10; cf. Rom. 5.12.

[20] The state of sin entails "slavery of the devil." Cf. Trent (ES 788).

[21] Cf. *De voc.* 1.8 (ACW 14.35).

[22] Cf. 1 Tim. 2.5; Rom. 5.15, 18.

[23] Preceded: both Pelagians and Semi-Pelagians (*initium fidei* without grace) held the contrary.

[24] Compare *Resp. cap. Gall.* 11; there God is said to compel man to sin, here that He is the cause of sin because He creates nature evil.

[25] The objection twists the doctrine of original sin, as though this meant that God creates an evil nature.

[26] Answer: God is the author of nature, which is good, not of sin, which is evil.

[27] Cf. Gen. 3.5f.: Eve (and Adam) believed the devil, and not God.

[28] 2 Cor. 5.17.

[29] Col. 3.10.

[30] Cf. Rom. 5.12, 17.

[31] Cf. Rom. 6.10.

[32] Acts 4.12.

[33] Another parody of original sin, as though God created men with a will bent on evil (= devilish). Man's will actually is inclined to evil in consequence of original sin, not in consequence of its creation.

[34] 1 John 5.19.

[35] Matt. 12.34.

[36] John 8.44.

[37] *Ibid.*

[38] *Ibid.*

[39] Compare *Resp. cap. Gall.* 8: there, God does not wish all men to be saved; here, God wants a great number not to be saved.

[40] It is not God's will that men give up the desire to be saved.

[41] Ps. 144.41.

[42] Cf. Augustine, *De nat. et grat.* 26.29 or 43.50; cf. Trent (ES 804).

[43] Objection: God is the positive cause of evil—He not only allows it; repeatedly rejected by Prosper; cf., e.g., *Resp. cap. Gall.* 7.

[44] Objection: same idea applied to sin in general, not only to unbelief.

[45] This and the two following objections say that God predestines men to sin. Prosper answers: God only foreknows sin.

[46] Answer: predestination is only of what is good.

[47] Ps. 24.10.

[48] Ps. 34.23.

[49] 2 Cor. 13.7.

[50] Cf. Matt. 16.27; Rom. 2.6.

[51] Cf. Matt. 25.33, 41.

[52] A second example of crimes imputed to God's predestination; cf. n. 45 above.

[53] Temptation does not suppress a sinner's freedom and responsibility; if it did, giving way to it would be no sin.

[54] God foreknows but does not predestine (= will) evil; He does predestine and will the punishment of sin (which is a good).

[55] Cf. 1 John 3.10.

[56] 1 Cor. 6.19.

[57] 1 Cor. 6.15. More illustrations of what the supposed predestination to sin implies; cf. n. 45 above.

[58] Cf. *De voc.* 2.37 (ACW 14.152).

[59] Cf. *ibid.* 2.33 (ACW 14.216f. n. 309); Augustine, *De civ. Dei* 22.2: ". . . futura iam fecit."

[60] Rom. 11.29.

[61] 2 Tim. 2.19.

[62] Cf. Mark 3.27.

[63] Col. 1.13.

[64] 1 John 2.19.

[65] Cf. 2 Peter 2.22.

[66] Compare *Resp. cap. Gall.* 12—how predestination is supposed to cause sin.

[67] Answer: God is never cause of sin; cf. n. 43 above.

⁶⁸ Cf. John 5.17.

⁶⁹ The objection draws a consequence from positive reprobation: the prayer of the reprobate asking for final perseverance will not be granted.

⁷⁰ Answer: there is no predestination to sin.

⁷¹ Cf. John 15.5.

⁷² Cf. n. 42 above.

⁷³ Cf. n. 9 above.

⁷⁴ The objection formulates another conclusion from positive reprobation: God prevents the repentance of the reprobate.

⁷⁵ Answer: sin is the sinner's free choosing, repentance is not without grace.

⁷⁶ Ps. 76.11.

⁷⁷ 2 Tim. 2.26.

⁷⁸ The answer may seem rather unsatisfactory. Only by considering "sufficient" grace and the sinner's free refusal of the grace of repentance offered him would it become more complete. But this idea lay outside the perspective of Prosper, who considers only ever-efficacious grace. Cf. Intro. nn. 62f.

⁷⁹ Matt. 6.10.

⁸⁰ Another conclusion from positive reprobation, placing on a par God's will regarding sin and regarding its punishment.

⁸¹ John 6.39.

⁸² John 6.37.

⁸³ God's infallible foreknowledge of sin does not entail any necessity of sin or causality on God's part.

⁸⁴ Answer: by praying "thy will be done," future sinners ask, not that they may sin, but that they should be punished for their sin. The first is in no way willed by God, the second is.

⁸⁵ Matt. 25.31-34.

⁸⁶ Matt. 25.41.

⁸⁷ Cf. *ibid.* and 1 John 3.8.

OFFICIAL PRONOUNCEMENTS OF THE APOSTOLIC SEE

¹ The Latin title of this work is *Praeteritorum episcoporum sedis aposto-licae auctoritates de gratia Dei (et libero voluntatis arbitrio)*, according to Constant (ML 50.431) and the Ballerini (*S. Leonis opera* 2 [Venice 1756] 251f.). The bracketed words are not found in the MSS.; cf. Cappuyns, "L'Origine" 161 n. 2. The *auctoritates* were appended to the letter of Pope Celestine to the bishops of Gaul (cf. Intro. n. 26) and passed in tradition as "Celestian." Cappuyns, *art. cit.*, has established the Prosperian origin of the pseudo-Celestian capitula.

[2] The Semi-Pelagians are aimed at; they claimed and wished to remain Catholic and to have nothing in common with Pelagianism.

[3] These heretics are the Pelagians condemned in the African councils.

[4] Augustine especially is meant, though his name is not mentioned throughout the document. For the grievances of the Semi-Pelagians against his teachings, cf. Prosper's letter to Augustine and his answers to the two catalogues of objections.

[5] Cf. *Epist. ad August.* 2.3.

[6] Pelagianism.

[7] *Indiculo*: the document is also known as *De gratia Dei indiculus* (cf. ES 129); the same term is used for the lists of objections of the Gauls and of Vincent (cf. ML 51.156A, 177A). Cappuyns, "Premier représentant" 328, calls it a syllabus or countersyllabus in answer to the pamphlets of the Gauls and of Vincent.

[8] *Naturalem possibilitatem et innocentiam*: cf. Augustine, *De nat. et grat.* 40.47.

[9] *Epist. 29: In requirendis* 6 (ML 20.586B). St. Innocent was Pope from 401–17.

[10] The Council of Carthage of 416; cf. Augustine, *Epist.* 181; de Plinval, *Pélage* 303f.

[11] Other reading, followed in Quesnel's edition of St. Leo: *libero enim arbitrio ille perversus* (ML 51.205 n. a).

[12] Other reading: *huius ruinae latuisset* (instead of *iacuisset*), followed in Migne's text.

[13] *Epist. 29: In requirendis* 3 (ML 20.584B).

[14] *Posthac*: after what he said before about the Pelagians in the same letter (2).

[15] Cf. in the same letter, 181 among the letters of Augustine (ML 33 780–83), 4, a further development of this error: "Sed iam isti, qui tales sunt, nullam Dei gratiam consequentur, qui sine illo tantum se assequi posse confidunt, quantum vix ab illo postulant, accipere promerentur."

[16] Cf. ES 103.

[17] *Epist. 29: In requirendis* 6 (ML 20.586C).

[18] *Epist. 30: Inter caeteras* 3 (ML 20.591A).

[19] Council of Mileve (416).

[20] The freedom lost by original sin is not the freedom of choice (*liberum arbitrium*) but the ability to do good. And this is not fully restored by baptism: "concupiscence" remains after baptism (cf. ES 792).

[21] St. Zosimus succeeded St. Innocent and was Pope in 417–18.

[22] *Epist. tractoria* of the year 418; it was not preserved, except for a few fragments. Cf. Amann, "Zosime," DTC 15.2 (1950) 3708–16.

[23] Pope Zosimus attributes his idea of referring the question to the

judgment of the African bishops to an inspiration of grace: an example of a good movement that originates both from grace and from free will.

24 The letter was not preserved—only the fragment quoted here.

25 Prov. 8.35 (LXX).

26 Rom. 8.14.

27 Cf. John 15.5.

28 *Epist. tractoria;* cf. Amann, *art. cit.* 3713f.

29 Eph. 6.12 (other version than Vulgate).

30 Rom. 7.24f.

31 1 Cor. 15.10.

32 Of the year 418. Its canons (cf. ES 101ff.) were approved by Pope Zosimus in his *Epist. tractoria.* On this approval cf. Floëri, *art. cit.* (Intro. n. 48).

33 Mansi 3.811; ES 103.

34 Mansi 3.811; ES 104.

35 1 Cor. 8.1.

36 Ps. 93.10.

37 1 John 4.7.

38 Mansi 3.811; ES 105.

39 John 15.5.

40 Pelagianism.

41 Compare *De voc.* 1.12 (ACW 14.52).

42 *Lex supplicandi statuat legem credendi:* a maxim originated by Prosper that was to become renowned. For its history and meaning, cf. G. Löw, "Liturgia," EC 7 (1951) 1443f.

43 The similarity with our present-day solemn orations of Good Friday was noted in ACW 14.184 n. 178.

44 Col. 1.13.

45 Rom. 9.22f.

46 Compare *De voc.* 1.23 (ACW 14.71f.).

47 It is hardly necessary to note that this "casting out of the devil" does not refer to "possession" but to the "slavery of the devil" implied in the state of sin. Cf., e.g., Trent (ES 788).

48 John 12.31.

49 Matt. 12.39.

50 Mark 3.27.

51 Eph. 4.8.

52 The beginning of faith is from grace and not from unaided free will: against the Semi-Pelagian error.

53 Phil. 2.13.

54 Cf. *De voc.* 1.8 (ACW 14.35f.).

⁵⁵ A well-known Augustinian idea; cf., e.g., *Epist. 194 ad Sixt.* 5.19 (ML 33.880), sanctioned later by the Council of Trent (cf. ES 810).

⁵⁶ Cf. *De voc.* 2.26, 35 (ACW 14.134f., 149f.).

⁵⁷ Ps. 102.3f.

⁵⁸ Matt. 6.13.

⁵⁹ In Prosper's mind, these obscure and difficult points are those concerning predestination (with the discrimination between elect and non-elect) and its connection with the universal salvific will.

⁶⁰ As noted, n. 4 above, Augustine, chief among the opponents of the Pelagians, is not mentioned by name, apparently because of the connection of his name with predestination, which Prosper, on set purpose, leaves out of his document.

⁶¹ As said in the introductory paragraph to the *Auctoritates*, Prosper's purpose was to state the doctrine of the faith on the question of grace.

⁶² Prosper feels confident of having stated nothing but what pertains to the faith, as taught by the Apostolic See, whether in direct statements emanating from popes, or in decisions approved by them, or in the "law of prayer" as kept, with their approval, in the universal Church.

INDEXES

INDEXES

1. OLD AND NEW TESTAMENT

2. AUTHORS

243

3. GENERAL INDEX

Abimelech, 88
Adam's sin, 31, 39, 53, 59, 82, 91–96, 104 f., 113, 129, 132, 140 f., 166 f., 170, 179, 214, 220, 224; before, 92–95, 132
adoption, 59
Africa, Church of, 23; Councils of, 22 f., 82, 133, 178, 198
angels, two, 104, 108
anti-Augustinians, 3, 7 f., 223
Apostolic See, 22, 70, 82 f., 136, 163, 178, 182 f., 185, 235
Augustinians, 3, 7, 10

Baius, 195
Balaam, 88
baptism, 11, 13, 26, 30 ff., 34, 39, 42 f., 140 f., 150, 157, 164, 179 f., 184, 201, 226, 230, 233; ceremonies of, 184
beginning, of faith, 13 f., 84, 106, 111, 126, 184, 199 f., 220 f., 234; of good will, 74, 78–82, 112 f., 123 f., 127 ff.; of good works, 79, 112, 127; of salvation, 45, 62 f., 73, 103, 204; of virtues, 106 ff., 113 f.
believers, 26, 33, 55, 120, 123
Body of Christ, 21, 24, 38, 123, 150
Boniface, St., Pope, 133 f., 137, 221
Britain, 134

Camille, 7, 49
Carthage, Councils of, 13, 179, 182, 198, 210, 212, 215, 218, 226, 233
Catholics, 22, 53, 76, 82, 84, 111 f., 114, 125, 166, 169, 174, 178
Celestius, 82, 99, 134, 178, 210
centurion, 10, 118, 121, 123, 131; Cornelius, 26, 199
charity, 27 f., 109 f.
Christ, Saviour and helper, according to Cassian, 123 f., 125, 131 f.
commandments of God, 98 f., 118, 183
conversion, 76 f., 86 f., 169

creation, gift of, 21; contemplation of, 86

damnation, eternal, 141, 165
David, 60, 100 ff., 116, 217
death, good, 39; eternal, 42, 109, 141, 173 f., 176; different comments on, 141 f.
delays, divine, 32, 34, 43, 204, 227
demerit, 149
Diospolis, Council of, 198, 221
discrimination, in God's call, 75, 210
diversity in grace, 88

elect, 28, 33, 38 ff., 50, 54 f., 65, 76, 159, 235; fixed number of, 4, 16, 44, 195, 200, 228
election, divine, 42 f., 49 f., 54, 58, 63, 146
Ephesus, Council of, 210
Esau, 49, 51

faith, gift of God, 7, 26 f., 49 f., 51, 53, 56 ff., 61 f., 64 f., 102, 107, 144 f., 148 f., 158, 162, 224; no gift, according to Cassian, 10, 119–22; according to Pelagians, 22, 56 f.; according to Semi-Pelagians, 44, 52; of the Church, 89 f.; call to, 143 f.
Fall, 4 f., 10, 13 ff., 18, 52, 92, 103, 195, 214, 216, 223
fatalism, 4 f., 11, 23, 35 f., 140, 199, 202 f., 223
foreknowledge, God's, 43, 46, 61 f., 232; and predestination, 47, 204 f., 224 f., 227; see prescience
forgiveness, 169
free will, and grace, 14 f., 25 f., 28 f., 34 f., 88 f., 95 f., 118, 179 f., 219; without grace, 110, 114 f., 132; and predestination, 11, 144; and beginning of grace, 75; and original sin, 94 ff., 167 f., 179 f., and God's decree, 146 f.; Pelagian concept of, 21 f., 203, 217, 224

245